P9-CFZ-109

TOEING THE LINES

Women and Party Politics in English Canada

In the power structure of Canadian politics, as in industrial and financial power structures, women at the top are hard to find. In this study, Sylvia Bashevkin analyses the experiences of women in English-Canadian political parties. From extensive archival material she has traced the history of women's participation in partisan politics. From in-depth interviews and surveys of contemporary women, she demonstrates how little progress has been made. Today's major parties are organized with a gender-based division of labour; women remain vastly underrepresented in the upper echelons of power and influence.

Bashevkin identifies a continuing dilemma for Canadian women: they struggle with conflicting loyalties – to their independence on the one hand, and to partisanship on the other. This ambivalence serves to limit the political mobility of women as a group, a situation aggravated by party organizations that foster discriminatory attitudes and practices. Recent feminist activity, however, has had some impact on party involvement. Bashevkin highlights the development of affirmative action policies and leadership campaigns designed to raise the level of female participation.

In examining the political condition of women in English Canada within a comparative context, she makes an important contribution to ongoing debates on feminism and contemporary democratic practice.

SYLVIA B. BASHEVKIN is Assistant Professor of Political Science at the University of Toronto and a frequent commentator on issues of women and politics.

SYLVIA B. BASHEVKIN

Toeing the Lines: Women and Party Politics in English Canada

UNIVERSITY OF TORONTO PRESS
Toronto Buffalo London

© University of Toronto Press 1985
Toronto Buffalo London
Printed in Canada

ISBN 0-8020-2557-9 (cloth)
ISBN 0-8020-6576-7 (paper)

HQ
1236.5
.C3
B37
1985

Canadian Cataloguing in Publication Data

Bashevkin, Sylvia B.
  Toeing the lines

  Includes index.
  ISBN 0-8020-2557-9 (bound) – ISBN 0-8020-6576-7 (pbk.)

  1. Women in politics – Canada.   2. Political
  parties – Canada.   I. Title.

HQ1236.5.C3B37 1985   305.4'332'0971   C85-098545-5

This book has been published with the help of a grant from the Social Science
Federation of Canada, using funds provided by the Social Sciences and
Humanities Research Council of Canada. Publication has also been assisted
by the Canada Council and the Ontario Arts Council under their block
grant programs.

DEC   6 1985

FOR A.L.

Contents

viii Contents

6
Comparative perspectives on women and party politics 120

7
Epilogue: Prospects for political representation in English Canada 156

Illustrations

Acknowledgments

This book grew out of a dissertation project on women's political attitudes in France, Canada, and the United States, which illustrated the limited background material available on the English-Canadian case. Since one study can only begin to address the political history, beliefs, and involvement of English-Canadian women, I hope that this book will stimulate new research in what remains a significant and long-neglected area.

I am very grateful to a number of friends, colleagues, and funding sources for their generous support of this project. In particular, Professor Naomi Black has long encouraged my work in the field of women and politics, as have Professors Jill Vickers, Thelma McCormack, Sandra Burt, and Janine Brodie. Marianne Holder shared her first-hand experiences in the 'real world' of women and politics and contributed a careful reading of the final manuscript. Most recently, this study has benefited from the editorial direction of Virgil Duff at the University of Toronto Press.

On a financial level, I wish to thank the Social Sciences and Humanities Research Council of Canada, which granted doctoral and post-doctoral fellowships as well as a subvention in aid of publication through the Social Science Federation of Canada. During 1981-3, the Institute for Behavioural Research at York University and Department of Political Science at McMaster University offered institutional 'homes' for my post-doctoral research and, since 1983, Erindale College has provided a most congenial setting. I am especially thankful to Principal Paul Fox and Dean Len Brooks at Erindale, whose willingness to commit university resources to a young and, at the time, sessional instructor is both exceptional and deeply appreciated. I also wish to thank the Humanities and Social Sciences Committee at the University of Toronto, whose faculty grant-in-aid during 1983-4 helped to finance the preparation of the manuscript. Fjola Burke and

Joanna Collins contributed their expertise and enthusiasm to this task, for which I am most grateful.

A less visible contribution to this study has been made by the political activists who agreed to be interviewed and prodded for data (both qualitative and quantitative) on female participation. I am very thankful to the many informants (most of whom are identified by name in appendix B) who shared their knowledge of this subject, since without their cooperation and interest, the book simply could not have been written.

Finally, in any study of politics and especially party politics, the predispositions of the author need to be clearly and carefully acknowledged. It may be helpful for the reader to know that prior to beginning research for this study, I briefly held office on the executive of the Ontario NDP Women's Committee and worked in a number of routine capacities in provincial and federal NDP campaigns in the Toronto area. This involvement offered useful first-hand exposure to many of the problems faced by women in Canadian party organizations, thereby informing on a practical level much of the discussion which follows.

Above all, this study has benefited from the insight and encouragement of my husband, Alan Levy.

All remaining errors of fact and judgment are my own.

Preliminary versions of some of this material appeared in *Journal of Canadian Studies* (Summer 1982); *Comparative Political Studies* (July 1983); *International Journal of Women's Studies* (January / February 1984); and *British Journal of Political Science* (January 1985). I am grateful to the editors of these journals for their kind permission to reprint various passages.

Preface

It has become a commonplace observation that relatively few women in
Canada are major party leaders, cabinet ministers, provincial legislators,
members of parliament, or backroom party strategists. Yet little is known
about why women are, or appear to be, so distant from formal positions
of political power. What is the historical background to women's participation in Canadian politics? How have females responded to their lack
of direct political influence? Until recently, political scientists have generally neglected these and other questions which concern the status of
women. Believing that such issues were private and hence apolitical,
researchers tended to overlook this area and, as a result, 'political man'
became a common synonym for 'political participant' in much of the
discipline.[1]

Since the late 1960s, however, growing attention has been devoted to
the social and political status of Canadian women. Historians, for example, have examined the background to early suffragist activities as well
as subsequent efforts by women to introduce major reforms in social
legislation.[2] Similarly, sociologists and economists have recently considered the dimensions of family roles and labour force participation by
women in Canada, while a number of political scientists have explored
the dimensions of female political attitudes and involvement.[3] The present
study forms part of this developing literature on women and politics in
Canada. In particular, it begins to address the complex relationship between women and major party organizations in English Canada, focusing
upon the historical as well as the contemporary dimensions of this subject.

Our discussion opens in chapter 1 with a review of the political history
of women in English Canada. Using the tension between political independence and partisanship as an organizing theme, we address the growth

of the early suffrage movement as well as developments after enfranchisement which affected social welfare legislation and the specific right of women to hold public office. Furthermore, we trace the emergence of contemporary feminism and maintain that a dilemma between independence and partisanship continues to shape the relationship between women and politics in English Canada.

What are the political implications of this historical background? On an attitudinal level, as discussed in chapter 2, we propose that circumstances surrounding female enfranchisement and the more recent growth of contemporary feminism may have contributed to particular trends in female politicization and partisanship. Using existing data from 1965 and 1979 national surveys, we re-evaluate older Canadian studies of female public opinion and consider the attitudinal implications of women's political history in English Canada.

Chapter 3 examines the actual participation of women in mainstream party organizations, including local constituency associations, party conventions, and campaign activities. Drawing on longitudinal data from federal- and provincial-level (especially Ontario) politics, it suggests that while women's involvement has tended to increase in recent years, there remain few females at elite levels of party activism. This problem of underrepresentation is particularly apparent in competitive political environments, where parties hold or are in a position to challenge the reins of government. Moreover, we demonstrate that many women continue to perform stereotypically feminine types of party work, including clerical or 'pink-collar' roles within local constituency associations.

In chapter 4, our focus shifts somewhat in order to consider contemporary responses to female underrepresentation within party organizations. Aside from broader societal changes in gender role socialization and the distribution of household and child-rearing responsibilities, there remain at least two approaches which have been attempted inside Canadian party organizations. The first of these involves formal affirmative action policies, which vary widely across parties and levels of government. A second approach, less formalized than the first, begins with the nomination of women as party leadership candidates, where such campaigns for leadership function as a catalyst for increasing female visibility and influence within the larger party organization. In chapter 4, we examine both of these responses and evaluate their impact upon the political status of women in English Canada.

How does this status compare with the partisan roles of women outside the mainstream Canadian party organizations, and in other North American and Western European party systems? Chapter 5 addresses the development of women's auxiliaries and associations as well as newer caucuses, committees, and commissions in the major English-Canadian parties. We compare the goals and accomplishments of these various groups and conclude that while some traditional women's affiliates continue to provide an important support structure for mainstream party organizations, these older associations are gradually being replaced by more explicitly pro-feminist women's groups. That is, newer women's organizations within the parties appear to operate according to a mandate which is clearly distinguishable from that of their predecessors, involving demands for both increased numerical representation of women in party activities and increased attention to so-called women's issues in party policy.

Similar types of changes are also under way in other contemporary party systems, including those of the United States, Quebec, France, Great Britain, and Australia. In chapter 6, we compare developments in English Canada with data on the history, attitudes, and participation of women in similar party environments, and outline a number of areas which deserve more careful consideration by students of both Canadian and comparative politics. Overall, we conclude that even though increased numbers of women in English Canada and elsewhere are involved in politics and concerned about their position within the parties, most remain distant from power and policy influence. We thus suggest that women as a group are frequently 'toeing the lines' in Western party organizations, rather than participating in strategic, legislative, and policy work which would transcend their conventional maintenance (including clerical) roles.

One brief note before turning to the political history of women in English Canada: Quebec has been excluded from the main focus of this study for a number of reasons, many of which will become apparent in chapters 1, 2, and 6. First, female enfranchisement in Quebec was strongly opposed by clerical and political interests which were preoccupied with maintaining French-Canadian identity in the face of a perceived threat from neighbouring Anglo-American culture. Throughout the first four decades of this century, approximately, women in Quebec were denied many rights which had already been obtained by their sisters elsewhere in Canada, including the right to vote in provincial elections.[4] Therefore, the background to suffrage in Quebec suggests a distinctive political history, as well as a disparate set of attitudes and participatory behaviours, which are best served by a separate study. In fact, if incorporated within a comparative framework, the political history of women in Quebec might be included most appropriately in a study of France, Italy, and other Catholic cultures.[5]

Second, in more contemporary terms, the political experiences of women in Quebec are shaped by a social and partisan environment which differs clearly from conditions prevailing elsewhere in Canada. For example, the development of modern feminism during the late 1960s and following coincided with the emergence of a strong independentist movement, and with the exacerbation of tensions between Francophones and Anglophones, separatists and federalists, in the province.[6] Many of the same political organizations which are significant elsewhere in Canada, particularly the Conservatives and New Democrats, have until recently remained marginal or irrelevant within this context. Similarly, efforts during the 1970s to increase the numerical representation of women in government at the federal level in Quebec were distinctive because of the virtual political monopoly of the Liberal party, which held relatively centralized and hierarchical control over nominations to the House of Commons.

These factors indicate that the historical as well as contemporary dimensions of women and party politics in Quebec deserve more careful and thorough examination than is possible in a single-volume study of this type.

Abbreviations

BNA Act	British North America Act
CACSW	Canadian Advisory Council on the Status of Women
CCF	Co-operative Commonwealth Federation
CDU	Christian Democratic Union (West Germany)
CEW	Committee for the Equality of Women in Canada
CFUW	Canadian Federation of University Women
CSA	Canadian Suffrage Association
IODE	Imperial Order Daughters of the Empire
LPC	Liberal Party of Canada
LPC(O)	Liberal Party of Canada (Ontario)
LPO	Liberal Party of Ontario
MLA	Member of Legislative Assembly
MP	Member of Parliament
MPP	Member of Provincial Parliament (Ontario)
NAC	National Action Committee on the Status of Women
NCWC	National Council of Women of Canada
NDP	New Democratic Party
NEFU	National Equal Franchise Union
NFLW	National Federation of Liberal Women
NLWV	National League of Women Voters (U.S.)
OLP	Ontario Liberal Party
ONDP	Ontario New Democratic Party
OPCAW	Ontario Progressive Conservative Association of Women
OWLA	Ontario Women's Liberal Association
PC	Progressive Conservative
PCF	Parti Communiste Français
PLQ	Parti Libéral du Québec

POW	Participation of Women Committee (federal NDP)
RCSW	Royal Commission on the Status of Women
SPD	Social Democratic Party (West Germany)
SUPA	Student Union for Peace Action
TWLA	Toronto Women's Liberal Association
UFA	United Farmers of Alberta
UFO	United Farmers of Ontario
VOW	Voice of Women
WCTU	Woman's Christian Temperance Union
WLC	Women's Liberal Commission
WPA	Women for Political Action
YWCA	Young Women's Christian Association

TOEING THE LINES

*of - Fulenwider :
(women's) movements need
to maintain a creative
tension between their
politics + their vision*

1

Independence versus Partisanship: Dilemmas in the Political History of Women in English Canada

The Women's Good Government League ... stands on the principle of cooperation and is assured that women can best serve their country by keeping out of parties and away from the party machines.
Woman's Century, 1918[1]

I couldn't open my mouth to say the simplest thing without it appearing in the papers. I was a curiosity, a freak. And you know the way the world treats freaks.
Agnes Macphail, 1949[2]

The political experiences of women in Canada have been shaped by many influences, some of which are related directly to women, and others of which emanate from broader political processes and structures. Existing research on female political involvement has interpreted these experiences in reference to two main sets of factors, one psychological, including conventional patterns of gender role socialization, and the second structural, involving discriminatory practices within party organizations.[3]

While this prevailing focus upon role constraints and structural limitations reveals some of the obstacles to female political activity, it has obscured an important historical dimension within the political development of English-Canadian women. Boldly stated, the ideological and organizational dilemmas surrounding female enfranchisement in English Canada provide a critical and widely neglected perspective on subsequent political experiences in this culture. In the following discussion, we shall argue that early feminism and suffragism in English Canada were part of a broader progressive challenge to the traditional two-party system and, furthermore, that these movements became locked in the horns of a trying political dilemma: on the one hand, early women's groups were attracted toward a position of political independence, which could guarantee both organizational autonomy and purity; on the other hand, they were drawn toward conventional partisanship, which might better ensure their political influence and legislative success. Taken together, this tension between independence and partisanship within the context of a changing party system helped to define the parameters of women's political history in English Canada for many decades. A similar dilemma, in fact, continues to shape the development of contemporary English-Canadian feminism, as well as the broader relationship between women and the present party system.

In practical terms, this tension between independence and partisanship has limited the exercise of effective political power by women in English Canada.[4] Ironically, even though females in some regions had the right to vote – primarily in local school board elections – as early as the eighteenth century, and although many were organized into such party affiliates as the Toronto Women's Liberal Association prior to the formal extension of the franchise, few entered the electorate as politically skilled or equal participants.[5]

This situation resulted in part from the ideological position adopted by mainstream suffragists, which began with the assumption that females would spread a mantle of purity from their private domestic sphere to the public, political domain. In the words of the *Woman's Century*, quoted above, new women voters were advised to avoid the corrupting, immoral party organizations and to adopt an independent, non-partisan route to national influence. The limitations of this strategy, as applied within an essentially partisan, parliamentary system, combined with women's cooptation into separate auxiliaries within the two major parties, are reflected clearly in Agnes Macphail's commentary on life in the House of Commons. More than fifteen years after the formal extension of the federal franchise, Macphail remained the sole female member of parliament, a 'freak' who reluctantly symbolized a continuing distance between women and political power in Canada.

What was the organizational and ideological background to this dilemma between independence and partisanship? To what extent has the subsequent political history of women in English Canada been shaped by early feminist experiences? And how have women recently begun to question and to challenge their lack of political and especially partisan influence? These are the main questions which inform our discussion of the political history of women in English Canada.

ORIGINS OF THE MOVEMENT

The formal beginnings of the suffrage movement in English Canada are generally dated from the founding of the Toronto Women's Literary Society in 1877.[6] Composed primarily of well-educated and professional women of the Protestant middle classes, the Literary Society disguised its suffragist leanings until the 1880s, when Dr Emily Stowe, her daughter (Dr Augusta Stowe-Gullen), and a number of other activists established the Canadian Woman Suffrage Association and a series of similarly directed organizations.[7]

Much of the ideological and organizational strength of English-Canadian suffragism developed as a result of ties between this movement and other reform groups which operated during the turn-of-the-century period. As indicated by Carol Bacchi's (1983) research on major suffragist leaders, the movement attracted many men and women who were also affiliated with temperance, urban improvement, and civic education activities. Organized pressure for the vote was thus allied with a broader reformist response to the rapid pace of industrialization, urbanization, and the perceived decline of traditional values in many Western societies, including Canadian.

In addition, women in Toronto and the western provinces were particularly influenced by feminist and suffragist initiatives in other Anglo-American democracies; they frequently merged elements of the American and British movements with an essentially moderate, non-militant approach which was reflective of English-Canadian culture more generally.[8] Moreover, Canadian feminists also benefited from the increasing opportunities available to middle-class women in education, professional employment, and volunteer work, and thus shared a growing international commitment to broadening their own political rights.[9]

What rationale did English-Canadian suffragists offer in pursuit of the vote? The historical literature on this subject demonstrates a number of important divisions within the movement, particularly along generational and ideological lines. As in the American case, English-Canadian activists included an older 'hard-core' minority which sought to challenge the discriminatory treatment of women in virtually all facets of social life, including education, employment, political rights, and, most importantly, the family.[10] Believing that females justly deserved the same degree of individual independence that had accrued to males, 'hard-core' feminists, such as Flora MacDonald Denison, campaigned outside the more moderate, reformist mainstream of 'social feminism' in English Canada.[11]

TABLE 1.1
Legislative changes affecting the political status of women in Canada

Jurisdiction	Date of female enfranchisement[a]	Legislative sponsor	Date of eligibility to hold office	First woman elected
Manitoba	28 January 1916	Liberal gov't	28 January 1916	29 June 1920
Saskatchewan	14 March 1916	Liberal gov't	14 March 1916	29 June 1919
Alberta	19 April 1916	Liberal gov't	19 April 1916	7 June 1917
British Columbia	5 April 1917	Liberal gov't	5 April 1917	24 January 1918[b]
Ontario	23 April 1917	Conserv. gov't	4 April 1919	4 August 1943
Canada	24 May 1918, full female franchise[c]	Union gov't	7 July 1919	6 December 1921
Nova Scotia	26 April 1918	Liberal gov't	26 April 1918	7 June 1960
New Brunswick	17 April 1919	Liberal gov't	9 March 1934	10 October 1967
Prince Edward Is.	3 May 1922	Liberal gov't	3 May 1922	11 May 1970
Newfoundland	13 April 1925[d]	Conserv. gov't	13 April 1925	17 May 1930[b]
Quebec	25 April 1940	Liberal gov't	25 April 1940	14 December 1961

a Denotes date of royal assent.
b Denotes victory in by-election.
c The Military Voters Act and the Wartime Elections Act, which both received royal assent in September 1917, enfranchised women who were British subjects and who had served in any branch of the military, or who had a close relative serving in the armed forces of Canada or Great Britain.
d According to this 1925 legislation, female voters had to be age 25 or over to vote, while men could vote at age 21. This disparity was rectified by the Terms of Union of Newfoundland with Canada, 1948.
Sources: Catherine L. Cleverdon, *The Woman Suffrage Movement in Canada* (Toronto: University of Toronto Press, 1974) and Terence H. Qualter, *The Election Process in Canada* (Toronto: McGraw-Hill, 1970), 9, 52

The ideological and organizational pivot of Canadian suffragism thus resembled its 'social feminist' counterpart in the United States, which linked 'suffrage and temperance and other crusades, such as civil service reform, conservation, child labor laws, mothers' pensions, municipal improvements, educational reform, pure food and drug laws, industrial commissions, social justice and peace.'[12] 'Maternal' or 'social' feminism in English Canada was, as its name suggests, predicated upon a fundamental belief in the necessity for social reform and for women's participation in this process. Unlike more radical 'hard-core' arguments, it elevated Protestant social reform above demands for legal emancipation and claimed that the granting of the vote to women was essential for general social improvement.[13]

The manner in which organized feminism developed held important implications for women's relationship to the Canadian political system. For much of its history, the core of the movement remained in Toronto, which served as the headquarters for such groups as the Dominion Women's Enfranchisement Association and the Canadian Suffrage Association. While claiming to be nationwide, these organizations actually 'had few affiliates and even less control outside Toronto' – where, ironically, the initial legislative successes of the movement were achieved (see table 1.1).[14]

The regional divisions and conflicts which characterized other Canadian social movements thus affected suffragist organization in an especially damaging manner, since the latter needed to operate on a region-by-region basis in order to secure the provincial franchise, while it also required an image of national influence in order to achieve the vote federally. These organizational demands were not easily reconcilable; as Catherine L. Cleverdon (1974) points out: 'The small but valiant bands of women found it necessary to concentrate their political efforts upon their provincial governments, and this undoubtedly militated against the successful formation of any truly nation-wide suffrage association.'[15] Indeed, in the absence of such a national organization, suffragists relied heavily upon alliances with older, established, and generally conservative women's groups, including the Woman's Christian Temperance Union (WCTU), the Federated Women's Institutes, and the National Council of Women of Canada (NCWC).[16] Particularly in the case of the NCWC, which formally endorsed enfranchisement in 1910, suffragists gained an important element of national visibility and credibility, at the same time as they became dependent upon increasingly moderate, social feminist strategies which were acceptable to the NCWC leadership and similar coalition partners.

The organizational features of Canadian suffragism thus held important consequences for the momentum of the movement. Cleverdon's historical study offers abundant evidence regarding its episodic or 'fits-and-starts' development; enfranchisement organizations were established, activated, and then receded into dormancy and were reactivated with great frequency. As rapid legislative progress was made in one region, particularly in the western provinces during the years 1914-17 (see table 1.1), it was expected that a growing momentum would carry the cause from coast to coast. This sense of momentum, however, overshadowed the fact that the women's movement remained small and weak in national terms. Moreover, its affiliates in Francophone Quebec and Atlantic Canada were particularly slow to develop, meaning that the organizational strength of the movement existed outside of those areas where women's traditional roles were most constraining and, in the view of many activists, most in need of legislative reform.[17]

SOCIAL FEMINISM AND THE PARTIES

The major political effects of early feminist history in English Canada, however, concern women's relationship with the established party system. In common with other reformist movements of the early twentieth century, including those which embraced labour and agrarian interests in the western provinces, major streams within Canadian suffragism rejected the evils of 'partyism' in favour of an independent, virtually suprapolitical posture.[18]

This rejection of conventional partisanship grew out of a broader distrust of established political structures, which was reflected quite generally in Western Canadian progressivism. As described in the classic study by W.L. Morton (1967), leading progressive farmers and trade unionists supported direct or populist democracy, based upon citizen-initiated legislation, referenda, and recall propositions.[19] Many progressives believed that political corruption and the absence of regional and group representation under existing arrangements resulted from party control over political nomination and election procedures. In the words of Morton, progressives endorsed a populist system to replace conventional representative democracy, in order to 'break the hold "bosses" and "machines" serving the "invisible government" of the "interests" were alleged to have on the government of the country.'[20] Many suffragists, especially in Western Canada, shared this belief in the intrinsically corrupting, immoral, and impure character of established party institutions.

One of the most vocal critics of this system was Nellie McClung, a nationally prominent suffragist and social feminist who was especially active in both Manitoba and Alberta. McClung's diary recorded her initial impressions of party politics, gathered during a Liberal campaign meeting which she attended in rural Manitoba during the 1880s. Women in the audience were exhorted by provincial Premier Thomas Greenway 'to see that their menfolk voted and voted right and this he said (so even we could understand) meant voting Liberal.'[21] After two questions regarding women's rights were ignored by the chairman, McClung left the meeting with a firm belief that politics was 'a sordid, grubby business ... I do not want to be a reformer.'[22]

McClung's subsequent exposure to WCTU activities and to Women's Press Club and Local Council work in Winnipeg led toward a reversal of this early view regarding reform. As a suffrage activist in the Political Equality League during later years, however, McClung reflected many elements of her older anti-party attitude. In fact, like many American social feminists, she merged a progressive critique of party politics with social reform arguments in favour of female enfranchisement: 'If politics are corrupt, it is all the more reason that a new element should be introduced. Women will I believe supply that new element, that purifying influence. Men and women were intended to work together, and will work more ideally together, than apart, and just as the mother's influence as well as the father's is needed in the bringing up of children and in the affairs of the home, so are they needed in the larger home, – the state.'[23] Politics was thus perceived by McClung and many of her allies as housekeeping on a grand scale. If women could introduce order, morality, and purpose to the domestic household, then they could surely extend this positive influence to 'the larger home, – the state.' The evils of partyism would finally be superseded, following female suffrage, by a reform-oriented system of good government.

Aside from the utopian expectations which were generated by this approach, and which were particularly significant in the decades after 1918, McClung's argument was important because it cemented the alliance between mainstream social feminism, on the one hand, and parties which were anxious to co-opt progressive interests – including women – on the other. In the Prairie region, which is useful for illustrative purposes, McClung established what might be termed an 'arm's-length alliance' with the pro-reform Manitoba Liberals in 1914, on the basis of an agreement that the latter would introduce suffrage legislation once they defeated the governing provincial Conservatives. The Liberals lost the subsequent election despite the efforts of McClung (who noted that she 'never even took car fare from the Liberal party ... I am a freelance in this fight') and others, but later won power in 1915.[24] The party indeed sponsored suffrage legislation following its election, as did the Alberta Liberals for whom McClung campaigned successfully as a provincial candidate in the 1917 elections.

Perhaps the most troubling aspect of this alliance was its effect upon newly elected suffragists: McClung, for example, grew increasingly uncomfortable in her role as an 'independent' MLA within a distinctively partisan caucus and legislature. Believing in the need for non-partisanship, however, McClung voted her conscience in the Alberta house, which generally meant crossing party lines to support government (UFA)-sponsored legislation. The frustration which greeted this direct exposure to political and especially parliamentary decision-making, combined with McClung's defeat in the subsequent provincial election, was echoed across Canada as other suffragists and similarly minded reformers entered the party-dominated system, only to find that their broader structural and issue (especially prohibitionist) objectives were marginalized by the very parliamentary system which they had set out to transform. Despite their formal commitments to political independence, therefore, suffragists soon discovered that they were wedged within the same partisan political system which they had earlier promised to eliminate, or at least transcend.

THE FEDERAL FRANCHISE

The difficulties associated with operating within an established party system and, at the same time, maintaining a critical distance and independence from that system are evidenced clearly in events surrounding the granting of the federal franchise. While legislation to enfranchise widows and unmarried women was presented as early as 1883 by Sir John A. Macdonald, it was not until after provincial suffrage was enacted in Ontario and the western provinces that this issue received serious consideration on the federal level.[25] Suffrage thus reached the national agenda at the same time as women's contribution to the World War I effort was becoming increasingly evident, and when the Union government of Prime Minister Robert Borden faced a major electoral and political challenge concerning the issue of conscription.

While the basic facts of the conscription crisis are relatively well known, only limited attention has been given to the organizational dynamics of Canadian suffragism during this period and their relationship to wartime legislation. One source of internal conflict among English-Canadian feminists existed long before 1917, since it dated back to older generational and ideological differences between radical 'hard-core,' represented by the Canadian Suffrage Association (CSA), and more moderate 'social,' including the NCWC, WCTU, and National Equal Franchise Union (NEFU), elements in the movement.

Racism, conscription, and the war itself further divided feminist ranks during the period of World War I. As demonstrated in historical research by Gloria Geller (1976) and Bacchi (1983), the political or hard-core stream represented by the CSA generally resisted appeals to Anglo-Saxon superiority and purity which were inherent in government-sponsored legislation to permit a limited female franchise in 1917.[26] CSA activists also tended to be urban pacifists who remained suspicious of the government's motives in introducing the Wartime Elections Act. In the words of the CSA president, Dr Margaret Gordon, this proposal constituted 'a win-the-election measure ... it would be direct and at the same time more honest if the bill simply stated that all who did not pledge themselves to vote Conservative would be disfranchised. This might be satisfactory to some but it is not a Canadian-born woman's ideal of free government, nor can anyone who approves of this disfranchise bill claim to represent Canadian suffragettes.'[27]

By way of contrast, the more conservative mainstream of English-Canadian feminism – and particularly the members of its elite – were more willing to adopt racial and patriotic (that is, pro-war) arguments in their pursuit of the franchise. Bacchi (1983:141) points out that the four activists who surveyed women's opinions regarding full versus partial federal suffrage (on behalf of the prime minister) were all married to Conservatives. In addition, it is notable that such pro-reform Liberal women as Nellie McClung agreed with limited enfranchisement and expressed racial and patriotic views in support of this legislation.[28] Mainstream social feminists, and most notably the presidents of the NCWC, NEFU, Imperial Order Daughters of the Empire (IODE), and the Ontario WCTU, thus endorsed what Cleverdon (1974) terms 'one of the most bitterly debated and controversial measures in Canadian history.'[29]

The Wartime Elections Act, which received royal assent on 29 September 1917, ultimately enfranchised only those women who were British subjects of age 21 and over, and who had a close family member serving in the Canadian or British armed forces. In political terms, the effects of this bill were as predicted, since newly enfranchised women helped to re-elect the pro-conscription government of Prime Minister Borden. Furthermore, once established in its new term, the Union government convened a Women's War Conference in Ottawa and enacted full suffrage legislation in 1918.[30]

While these developments suggest that Canadian women made successful use of the federal party system, it is important to recognize that their 1918 victory entailed major political costs. First, and probably most important for the future relationship between women and political power in Canada, the key arguments of both hard-core (equal rights on the basis of political justice) and social feminists (social reform incorporating the vote) were marginalized in the federal debate, which centred more directly around conscription and the electoral viability of Borden's Union government. Therefore, both the women's rights and social reform concerns of Canadian feminism were wedged outside the main national agenda, such that federal suffrage was largely achieved through a series of political choices made by, and in the interests of, the government of the day. Suffragists thus found themselves formally empowered within, but substantively distant from, the very system of national party government which they had long distrusted.

Second, the federal victory and subsequent enfranchisement bills in Atlantic Canada left organized feminism with no clear strategy for future action. It is to these post-enfranchisement dilemmas that we now turn our attention.

THE AFTERMATH OF SUFFRAGE

As in the United States, many women voters in English Canada entered the electorate expecting a social and political millennium. The ideology of social feminism, which emphasized the pure reformist motives of women, promised a restoration of traditional moral values in both the home and the state. This commitment to uplifting was not easily translated into practical action on a mass scale, however. As Nellie McClung reflected during the 1930s, 'We were obsessed with the belief that we could cleanse and purify the world by law. We said women were naturally lovers of peace and purity, temperance and justice. There never has been a campaign like the suffrage campaign ... But when all was over, and the smoke of battle cleared away, something happened to us. Our forces, so well organized for the campaign, began to dwindle. We had no constructive program for making a new world ... So the enfranchised women drifted. Many are still drifting.'[31]

As McClung observed, the divisions within suffragist ranks which had existed throughout the early decades of the twentieth century deepened during subsequent years. In many regions, feminists and other newly enfranchised women split politically along demographic lines which had conventionally divided men. In this manner, class, ethnic, occupational, regional, and rural / urban differences shaped female political perceptions and often obscured earlier visions of a single emancipated womanhood, united in its goals and experiences.

On an organizational level, these internal cleavages became increasingly visible. Research by Bacchi (1983), for example, reveals the fragmentation surrounding Canadian efforts to establish a separate woman's party in the years immediately after federal suffrage.[32] In 1918, a number of social feminists in the NEFU founded this party, with the stated goal of extending their political gains as enfranchised women. While the objective of consolidating earlier achievements was probably shared by many feminists, a separate party strategy under the leadership of pro-war, anti-labour, and generally Conservative-affiliated women from Toronto met with less than solid support. Not surprisingly, the Woman's Party was frequently condemned as being urban, elitist, and a Conservative front group. Its failure to develop as a viable and autonomous political organization paralleled the fate met by a similar National Women's Party in the United States, where females were also wedged by established lines of party organization, political ideology, and social class.[33]

What distinguished English-Canadian from American feminism, however, was the absence of strong national organization following enfranchisement. Mainstream social feminists in the United States recognized the importance of political education and a cohesive social reform lobby at the state and federal levels; in 1920, they launched the non-partisan National League of Women Voters (NLWV) to fulfil this mandate.[34]

With the important exception of British Columbia, English-Canadian suffragists established few ongoing organizations following enfranchisement, and women generally floundered politically as a result. It was widely believed, including by such prominent social feminists as Nellie McClung and Louise McKinney, that Canadian women voters should return to their homes after World War I and, using their domestic environment as a base, work to mobilize public opinion around such issues as the minimum wage and industrial working conditions.[35] Unfortunately, the organizational structures necessary to achieve systematic results were generally lacking.

One notable exception to this pattern developed in British Columbia, where social feminists continued to remain active in politics following provincial enfranchisement. As a group, BC suffragists employed their alliance with the provincial Liberals in order to retain significant legislative influence through the late 1920s. In fact, the path adopted by BC feminists, which involved transforming the suffragist Political Equality League (established in 1910) into the post-suffragist New Era League, coincided with similar national efforts in the United States, where the pro-vote National American Woman Suffrage Association became the League of Women Voters following 1920.

Many of the major policy concerns of the New Era League paralleled those which had motivated earlier suffragist activities. As summarized by Elsie Gregory MacGill (1981) in the story of her mother's social feminist involvement, the main priorities for reform legislation in BC included prison and family law reform; infant protection; industrial health and safety; minimum wage legislation for women; mothers' pensions; a Juvenile Courts Act; and improved public health, library, and education systems.[36]

The ability of BC feminists to ensure government sponsorship and passage of this legislation was related to two factors: first, a number of active suffragists, including 'high Tory' Helen Gregory MacGill, became party members after the provincial Liberals adopted woman suffrage in their platforms of 1912 and following.[37] In addition, the fact that Liberals in the Prairie provinces also favoured and ultimately enacted female enfranchisement legislation (see table 1.1) led active suffragists to join the party and to establish the BC Women's Liberal Association during this same period.[38]

Second, alongside their partisan ties, social feminists in BC retained an independent women's network through such groups as the New Era League. After a prominent suffragist and founder of the Women's Liberal Association, Mary Ellen Smith, was elected to the provincial legislature in 1918 and later appointed Minister without Portfolio in 1921 (thus becoming the first female cabinet minister in the British Empire), feminists outside the legislature began to channel their reformist concerns through Smith to the provincial government.[39] Smith's position in the Liberal cabinet, combined with the ability of social feminists in BC to retain some organizational continuity following enfranchisement, thus ensured the passage of significant reform measures, including mothers' pensions and a Minimum Wage Act.[40]

With their active ally inside the chambers of government, social feminists in BC found that many reform bills received favourable reception during the critical first decade after suffrage. However, this successful combination in BC of partisan alliances, including the election and cabinet appointment of an active feminist woman, with politically independent and effective women's organizations became the exception rather than the rule for many years following 1918. Indeed, as evidenced on the federal level during the 1920s, women's rights to vote and to hold public office generally had minimal effects on the broader political system.

THE PROBLEM OF PUBLIC OFFICE

Despite the early successes of the Dominion Women's Enfranchisement
Association in electing two women to the Toronto School Board in 1892,
the election of females to public office was not a high priority for mainstream social feminism in English Canada. According to Bacchi (1983),
efforts to elect women faltered as older hard-core feminists became increasingly outnumbered by moderate social reformers, who attached relatively little importance to candidacy and office-holding. In fact, many
social feminists questioned how the bulk of married, child-rearing women
could devote themselves to any career outside the home, including politics.
In the words of one activist, there were 'plenty of "unmarried women and
widows, and married women with grown-up children" ' to work in elections and run for office.[41]

In light of this prevailing view, it is not surprising that relatively few
women contested public office, and even fewer held elective office, in the
years following formal enfranchisement. On the federal level, for example,
only four women were nominated as candidates in the 1921 general elections, representing 0.6% of the total federal candidates for that year.[42]
The sole woman elected to the House of Commons in 1921 was Agnes
Macphail, a 31-year-old unmarried schoolteacher who represented the
rural Ontario riding of South-East Grey.

Macphail's political career, including her experiences as an MP and
subsequently as an Ontario MPP, is important not only because it confronted many of the psychological and structural obstacles generally faced
by women in politics, but also because it reflected a more specific tension
between partisanship and independence in the political history of women
in Canada. In terms of general barriers to elite level participation, the
nomination, election, and legislative tenure of Agnes Macphail had much
in common with the experiences of other women in Canada and elsewhere.
For example, like many female candidates in competitive ridings, she had
to defeat ten males to win nomination initially, and then withstood strong
protests from both the constituency organization and electorate at large
because of her gender.[43] In Macphail's own words, 'It took strenuous
campaigning for two months just to stop people from saying, "We can't
have a woman." I won that election in spite of being a woman.'[44]

Once she had defeated the incumbent Conservative MP in South-East
Grey, Macphail's entrance to the House of Commons was treated on the
social or women's pages of the Canadian press, where her wardrobe and
personal style were closely scrutinized.[45] This treatment as a new MP
encouraged Macphail to adopt an increasingly critical perspective toward

her own political experiences, even though she had not been active previously as a feminist or suffragist.[46] First, and very importantly, Macphail's
legislative work suggested to her that progressive men were not immune
to the general biases of males against females in politics, since J.S.
Woodsworth (at the time a Labour MP from Manitoba) once confessed:
'I still don't think a woman has any place in politics.'[47] Second, Macphail
learned that few policy concerns raised by Canadian feminists received
serious attention within legislative bodies. She therefore worked diligently
on family allowance, equal pay, and women's prison issues, even though
her initial priorities had concerned the rights of Ontario farmers.

Third, Macphail's experiences as a provincial and federal legislator led
her to speak publicly about continuing obstacles to female political involvement. During the 1930s, she rejected at least one proposal which
would have guaranteed female representation on all new CCF committees,
arguing that women could not demand special considerations on the basis
of gender.[48] Nevertheless, she believed strongly that males would not
easily concede or even share control over political decision-making. In a
1949 article entitled 'Men Want to Hog Everything,' Macphail foreshadowed the more recent observations of Liberal MP Judy LaMarsh: 'The
old ideas of chivalry justify men in thinking of women as a rather poor
choice in human beings. Put her on a pedestal, then put pedestal and all
in a cage.'[49]

What was specifically Canadian about Macphail's experiences, however, was the extent to which her own career reflected ongoing political
tensions between partisanship and independence. Most notably, Macphail
was elected on the platform of the United Farmers of Ontario, a primarily
agrarian-based rural organization which rejected conventional 'partyism'
in favour of direct group representation in the House of Commons.[50] Her
role as a parliamentarian was therefore independent of the two established national parties, which did not elect woman members other than
the spouses of former (male) MPs until the 1950s, at the same time as it
was related to ongoing efforts to challenge Liberal and Conservative dominance through a progressive labour / agrarian coalition at the federal
level. Ultimately, the parliamentary alliance with which Macphail was
associated formed one basis for the Co-operative Commonwealth
Federation, established in 1932.

Macphail's political impact as a legislator was thus constrained by
many of the same factors which had affected early feminist activism in
English Canada. Like the suffrage movement itself, Macphail rejected
conventional partisanship and established her legislative career outside

the parameters of mainstream party politics. While this 'anti-partyism' was consistent with Macphail's progressive beliefs, just as it coincided with the reformist tenor of Canadian suffragism, such a position tended to limit her influence within an essentially partisan, parliamentary system.

On the other side of the coin, Macphail's commitment to political independence was complicated by a need to form coalitions in order to challenge conventional two-party dominance in English Canada. In Macphail's case, a parliamentary alliance with pacifists and Western Canadian socialists eventually cost her the seat in South-East Grey, since the constituents of this rural riding were unsympathetic toward many of the political partnerships and causes with which their MP was associated.[51]

Moreover, Macphail's ability to fashion an independent position around the rights of women was hampered by both consciousness and organization during this period: not only was there limited understanding of gender inequality and its implications, but also most established organizations of Canadian women were ideologically opposed to the broader political views held by Agnes Macphail. Notably, Macphail was generally viewed as an agrarian progressive and, ultimately, as a leading Canadian socialist and pacifist. Her statements in support of the Glace Bay miners and against Canadian military academies, for example, were vehemently denounced by IODE, the Women's Canadian Club, and other established groups which had staked out a role as the legitimate and representative voices of Canadian women.[52]

It was not until the relatively legalistic matter of female appointment to the Senate was broached that Canadian women began to overcome these internal differences and to pursue a more unified, coherent political strategy. In fact, the judicial victory associated with the Persons Case in 1929 resembled closely the efforts to establish a royal commission on the status of women nearly forty years later, as well as the subsequent constitutional changes won by Canadian women in 1981. It is to the issue of Senate appointments that we now turn our attention.

THE 'PERSONS CASE'

The issue of women's eligibility for Canadian Senate appointments, which centred around legal interpretations of the word 'persons,' came to public attention during the year following full federal enfranchisement. In 1919, the first president of the Federated Women's Institutes of Canada, Edmonton police magistrate Emily Murphy, received unanimous support from her organization for a resolution which encouraged the government of Canada to appoint a woman to the Senate. The NCWC and the Montreal Women's Club passed similar resolutions, which were subsequently rejected by the federal Conservative government on the basis of a narrow constitutional reading of the word 'persons.'[53] A specific nominee to the Senate was suggested by the Montreal Women's Club, which endorsed Judge Murphy on the basis of her suffragist and social feminist efforts in co-ordination with Nellie McClung, Henrietta Muir Edwards (an activist in the Alberta branch of the NCWC), and provincial UFA legislators Irene Parlby and Louise McKinney.

One difficult problem which confronted Murphy and her supporters grew out of partisan divisions among Canadian women. According to Rudy Marchildon (1981), attempts to have the 'persons' issue raised at major party conventions during the 1920s were unsuccessful, largely because many women's groups (including the Montreal Women's Club) were composed primarily of Liberals who objected to petitioning the then-Conservative government. Once the Tories were defeated federally, fears that a newly elected Liberal government might appoint British Columbia MLA Mary Ellen Smith to the Senate prevented many Conservatives from actively pursuing the 'persons' issue.[54]

Fortunately for the cause of female senators, Emily Murphy learned in 1927 of an obscure provision in the Supreme Court Act which permitted interested parties to request constitutional interpretation of points under the BNA Act. She then enlisted the support of her four suffragist colleagues from Alberta and, on 19 October 1927, all five women petitioned the Supreme Court of Canada. Since their legal expenses were assumed by the federal government, Murphy's group selected a prominent Toronto lawyer, Newton Wesley Rowell, to present the case both in Ottawa and, subsequently, before the Privy Council in London. Rowell had strongly supported woman suffrage during his term as Liberal Opposition leader in Ontario, and his wife had served during that same period as the first president of the Toronto Women's Liberal Association.[55]

Despite the well-sustained arguments presented by Rowell in Ottawa, all five Supreme Court justices who heard the case concurred in the following judgment, delivered on 24 April 1928: 'Women are not "qualified persons" within the meaning of Section 24 of the BNA Act, 1867, and therefore are not eligible for appointment by the Governor General to the Senate of Canada.'[56] The solicitor-general in the federal Liberal government, Lucien Cannon, supported by Quebec special counsel Charles Lanctot, had successfully argued that the original intent of the BNA Act was strictly for men, as 'qualified persons,' to be appointed to the Senate. The federal government position also maintained that if a more liberal and contemporary interpretation were to be attached to 'persons,' then such changes would require legislative rather than judicial action.

Undeterred by this defeat in the Supreme Court of Canada, and by the failure of the federal justice minister to introduce amending legislation as promised during the 1928 parliamentary session, Judge Murphy made plans to present her case in London. On 18 October 1929, approximately two years following an initial petition to the Supreme Court of Canada, the Judicial Committee of the Privy Council announced its decision that women were indeed persons and thus eligible for appointment to the Senate. This decision was greeted with 'much gratification' by Judge Murphy and her allies, who believed that the 'Persons' judgment at last conferred 'full political rights' upon the women of Canada.[57]

In the years following 1929, neither Emily Murphy nor any of her four colleagues was appointed to the Senate. Apparently, their feminist activities and, in the case of Murphy, Conservative family connections eliminated them from consideration by a Liberal government which was unwilling to risk the political costs which might be attached to such nominations, especially in the province of Quebec. The Senate thus became for women what it had long remained for men, namely a regionally and religiously balanced Upper House which rewarded loyal party activists rather than non- or minimally partisan social reformers.

Not surprisingly, then, the first woman to be appointed to the Senate was a well-known Ontario Liberal, Cairine Wilson, who was nominated in 1930 by the King government. Unlike Murphy, McClung, or other feminist women who had entered into alliances with the Liberals, Senator Wilson was a seasoned and reliable partisan who had led the Eastern Ontario Liberal Women's Association, the Ottawa Liberal Women's Club, and the National Federation of Liberal Women. Her father was a wealthy Laurier Liberal from Montreal, who had also held a Senate seat.

Aside from these obvious political credentials, Senator Wilson was an uncontroversial social choice as the first woman in the Upper House. She had raised a large family, was active in church and charity work, and believed firmly in traditional moral and family values. For example, when asked in one interview about her interest in serving on the Senate divorce committee, Wilson replied 'that she had no such ambition, and that she had been so busy with her home and her babies she hadn't time to think about divorce.'[58]

The press response to Wilson's appointment echoed conventional views regarding the civilizing influence which women would bring to public life. The new senator was predicted to become 'a charming and hospitable hostess' in Ottawa, a welcome 'adornment' to the city and the nation's Upper House.[59] In the words of a *Maclean's* journalist, Senator Wilson was 'for all of her wealth and social prestige and political distinction ... first, last, and always a woman – a wife and mother of eight children.'[60]

The second woman appointed to the Senate was also a party stalwart who had served on the national executive of the Conservative Women's Association; Iva Fallis, from Ontario, was nominated in 1935 by the Tory government of R.B. Bennett. It was not until 1953 that additional women were appointed to the Senate, and not until the 1970s that two publicly prominent women, Thérèse Casgrain and Florence Bird, were named on the basis of their independent, non-partisan contributions to improving the status of women. The latter appointments were more closely related to the second wave of women's rights activism in Canada, discussed below, than to the premature expectations of political equality which accompanied victory in the Persons Case.

BETWEEN THE MOVEMENTS

In the years following federal enfranchisement, social reform legislation during the 1920s, and the Persons Case, most Canadian women reassumed the traditional domestic responsibilities which they had performed prior to World War I. The world Depression played a major role in limiting the number of jobs available to either men or women, and prevailing beliefs that whatever work existed should go to male breadwinners had an especially devastating effect upon female employment throughout the 1930s.

As women re-entered the home, frequently with the blessings of such prominent feminists as Nellie McClung, they helped to shape a society which was considerably different from that of earlier years. Perhaps the most significant change affecting women after 1920 was the increased level and acceptability of both female education and employment. As Mary Vipond (1977) demonstrates, growing numbers of single girls – and especially those of the middle classes – were encouraged during this period to develop career goals for the years prior to their marriage. A sound formal education was viewed as one critical element in such development since, over the longer term, 'a well-educated woman would be a more capable, more self-confident, and therefore a *better* wife and mother.'[61]

The household itself was also transformed during this period, as manufacturers introduced new 'labour-saving' inventions to the marketplace. A wide array of new devices, from electric irons and toasters to dishwashers and sewing machines, was advertised as the cure for domestic drudgery. Married women could thus devote the bulk of their energies to the family, and particularly to the declining numbers of children who were born following 1920. As reflected in mass circulation magazines of the day, women were expected to develop a more trained and intense approach to their child-rearing responsibilities.[62]

This modernization of the domestic household, combined with increased opportunities for female employment and education, held differing political implications for middle- and working-class women. In the former case, the inter-war years were generally characterized by organizational continuity within such groups as the NCWC (established in 1893), the YWCA (established in 1894), and the Canadian Federation of University Women (CFUW, established in 1919). These voluntary associations, along with the newer Canadian Federation of Business and Professional Women's Clubs (established in 1930), remained actively committed to the social reformist goals which had earlier motivated mainstream English-Canadian feminism. Similarly, the various women's associations within the two older political parties continued to operate through the 1930s, and to promote in general an auxiliary or supportive role for women in politics (see chapter 5, below).

By way of contrast, these same years were a time of considerable ferment within the Canadian left, and particularly among women on the left. Research by John Manley (1980) on the Ontario CCF, for example, suggests that some working-class women rejected both the conventional feminist model of moderate social reform, as well as the traditional partisan model of women as ancillary political workers and primary social and fund-raising organizers.[63] The Women's Joint Committee, which existed in Toronto for approximately six months during 1936, was a forerunner of more recent efforts to establish politically assertive women's groups within the major parties. Although the committee was weakened organizationally by a willingness to co-operate in 'united front' activities, it strongly endorsed leadership training programs for party women, publicly accessible birth control clinics, equal pay statutes, and other progressive positions on policies of specific relevance to Canadian women.[64]

This ferment among women on the left, as well as the expansion of voluntary organizations among middle-class women, was temporarily interrupted by the events of World War II. Wartime mobilization drew hundreds of thousands of Canadian women into the armed forces, defence industries, service sector, and agriculture.[65] Child-care facilities and special tax provisions were established to encourage married women in particular into the wartime labour force.

Following the end of hostilities, when women's employment was no longer deemed to be 'of national importance,' most day-care centres were closed and federal tax statutes reverted to their traditional format.[66] As in the years after World War I, women were expected to surrender their jobs to returning veterans – an arrangement to which most willingly consented – and to resume their domestic duties. Therefore, despite assumptions that wartime employment would permanently alter the status of women in Canada, it generally served as only a temporary break with conventional gender role norms and expectations.[67]

An important new influence upon the experiences of post-war women, however, was the economic prosperity and sense of confidence which pervaded North American society during these years. As in the decade after World War I, middle-class women in particular were pressured to consume on behalf of their households, and to provide emotional and personal comforts to their upwardly mobile husbands and 'baby boom' offspring.

The conflict between these domestic pressures and conventional role responsibilities, on the one hand, and the social experiences and expectations of women outside the home, on the other, held important political consequences for later years. That is, as middle-class women were exposed to broadened educational and occupational opportunities, many of which resulted from an enlarged service sector necessary to operate the modern welfare state, they confronted an official as well as informal ideology which was grounded in older, increasingly outdated social values. This contradiction between the post-war 'feminine mystique' of contented and conventional domesticity and a growing sense of personal restiveness and questioning provided one basis from which the second wave of women's rights activism developed in English Canada.[68]

A renewed feminist movement also grew out of post-war activities on the Canadian left, where the gap between egalitarian socialist ideology and internal party practices – noted earlier by Agnes Macphail and others – continued to widen. As highlighted by Dean Beeby (1982) in his study of the Ontario CCF, relatively few members of the party's political elite were females, even though the organization claimed to represent the interests of all women (notably, the provincial caucus became the first in

Canada to introduce equal pay legislation, in 1949).[69] Moreover, the CCF in Ontario employed the bulk of its female membership in social, fundraising, canvassing, and publicity work, a pattern which was reinforced following the appointment in 1942 of a separate women's committee. While the professed goal of this committee and a subsequent Status of Women Committee (established in 1947) was to increase female party involvement at all levels, such groups frequently evolved into auxiliary-type associations which specialized in consumer price monitoring, bazaars, cookbook projects, and other activities of a stereotypically feminine nature.[70]

This continuation of conventional role norms and power arrangements within the organized left provided an important groundwork for subsequent radical and socialist feminist movements in English Canada.

THE RENEWAL OF CANADIAN FEMINISM

The renewal of organized feminism in English Canada is often linked with the establishment in 1960 of Voice of Women (VOW), a non-partisan, grass-roots association which was formed to oppose nuclear arms testing and weapons proliferation. From the outset, VOW remained a loosely organized group whose main goal was 'to unite women in concern for the future of the world.'[71] The membership of VOW reached approximately 5,000 in 1961, and its leadership included a number of women who were later instrumental in efforts to establish a royal commission on the status of women (Helen Tucker, Thérèse Casgrain) and to pressure for implementation of the commission's recommendations in a national action committee on the status of women (Kay Macpherson).

While VOW thus provided 'a significant training ground' for future status of women activists, it also offered valuable lessons in the political tensions which continued to confront independent women's organizations.[72] In 1963, when Prime Minister Lester Pearson reversed his position on the stationing of Bomarc missiles in Canada, VOW split internally over a response to his decision. Activists asked:

Could one swallow the Liberal decision and still campaign against nuclear weapons without its constituting an attack on the party? The majority decided that such a swallow would gulp away VOW credibility. The organization attacked the policy ... Many members disagreed; some because they wished to support and vote for Liberals, some because they were convinced that the loss, apparent or real, of an apolitical posture would destroy VOW's effectiveness. Others argued

TABLE 1.2
The establishment of major Canadian women's organizations, 1960–83

Date	Organization	Main purpose
July 1960	Voice of Women (VOW)	'To crusade against the possibility of nuclear war'[a]
April 1966	Fédération des Femmes du Québec (FFQ)	To pressure for legislative reform and a Council of Women
June 1966	Committee for the Equality of Women in Canada (CEW)	To pressure for establishment of a royal commission on the status of women
February 1967	Royal Commission on the Status of Women (RCSW)	'To inquire into and report upon the status of women in Canada'[b]
March 1969	New Feminists, Toronto	'To awaken the consciousness of women as to the nature and extent of their oppression as women'[c]
September 1970	Report of the Royal Commission on the Status of Women	'To recommend what steps might be taken ... to ensure for women equal opportunities'[d]
January 1971	National Ad Hoc Committee on the Status of Women in Canada	To pressure for implementation of Royal Commission recommendations
April 1972	National Action Committee on the Status of Women in Canada	(Replaced Ad Hoc Committee)
February 1972	Women for Political Action (WPA)	To increase female political participation and political education at all levels of government
May 1973	Canadian Advisory Council on the Status of Women (CACSW)	To report on women's concerns to the Minister Responsible for the Status of Women
February 1979	Feminist Party of Canada	To establish a political party with a feminist perspective
January 1981	Ad Hoc Committee of Canadian Women	To achieve equality for women in the Canadian Charter of Rights and Freedoms
January 1983	Canadian Coalition against Media Pornography	To protest the portrayal of women in First Choice Pay TV

a Kay Macpherson and Meg Sears, 'The Voice of Women: A History,' in Gwen Matheson, ed., *Women in the Canadian Mosaic* (Toronto: Peter Martin, 1976), 72.
b Terms of Reference, reprinted in *Report* of the Royal Commission on the Status of Women in Canada (Ottawa: Information Canada, 1970), vii.
c Lynne Teather, 'The Feminist Mosaic,' in *Women in the Canadian Mosaic*, 331.
d Terms of Reference, vii.

that it was one thing to oppose policies in general, but quite a different and disturbing thing to oppose particular leaders on specific matters. To these latter, open disagreement with father-figures was a new and terrifying sensation.[73]

Voice of Women's external credibility and internal unity suffered a great deal because of this split, since what survived of the organization was increasingly labelled as politically marginal, a captive of the radical left. Despite its claims to political independence, therefore, VOW became wedged by broader partisan conflicts which shaped the debate over war, peace, and specifically the Bomarc missiles. The transcendence of party politics, promised during the first decades of this century by mainstream suffragists, thus remained problematical within VOW during the 1960s.

The apparent lesson which was drawn from VOW's internal fragmentation was that Canadian women could best coalesce around one carefully circumscribed, relatively non-partisan concern, namely an official inquiry into the status of women. Demands for such an inquiry came to light publicly on 5 January 1967, when CFUW president Laura Sabia was quoted on the front page of the Toronto *Globe and Mail* as threatening to march some two million women on Ottawa, unless the federal government agreed to establish the Royal Commission on the Status of Women (RCSW).[74] Despite this seemingly sudden and, particularly for Canada and Canadian women, provocative statement, the discussion of women's status had continued for a number of years within older, middle-class women's associations, including CFUW, the YWCA, and Business and Professional Women's Clubs.[75]

As in the earlier example of the Persons Case, events surrounding the royal commission suggest that disparate groups and individuals could indeed organize around one narrow, well-defined objective. As summarized by Cerise Morris (1980), Laura Sabia employed her position as CFUW president to call together the representatives of some thirty-two other groups, who agreed in June 1966 to form 'a new national women's organization concerned solely with the status of women – Committee for the Equality of Women in Canada (CEW) and, through this vehicle, to press for the establishment of a royal commission.'[76] Supported by a strong editorial which appeared in the July issue of *Chatelaine*, a leading women's magazine, and by the broad-based coalition represented in CEW (which included VOW, NCWC, IODE, YWCA, Business and Professional Women, and the newly formed Fédération des Femmes du Québec), Sabia and sixty-four of her colleagues presented the Liberal minority government with a brief requesting the formation of such a commission in September 1966.[77]

During this same period, both women who then held seats in the House of Commons pressured the Liberal cabinet to establish a royal commission. One was New Democrat Grace MacInnis, the daughter of former party leader J.S. Woodsworth, who had modelled herself as a youth after Agnes Macphail.[78] When MacInnis probed the government's plans on the floor of the House, she generally received facetious and non-committal replies to her questions.[79]

A considerably more influential MP in these matters was Judy LaMarsh, who held the secretary of state portfolio in the Pearson cabinet. Like Agnes Macphail during the 1920s and 1930s, LaMarsh reluctantly became a consistent supporter and initiator of women's rights legislation: 'No matter how little a suffragette by temperament, circumstances gradually forced me into the role of acting as spokesman and watchdog for women. If there had been a dozen women in the Cabinet, that wouldn't have been necessary, but I had to carry out this dual, unasked for, entirely unofficial, and unpaid role.'[80] LaMarsh's pressures within Cabinet, combined with Sabia's organizational abilities and statements to the press, began to take effect by the winter of 1967. On 3 February 1967, Prime Minister Pearson announced the formation of a commission, to be headed by well-known journalist Anne Francis (Florence Bird).[81]

Despite numerous doubts about its usefulness and, particularly in the case of LaMarsh, its legislative impact, the royal commission was critical in helping to define publicly the issue of women's status in Canada.[82] Many academic researchers, older women's associations, newer status of women groups, and private individuals contributed to the hearings and final report; approximately 470 briefs in total were presented during the four years following its establishment. Press coverage of the commission process also ensured its visibility, as did the publication of a well-written, well-organized *Report* which provided one of the first systematic overviews of the contemporary female condition in Canada.[83] In all, 167 recommendations were listed in the final version, which was presented to Prime Minister Trudeau in December 1970.

In historical terms, it is difficult to distinguish the impact of the RCSW from the influence of concurrent developments on the Canadian left. Unlike women's rights activists associated with the royal commission, many of whom were middle-aged members of older voluntary organizations, females who were attracted to the Canadian left during the 1960s tended to be younger, more politically radical, and more doubtful regarding the significance of formal legislative reform. Few of the latter presented submissions to the RCSW, since a commonly held belief on the left was that the transformation of basic social and economic structures in Canada was necessary in order to eliminate what radical women increasingly identified as a problem of sexual oppression – in contrast to the prevailing liberal conception of unequal opportunity.[84]

The emergence of a more radical, women's liberation movement in Canada can therefore be linked to the experiences of females on the left and, more specifically, to their treatment within such new left groups as the Student Union for Peace Action (SUPA).[85] In common with some CCF women of the 1930s and following, female SUPA activists took issue with their assignment to clerical and fund-raising tasks, in light of the fact that men were deployed as leading political strategists, speakers, and decision-makers on the left. This rejection of conventional role norms by younger women produced a variety of practical and philosophic responses, ranging from radical feminism, which identified the origins of female oppression in biologically determined gender roles, to socialist and Marxist feminism, which generally focused upon the relationship between class structures and the institutions of the left, on the one hand, and women's social and economic position, on the other.[86]

Throughout most of the late 1960s and early 1970s, older women's rights and newer women's liberation groups competed for media attention, social legitimacy, and the loyalties of Canadian women. Signs of a possible rapprochement between the two sides appeared in 1972, however, at the Strategy for Change conference which formally established the National Action Committee on the Status of Women (NAC).[87] As an umbrella organization embracing widely disparate groups, NAC set out to see that the major recommendations of the royal commission were implemented, and that the various concerns of its constituent members were presented to parliamentary committees, task forces, and the public at large. From the outset, NAC's mandate was explicitly non-partisan; it was to argue forcefully and independently on behalf of Canadian women.

In the following year, the Canadian Advisory Council on the Status of Women (CACSW) was established. As suggested in the *Report* of the royal commission, this council was charged with the task of undertaking research, developing programs and legislative proposals, and consulting with existing organizations in the area of women's rights. However, contrary to the commission's recommendation, CACSW was made responsible to a single cabinet minister, namely the Minister Responsible for the Status of Women, rather than to Parliament as a whole. This jurisdictional matter became the basis for a major conflict between the Liberal government and women's groups during constitutional discussions in 1981, when the ability of the advisory council to represent independently the concerns of Canadian women was called into serious question (see below).

THE PROBLEM OF POLITICAL STRATEGY

The *Report* of the royal commission, published in 1970, highlights a wide variety of inequalities affecting women in Canada. One of the most troubling of these was the relative absence of females in positions of political influence and, more specifically, the weak representation of women in Canadian provincial and federal legislatures.[88] As British Columbia MLA Rosemary Brown reflected in the wake of both this report and her own political experiences, 'to talk of power and to talk of women is to talk of the absence of power as we understand it today.'[89]

The organized response of Canadian women to this situation has been complex and at times conflictual, encompassing both politically independent and partisan strategies. One early effort to increase female representation at elite levels was the Toronto-based Women for Political Action (WPA), a non-partisan organization established in 1972. Following a series of articles in *Chatelaine* magazine which highlighted the obstacles facing women in politics, and which presented profiles of '105 potential women MPs,' a number of activists in Voice of Women (including Kay Macpherson) and the Ontario Committee on the Status of Women (including future MP Aideen Nicholson) established WPA as a focal point for the growing national network of politically active feminists.[90]

Although a key priority of WPA was the election of more females to public office, there were frequent disputes within the group regarding the best means toward this end.[91] In 1972, prior to the announcement of a federal election, many WPA members favoured the nomination of independent women candidates who, following their election, 'could independently set up a caucus in the House of Commons.'[92] This position in support of independent candidacies was in fact pursued by WPA in 1972, when the organization fielded two of its members in the Toronto federal ridings of St Paul's (Macpherson) and Rosedale (Aline Gregory). While both campaigns mobilized large numbers of newly active women and, particularly in the case of Rosedale, introduced feminist collective organization and consciousness-raising to federal electioneering, neither was successful in winning a parliamentary seat.

These electoral defeats, combined with the inroads which other women appeared to be making in established party organizations, led many WPA members away from political independence and in the direction of traditional partisanship. In the words of one activist in Aline Gregory's campaign, 'There were a lot of people who took the message from these experiences that we should all join the established parties, and become conventional political participants ... In the years following 1972, many women indeed joined parties.'[93] As more WPA members became active and committed partisans, however, the group's mandate to remain politically independent became increasingly irrelevant to its core constituency. Therefore, until about 1979, WPA existed as little more than a Toronto post-office box address, sponsoring occasional conferences (including a 1973 'Women in Politics' session with Rosemary Brown as keynote speaker) and campaign schools.[94]

The partisan identifications adopted by WPA veterans and other feminists who chose to participate in mainstream party politics were generally New Democratic and, particularly on the federal level, Liberal.[95] Within both parties, feminist activists made impressive gains by the mid-1970s, as task forces and new women's rights organizations were established (the NDP Participation of Women Committee and the Women's Liberal Commission were created in 1969 and 1973 respectively) and as more women became visibly influential, particularly as holders of major party and public office (see chapter 3).[96] Notably, in 1972 three Liberal women were elected to the House of Commons from Quebec; they included Monique Bégin, who had served as executive secretary to the royal commission and as an activist in the Fédération des Femmes du Québec. In 1974, five more Liberal women took office as federal MPs, including Aideen Nicholson, who had largely built her campaign organization within the Ontario Committee on the Status of Women.[97]

The mid-1970s was also a very hopeful period for women in the NDP. On the federal level, a 1974 women's convention in Winnipeg served as the starting point for a feminist-oriented leadership campaign by Rosemary Brown.[98] As a backbencher in the British Columbia NDP caucus, Brown made a strong and credible showing against interim federal leader Ed Broadbent (see chapter 4). In addition to marking the first campaign for major party leadership by a woman in Canada, this 1975 convention also elected Joyce Nash as the first female president of a major federal party organization. In short, the gains made by Liberal and New Democratic women during the early and mid-1970s suggested that political influence was indeed accessible to all hard-working and committed partisans, regardless of gender.

This promise began to fade, however, as growing numbers of feminists questioned the policy changes which had been effected during the decade since the establishment of the RCSW. Such issues as equal pay, pension reform, abortion, day care, and sex role stereotyping in education and the media remained largely ignored by both provincial and federal governments through the 1970s, even though detailed reports and legislative proposals had been prepared by status of women groups (including NAC) and internal party task forces and women's organizations.[99]

A sentiment thus began to build by the late 1970s that women's advisory councils, notably on the federal level (CACSW), as well as women's associations within the parties were too traditional in their composition and strategy to provide effective political leadership in these important issue areas. In addition, the partisan and personality conflicts which developed in such groups as NAC suggested that a systematic, coherent response to government inaction was unlikely to develop within 'independent' women's organizations.[100]

Alongside these frustrations regarding policy influence, Canadian feminists also questioned the progress which had been made in electing women to public and party office. The weak showing of Conservative leadership candidate Flora MacDonald was particularly disappointing, since MacDonald had received considerable moral and financial support from many women who were not Conservatives (see chapter 4). While her campaign thus captured the imagination of many politically minded feminists, its sixth-place finish at the 1976 leadership convention suggested that major obstacles continued to impede women's participation in elite-level politics.

The establishment in February 1979 of the Feminist Party of Canada, coinciding with the revival of Women for Political Action and early discussions regarding a women's bureau in the federal Conservative organization, reflected the extent to which politically active women had begun to reconsider their accomplishments. One early statement by the Feminist Party expressed this malaise in terms of developments during the sixty years following federal enfranchisement: 'Since that time, women have indeed increased their attempts to become elected representatives – the number of women seeking federal office rose from 4, in 1921, to 137 in 1974. But the number of women who won seats in those 53 years rose only from one to nine. The dismal prognosis is that, at this rate, we will need another 842 years to achieve equal representation at the federal level.'[101] The response of Feminist Party founders was to create their own 'political party with a feminist perspective.'[102] This goal was complicated early on by fragile internal alliances (that is, Conservative status of women activists combined with radical feminists in a single organization), and by the announcement of two federal elections within approximately one year of the new party's establishment.

Ultimately, the Feminist Party was a short-lived coalition which made little direct impact upon female participation in Canadian politics. Like the activities of Women for Political Action in 1972, however, its establishment symbolized the continuing attractiveness of independent women's organizations to many feminists, including those who only later recognized their limitations within a partisan, parliamentary system. Moreover, the existence of WPA, the Feminist Party, and other similar groups pointed toward an underlying discontent among many women regarding their numerical representation and policy impact within the Canadian political process.

WOMEN AND THE CONSTITUTION

The longstanding political discontent of many Canadian women crystallized around a single issue – constitutional change – during the years 1980-2. Some English-Canadian feminists felt a particular stake in the renewal of constitutional federalism, since they had sent letters and telegrams of support to the 'Non' forces, and especially to activists in the 'Yvette' movement, during the 1980 Quebec referendum campaign.[103] The success of the 'Non' forces in this referendum, combined with the imminent defeat of the U.S. Equal Rights Amendment, suggested that Canadian women would need to play a major role in discussions over future constitutional arrangements.

Systematic input by women's groups into the constitutional process, however, came only after prolonged disputes with the federal government, and within these same women's organizations. Much of the public debate over women and the constitution followed a request by the Minister Responsible for the Status of Women, Lloyd Axworthy, that the federal advisory council (CACSW) cancel its planned conference on this subject. Axworthy advised that such a conference could prove politically damaging to the Liberal government, and a majority of council members – who were generally 'safe' Liberal appointees – supported his view. In the words of one approving member, 'I say that it's about time we started playing games the same way government plays games. We should start being nice to them. So if this conference is going to be an embarrassment, let's play it their way and cancel it.'[104]

Doris Anderson, who had worked previously as editor of *Chatelaine* and run unsuccessfully as a federal Liberal candidate in 1978, opposed Axworthy's intervention and resigned from the presidency of CACSW on 20 January 1981. Her unwillingness to cancel the conference provided an unexpected turn of events for Axworthy and his supporters, as well as for many women who had long doubted the value of the federal advisory council. On an organizational level, Anderson's resignation prompted the formation on 21 January of the Ad Hoc Committee of Canadian Women, which later held its own highly successful constitutional conference in Ottawa on 14 February.[105] The Ad Hoc Committee relied upon a diverse base of volunteer support, similar to that which had been employed earlier in the Persons Case and in efforts to create a royal commission. This visible core of support, which again developed around a single, well-defined political issue, later helped to ensure the inclusion of an equality rights clause in the new constitution (section 28).

In political terms, however, the 1981 constitutional crisis tended to exacerbate older tensions between partisanship and independence among Canadian women. Just as a number of Liberal activists felt betrayed by the resignation of Doris Anderson, [106] so many others who were less identified with the party believed that they (along with Anderson) were the victims of government – and especially Cabinet – manipulation.[107] These perceptions of betrayal and manipulation were deep-seated and spilled over into other organizations which were also associated with the constitutional process. In the National Action Committee, for example, one assistant to Lloyd Axworthy sponsored a contentious resolution on the Charter of Rights, which was approved after dubious political man-oeuvrings.[108] As retiring NAC president Lynn McDonald observed in the wake of these events, 'Women's organizations, with their fragile inter-party compositions, have been sorely tried by the Constitution debate.'[109]

Recent conflicts concerning a new federal constitution thus reflect the ability of Canadian women to form narrow issue coalitions across party lines, at the same time as they demonstrate the fragility and temporary nature of these alliances.[110] In fact, the decline of the Ad Hoc Committee following parliamentary approval of section 28 suggests that ideological unity and organizational continuity remain elusive goals in English Canada. Women's political history in the 1980s thus continues to be enmeshed in a complex and uneasy tension between non-partisanship and independent feminism, on the one hand, and the demands of a party-structured parliamentary system, on the other.

CONCLUSIONS

This chapter has examined the political history of women in English Canada, focusing upon a longstanding dilemma between non-partisan independence and more conventional political partisanship. Our discussion has emphasized the importance of this tension in shaping the suffragist and post-enfranchisement, as well as contemporary, political experiences of women in English Canada.

In order to evaluate the implications of this historical development for female political attitudes and participation, we shall introduce relevant empirical materials below in chapters 2 and 3.

2

Patterns of Female Politicization and Partisanship

If a Labour vote is a social novelty which the old, whose habits were fixed in an earlier period, adopt more reluctantly than the young, it may be that women lag behind because, in a changing world, their social contacts are more limited than those of men ... It is possible then that women's political conservatism results partly from a greater social isolation which makes them slower than men to change their opinions and attitudes.[1]

In the existing literature on public opinion and electoral behaviour in Canada, relatively little attention is devoted to the political attitudes of women. This neglect is particularly apparent in contemporary studies, which consider regional, class, and linguistic cleavages at length, at the same time as they give only limited consideration to the role of gender as either an independent or intervening influence upon attitude formation.[2]

Alongside the general neglect of gender is a problem of conceptual bias in those studies which do consider this variable. A number of efforts to explain patterns of female politicization rely upon arguments to the effect that 'traditional'[3] or 'parochial'[4] views result from women's 'isolation' in the domestic household.[5] One well-known political scientist has thus described the bulk of 'political barbarians' as women, who have limited appreciation of the dominant symbols and issues which inform political discourse in Canada.[6] Aside from the major conceptual problems which follow from their reliance upon an ahistorical and, in some cases, pejorative view of women's attitudes, such studies also reflect considerable empirical weaknesses.

In this chapter, we begin to explore the development of female politicization and partisanship in English Canada, using data from the 1965 Canadian National Election Study and the 1979 Social Change in Canada

Study.[7] Our purpose in employing these data is twofold: first, to examine critically the conceptual and empirical foundations of older research in this area; and second, to develop a more systematic approach to female politicization and partisanship, in light of historical materials presented in chapter 1.

Our discussion opens with an examination of conventional approaches to women's attitudes in Canada, in which we evaluate the conceptual and empirical groundings of this older literature. Next, we introduce 1965 and 1979 survey data in order to examine three major hypotheses which follow from the historical review presented in chapter 1. They concern the impact of pre-enfranchisement experiences upon subsequent patterns of female politicization, as well as the relationship between early and contemporary feminism, on the one hand, and partisan attitudes, on the other.

CONVENTIONAL APPROACHES TO WOMEN'S ATTITUDES

Established studies of public opinion and electoral behaviour in Canada have generally failed to consider women's political attitudes. Two brief discussions of this subject are offered in books by Peter Regenstreif (1965) and Mildred Schwartz (1967), both of which situate female public opinion in the context of limitations imposed by conventional domestic roles. According to Regenstreif, female political interest and participation are generally less than those of males; as well, women are 'disposed to favour the traditional [Liberal and Conservative] parties over the "radical" ones,' namely the New Democratic party.[8] These trends, along with impressionistic evidence that married women accept political direction from their husbands, indicated to Regenstreif that female behaviour was governed by 'the cultural norm that the place of women is in the home and not in the world of politics.'[9]

A more explicitly domestic explanation of political attitudes is presented in Schwartz (1967). *Public Opinion and Canadian Identity* quotes at length from a British discussion of lower female support for the Labour party (see the epigraph to this chapter), which suggests 'that women's political conservatism results partly from a greater social isolation which makes them slower than men to change their opinions and attitudes.'[10] Schwartz applied this argument in a Canadian context in claiming that within the Conservative and Liberal electorates, women 'appeared more parochial in their outlook' on national issues than men; therefore, 'like older respondents, women tend to be more traditional in their approach to national problems.'[11]

Echoes of this same domestic explanation of female attitudes may also be found in more recent empirical studies. For example, Jean Laponce's (1969) discussion of electoral behaviour in Vancouver-Burrard refers to the major constraints upon political awareness which are imposed by conventional domestic roles.[12] Similarly, statements presented by Rick Van Loon (1970) suggest that the limited social contacts of housewives, combined with traditional assumptions which regard politics as a masculine enterprise, have produced a lower level of politicization among Canadian women than men.[13]

On a conceptual level, older arguments to the effect that isolation in the domestic household shapes women's political attitudes deserve careful scrutiny. Drawing upon an older Aristotelian dichotomy between public (hence political) male and private (hence apolitical) female spheres, this approach suggests that, by definition, women are not equipped to be politically competent or active on a regular basis.[14] Rather, their isolation in the home and child-rearing responsibilities, frequently accompanied by greater religiosity and lower educational attainment than that of men, are seen as the source of attitudinal 'traditionalism' and 'parochialism.' The overall impression conveyed by conventional arguments is thus consistent with an impaired political outlook: Lacking meaningful ties with political institutions or with political history, women's views remain static, changeless, and, in the words of Thelma McCormack (1975), 'deviant' features of Western public opinion.[15]

A useful way of understanding the main lines of this argument is provided in figure 1, which presents a simplified version of the standard explanation. According to this perspective, women's political attitudes and participation are defined by the experience of domestic isolation, and by the absence of consistent political stimuli which motivate the presumably more active and aware lives of men in modern democracies.

On an empirical level, this approach is complicated by the absence of methodologically rigorous analyses. For example, if women's attitudes were indeed characterized by lower support for the NDP during the period considered by Regenstreif, and if this phenomenon was related at the time to domestic isolation and its various demographic correlates (including greater religiosity and lower educational attainment), then we could expect to find systematic documentation of these patterns in the existing literature. Unfortunately, such empirical evidence is generally not provided, since neither Regenstreif nor Schwartz introduces tabular controls which could help to establish that 'isolation' was the basis for female views. Moreover, Regenstreif's discussion does not offer a basic male-female breakdown in partisan attitudes.

FIGURE 1 Conventional model of women and politics

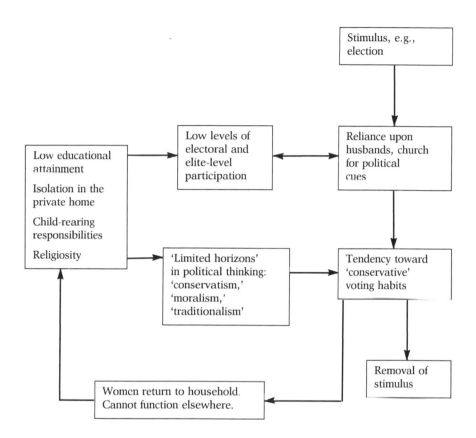

TABLE 2.1
Party identification of Anglophone Canadians, 1965[a]

	Women	Men
Liberal	42.3	37.2
Conservative	39.7	38.1
New Democratic	12.4	18.9
Social Credit	5.6	5.8
(N)	(804)	(728)

a Respondents were asked, 'Generally speaking, do you think of yourself as Conservative, Liberal, Social Credit, Créditiste, NDP, Union nationale, or what?' Non-identifiers were probed a second time, 'Well, do you generally think of yourself as a little closer to one of the parties than the others?' (If yes) 'Which one?' In this and the following tables, only English-speaking respondents from outside Quebec have been included (except where indicated), and all missing data are excluded.
Source: 1965 Canadian Election Study

These conceptual and empirical problems point toward the need for a careful reconsideration of established studies. In the following section, we introduce 1965 survey data in order to question whether, on a strictly empirical level, the conventional 'isolation' explanation provides a useful framework for the analysis of women's political attitudes in English Canada.

EMPIRICAL PERSPECTIVES ON THE LITERATURE

Our review of the older Canadian literature on women's political attitudes suggests two specific empirical hypotheses, one concerning the direction and the other, the correlates of female public opinion. First, in terms of direction, studies by Regenstreif (1965), Schwartz (1967), Laponce (1969), and others maintain that women are more politically traditional, particularly in terms of partisan preferences, than men.[16] This position may be evaluated in a fairly straightforward manner, using survey data from the mid-1960s to ascertain whether females were in fact more likely to identify with the older Liberal and Conservative parties, and less likely to identify with the newer NDP, than males.

Second, in reference to attitudinal correlates, established studies argue that the source of female 'traditionalism' or 'parochialism' rests in a condition of isolation within the domestic household. Given that female employment status was not ascertained in the 1965 study (which only probed the occupation of main wage earners in each household), we shall employ frequent church attendance and limited educational attainment as surrogate indicators of domestic 'isolation' in the following analyses.

TABLE 2.2
Ratings of NDP members of parliament by Anglophone Canadians, 1965[a]

	Women	Men
Pretty good	38.4	46.7
So-so	45.6	35.5
Not good	16.0	17.8
(N)	(636)	(712)

a Respondents were asked their opinions regarding MPs which each of the major parties
  had sent to Ottawa in the last few years.
Source: 1965 Canadian Election Study

To what extent were women's attitudes less radical, and more 'traditional' than those of men in 1965? Figures in table 2.1 indicate a 6.5%
gender difference in levels of NDP identification, with 18.9% of men and
12.4% of women expressing New Democratic partisanship.[17] The Liberal
party would appear to have benefited most directly from this difference,
since 42.3% of women and 37.2% of men stated Liberal identifications.
Data in table 2.2 provide additional evidence of somewhat less support
for the NDP among English-Canadian women in 1965: 46.7% of men and
only 38.4% of women gave favourable ratings to New Democratic members of parliament in that year.[18] As well, an additive measure of NDP
support (see note, table 2.3) which was constructed using seven items
from the 1965 survey shows significant differences in the mean scores of
women and men, with men being substantially more in favour of the party
than women.[19] These findings therefore suggest that, if defined in terms
of party support, the attitudes of English-Canadian women in 1965 were
less radical and more favourable toward the established parties (especially
the Liberals) than those of men.

When we turn to the correlates of partisanship in that year, however,
our results offer less than convincing support for conventional arguments.
As reported in table 2.4, male and female respondents in 1965 may be
divided into three categories of cultural 'isolation,' which represent high,
medium, and low levels of this phenomenon. Patterns of radical (defined
as NDP) partisanship can then be compared across categories, with the
expectation that secular, well-educated (or 'low isolate') respondents would
express relatively similar levels of NDP identification, while religious, less-
educated (or 'high isolate') ones would express more disparate views. In
particular, it was hypothesized that women in the 'high isolate' category
(that is, with frequent church attendance and low educational attainment)
would express particularly limited preference for the NDP.

TABLE 2.3
Comparison of mean scores of NDP support among Anglo-Canadian women and men,
1965 and 1979[a]

	1965			1979		
	Women	Men	t	Women	Men	t
NDP support	0.659	0.967	−3.42**	0.607	0.810	−3.22**
(N)	(882)	(842)		(1010)	(898)	
				**Significant at the .01 level		

a These additive measures were constructed by summing pro-NDP responses to the following 1965 items: party identification (weighted for strength of that identification);
identification with a different party in the past; party identification on the federal or
provincial levels if initial identification was not for both levels; party chosen in previous
provincial and federal elections if respondent always votes for the same party; 1963
federal party choice; 1965 federal party choice; party choice in last provincial election.
The items used for 1979 measure were: federal party identification, federal vote were
election held today, provincial identification, and provincial vote were election held today.
Sources: 1965 Canadian Election Study; 1979 Social Change in Canada Study

TABLE 2.4
NDP identification by level of cultural 'isolation' in English Canada, 1965[a]

	High		Medium		Low	
	Women	Men	Women	Men	Women	Men
NDP identification (%)	14.7	18.3	12.7	12.6	16.7	24.2
Difference (W − M)	−3.6		+0.1		−7.5	
(N)	(75)	(55)	(134)	(85)	(68)	(113)

a Categories of cultural 'isolation' were established as follows: high = elementary education, weekly church attendance; medium = secondary education, 1-3 times/month
church attendance; low = university education, few times/year or no church attendance.
Source: 1965 Canadian Election Study

Contrary to these expectations, data in table 2.4 show that the greatest
gender disparity in NDP support (7.5%) occurred among 'low isolates,'
who reported both advanced education and infrequent church attendance.
By way of contrast, the gender difference among 'high isolates,' who had
limited education and weekly church attendance, was less than half this
figure (3.6%), while that in the intermediate category was virtually nil
(0.1%).

Similarly, examining absolute levels of NDP support among both genders, we find that the 'isolation' argument would appear to be more applicable to males than to females. That is, the difference between 'high' and 'low isolates' was nearly 6% among men, compared with only 2% among women. Moreover, females in the 'high isolate' category, who were expected to identify least with the NDP, expressed slightly higher New Democratic partisanship than both men and women in the intermediate category. These results suggest that education and religious attendance had a less than profound impact upon the key group – women – to which the phenomenon of social isolation was assumed to be crucial.

Overall, then, we would conclude that although 1965 survey data indicate women's partisan attitudes to be more favourable toward the established or 'traditional' parties, and less supportive of the newer and more radical NDP than those of men, they do not reflect any systematic relationship between the phenomenon of NDP identification, on the one hand, and indicators of female cultural 'isolation' on the other. Moreover, by reporting a number of empirical trends which are the reverse of those predicted by conventional arguments (notably, greater gender differences in partisanship among 'low' versus 'high' isolates), our analysis suggests that the prevailing conceptual treatment of women's political attitudes in English Canada remains in need of serious revision.

THE IMPACT OF HISTORICAL INFLUENCES

Our review of conventional approaches to female public opinion in English Canada suggests that the 'isolation' explanation – particularly as applied to patterns of party support in 1965 – fails to offer an adequate account of this phenomenon. In the present section, we shall begin to develop an alternate view of women's attitudes, using the historical background presented in chapter 1 as a basis from which to re-examine the origins, direction, and correlates of female public opinion in English Canada.

One way of approaching these historical materials is to consider the circumstances surrounding the formal granting of political rights to Canadian women, and then to generate propositions regarding subsequent attitudinal developments. At least three general hypotheses follow from our historical review in chapter 1. First, the wedging of suffragism and feminism during the early decades of this century, particularly within the broader federal conflict over conscription, meant that women's formal political rights were granted as part of a larger legislative package – rather than following a national debate regarding the independent merits of enfranchisement. This pattern, combined with the fact that suffragism in English Canada was weak in terms of both national organization and ideological unity, suggests that women may have entered the political system with a collective sense of hesitation or ambiguity.[20] We shall employ empirical data on political interest and survey response in exploring the relationship between circumstances surrounding formal enfranchisement, on the one hand, and subsequent patterns of female politicization, on the other.

Second, it is notable that suffragism in Western Canada was associated with a larger progressive movement, which developed close political ties with provincial Liberal parties as well as with the agrarian and labour precursors of the CCF / NDP. In partisan terms, we could expect this alliance to be reflected empirically in relatively high levels of CCF / NDP and Liberal identification among older women in Western Canada, particularly among those who came of age politically during the suffrage period.

Third, our discussion of the development of contemporary feminism has highlighted the specific impact of this movement upon female involvement in the New Democratic and federal Liberal (LPC) parties. As outlined in chapter 1, many younger feminists who sought to exert influence upon established party organizations during the early 1970s and following joined the LPC and NDP organizations and worked to recruit additional support among other women for these parties. We would therefore hypothesize that younger women, and those attaching a high priority to women's rights concerns, would express relatively strong preference for the NDP and federal Liberals during the 1970s.

We shall now turn our attention to patterns of female politicization in 1965 and following.

PATTERNS OF FEMALE POLITICIZATION

In examining the impact of circumstances surrounding female enfranchisement in English Canada upon subsequent patterns of politicization, we shall employ 1965 and 1979 data on political interest and survey response. Although the 1965 figures were gathered approximately fifty years after the granting of suffrage to most English-Canadian women, they represent the earliest baseline year for which such data are available.

Turning first to figures on political interest in table 2.5, we find that English-Canadian women expressed considerably less interest in 1965 than comparable men, with 23.1% of females and 33.3% of males reporting

TABLE 2.5
Political interest of Canadian respondents, 1965[a]

| | Anglophones outside Quebec | | Francophones in Quebec | |
	Women	Men	Women	Men
Good deal	23.1	33.3	13.0	24.3
Some	45.7	43.2	36.4	48.9
Not much	31.2	23.5	50.6	26.8
(N)	(880)	(839)	(324)	(317)

a Respondents were asked, 'How much interest do you generally have in what is going
 on in politics – a good deal, some, or not much?'
Source: 1965 Canadian Election Study

a 'good deal' of interest in politics. Although these results support our hypothesis to the effect that circumstances surrounding female enfranchisement in English Canada tended to wedge women outside the mainstream political process, they also indicate that gender differences in English Canada were less than those which existed at the same time in Francophone Quebec. As reported in table 2.5, only 13.0% of Quebec Francophone females expressed a 'good deal' of interest, and a majority (50.6%) claimed to have 'not much' interest. The latter result, which differed by approximately 20% from both French-speaking males and English-speaking females, suggests that the exceptionally late date of provincial enfranchisement in Quebec (1940) had a major effect upon women's politicization through 1965. We would conclude, therefore, that by the mid-1960s, gender differences in political interest in English Canada remained substantial but considerably less than those in Francophone Quebec.

Comparable figures from 1979, presented in table 2.6, point toward a continued gender difference in political interest among both Anglophone and Francophone respondents. In 1979, the male / female difference among Anglophones residing outside Quebec remained in the 9% range: 61.9% of women and 70.6% of men claimed to be 'very' or 'fairly' interested in politics. By way of comparison, longitudinal figures from Francophone Quebec suggest an approximate doubling of gender differences over time, from slightly over 11% (13.0% versus 24.3% interested) in 1965 to about 23% (42.2% versus 64.9% interested) in 1979. While these findings may be influenced by divergent question wording in the two surveys, they would appear to indicate that, in English Canada, there was a general continuity over time in patterns of male and female political interest.

TABLE 2.6
Political interest of Canadian respondents, 1979[a]

	Anglophones outside Quebec		Francophones in Quebec	
	Women	Men	Women	Men
Very, fairly interested	61.9	70.6	42.2	64.9
Not very interested	28.8	22.6	41.4	25.8
Not interested	9.3	6.8	16.4	9.3
(N)	(1,003)	(893)	(351)	(382)

a Respondents were asked, 'How interested are you in politics and political events? Would you say ... Very interested, fairly interested, not very interested, or not at all interested?'
Source: 1979 Social Change in Canada Study

TABLE 2.7
Survey non-response of Canadian respondents, 1965 and 1979

	Anglophones outside Quebec		Francophones in Quebec	
	Women	Men	Women	Men
1965 party identification	8.9	13.5	20.7	20.4
1965 federal vote	17.1	18.2	29.3	22.2
Last provincial vote	26.9	22.4	28.4	20.6
(N)	(882)	(842)	(324)	(319)
1979 federal identification	18.2	18.6	22.2	24.3
1979 provincial identification	18.4	16.8	17.4	11.6
1979 federal preference	20.8	18.9	25.0	25.5
1979 provincial preference	20.1	19.7	21.2	19.2
(N)	(1,007)	(897)	(353)	(384)

Sources: 1965 Canadian Election Study; 1979 Social Change in Canada Study

A second indicator of politicization which is available in existing Canadian datasets concerns survey non-response, particularly on party identification and party preference items.[21] As reported in table 2.7, Anglophone respondents residing outside Quebec had relatively similar levels of non-response in both 1965 and 1979, with neither men nor women evidencing consistently higher levels of this phenomenon. Again, by way of contrast, Francophone females in Quebec had somewhat higher levels of non-response than Francophone males, suggesting once again that the considerably more recent and more bitter debate over enfranchisement in Quebec had important effects upon female politicization through the late 1970s.

To summarize this discussion of 1965 and 1979 survey data, we would conclude that the pre-enfranchisement experiences of women in English Canada may have contributed to somewhat lower levels of politicization, measured in terms of political interest, among females than males. The debate over woman suffrage was frequently wedged within broader systemic disputes involving progressive social reform, wartime mobilization, and particularly the federal conscription crisis. Combined with the organizational weakness and ideological disunity of suffragism itself, this background suggests that women gained formal equality in English Canada following limited independent discussion of their political rights. Compared with findings from Francophone Quebec, though, gender differences on measures of both political interest and survey non-response in English Canada are relatively small and suggest that the more recent and more bitter conflict over women's rights in Quebec generated more palpable political effects than the earlier struggle in English Canada. In the absence of older survey data, however, this comparison remains tentative.

We shall now turn to the question of party identification among English-Canadian women.

DIMENSIONS OF PARTY PREFERENCE IN 1965

A second hypothesis which was proposed above concerned the relationship between political alliances made by early feminism in Western Canada, on the one hand, and subsequent patterns of female partisanship, on the other. More specifically, we suggested that the coalitions built by Western progressives, including mainstream social feminists, with provincial Liberal parties and with the agrarian and labour precursors of the CCF / NDP contributed to relatively high levels of both CCF / NDP and Liberal identification among older women in Western Canada – and particularly among females who came of age politically during the suffrage period. This proposition is based upon a generational view of female partisanship, which maintains that the political experiences of various demographic groups (termed 'cohorts') help to shape their subsequent attitudinal development.[22] In this manner, it takes issue with older, less historical assumptions to the effect that domestic 'isolation' defines the political views of women as a group.

As was the case in our discussion of female politicization, we are limited to some extent in this section by the late beginnings of empirical political

TABLE 2.8
Party identification of Western Canadian respondents by birth cohorts, 1965[a]

	1931-45		1916-30		1901-15		Before 1900	
	Women	Men	Women	Men	Women	Men	Women	Men
Liberal	40.0	32.3	31.0	24.1	24.1	34.8	28.2	18.4
Conservative	36.6	30.2	43.7	28.7	44.4	26.1	33.3	59.2
New Democratic	11.7	29.2	6.9	30.6	13.0	29.0	15.4	10.2
Social Credit	11.7	8.3	18.4	16.6	18.5	10.1	23.1	12.2
(N)	(60)	(96)	(87)	(108)	(54)	(69)	(39)	(49)

a For exact question wording, see table 2.1.
Source: 1965 Canadian Election Study

research in Canada. That is, because the first major national election survey was conducted in 1965, we are faced with a smaller cohort of pre-enfranchisement respondents than might have been available prior to 1965. However, the number of older Western Canadian respondents in table 2.8 (N = 88) is sufficient to permit preliminary examination of our generational hypothesis.

As reported in table 2.8, Western Canadian women born before 1900, who came of age politically during the height of suffrage activism, reported considerably higher Liberal (28.2% versus 18.4%) and somewhat higher New Democratic (15.4% versus 10.2%) party identification than men of the same age. Notably, older men in Western Canada, particularly those residing in British Columbia, expressed substantially greater support for the Conservative party than older women (81.0% versus 37.5% Conservative in BC).

In comparison with other Western Canadian cohorts in table 2.8, we find that only among older respondents (that is, those born before 1900) did women report higher levels of NDP identification than men. In all four other groups included in this table, male New Democratic partisanship exceeded that of females, such that men born since 1900 were between two and four times more likely than women born during this period to report NDP identification. Similarly, it is notable that Western Canadian women in the enfranchisement cohort (that is, those born before 1900) had the highest level of NDP partisanship of any female cohort sampled.

This tendency for older Western Canadian women to report relatively high levels of identification with the Liberal and New Democratic parties may be attributed to their enfranchisement-period experiences and, more specifically, to the favourable treatment of women and women's rights by progressive political groups in the West during this period. In longitudinal terms, however, it is important to question how subsequent changes in Canadian politics and society, including changes in the status of women, may have shaped patterns of female partisanship.

One way of approaching this question is to trace roughly the evolution of the CCF / NDP, which sheds valuable light on the broader development of women's attitudes. It is widely argued that the CCF's emergence within a progressive 'social gospel' context encouraged the party to emphasize social concerns, particularly the elimination of 'injustice and inhumanity' in the words of the Regina Manifesto.[23] As Canadian society became increasingly urbanized and industrialized, however, this basic ideological focus tended to shift so that the 1961 Draft Program of the New Party, which was to supplant the CCF, opened with a discussion of economic priorities capped under the heading 'planning for abundance.'[24] In this manner, the CCF emerged in the western provinces as an outgrowth of social initiatives which included a strong commitment to women's political rights, and moved across time in an increasingly economic and 'masculine' direction – in the sense that women's status received diminishing attention within the organization, while the concerns of paid, employed, and, in particular, unionized men grew rapidly in prominence.[25]

In addition, as post-war affluence led to an expansion of the Canadian welfare state, Conservatives and especially Liberals began to adopt many social initiatives first proposed by the CCF / NDP, including government-sponsored health and unemployment insurance.[26] Women may have been drawn toward the older parties as a result, since the initial social priorities of the early CCF became more and more blurred with the passage of time. As well, it should be noted that the CCF / NDP remained a political-movement as well as a party, so that Canadian women who were so-cialized to the values of 'the feminine mystique' probably found it difficult to reconcile conventional role norms with the extensive political involve-ment expected of participants in such a movement.[27] In short, the attention paid to women's rights concerns and to social policy issues more generally tended to decline across time within the CCF / NDP, while the societal norms conducive to female involvement also receded. We would therefore propose that women who came of age politically following the enfran-chisement period, but prior to the contemporary wave of English-Canadian feminism, might express limited support for the party.

Preliminary support for this hypothesis is presented in table 2.9, which shows that New Democratic partisanship was lowest (9.1%) among women who came of age politically during the period of World War II (born 1916-

48 Toeing the Lines

TABLE 2.9
Party identification of Anglophone Canadian respondents by birth cohorts, 1965[a]

| | 1931-45 | | 1916-30 | | 1901-15 | | Before 1900 | |
	Women	Men	Women	Men	Women	Men	Women	Men
Liberal	48.5	42.8	42.0	36.3	37.6	35.7	36.2	27.4
Conservative	30.8	33.7	44.0	33.3	41.1	42.2	46.5	56.7
New Democratic	14.9	18.3	9.1	22.7	14.8	19.1	10.9	10.3
Social Credit	5.8	5.2	4.9	7.7	6.5	3.0	6.4	5.6
(N)	(259)	(218)	(268)	(250)	(159)	(166)	(110)	(88)

a For exact question wording, see table 2.1.
Source: 1965 Canadian Election Study

TABLE 2.10
Party identification among residents of union and non-union households, English Canada, 1965[a]

| | Union | | Non-union | |
	Women	Men	Women	Men
Liberal	44.4	40.3	41.7	36.1
Conservative	31.5	24.5	41.9	42.8
New Democratic	17.5	29.7	11.0	15.2
Social Credit	6.5	5.6	5.4	6.0
(N)	(169)	(185)	(635)	(543)

a Respondents were asked, 'Do you (or does the head of this household) belong to any
   of the following groups ... a labour union?' For exact question wording, see table 2.1.
Source: 1965 Canadian Election Study

30). By way of contrast, identification with the NDP was highest (22.7%) among men in this same cohort, which suggests that the political cues affecting male and female support for the NDP differed clearly in the period between female enfranchisement and the renewal of organized Canadian feminism. Combined with data in this same table which show that Liberal support grew systematically among younger female cohorts, our results would seem to indicate that the increasingly economic and 'masculine' focus of the CCF / NDP, coupled with the ability of the Liberals in particular to 'pre-empt' many of the former's social programs, worked to attenuate New Democratic identification among women who came of age politically through 1950.[28]

Another indication that a changing orientation in the CCF / NDP helped to produce gender differences by 1965 is reflected in data in table 2.10.

Comparing women's and men's support for the New Democrats in union-ized and non-unionized segments of the sample, we find that a 4.2% difference which obtains in the latter approximately triples in the former, such that 29.7% of males residing in union households in 1965 were New Democratic, while only 17.5% of females were NDP. This pattern, which exists in all four regions outside Quebec in 1965, is accompanied by a second, related trend: whereas 24.6% of Anglophone men who stated they were members of the working or lower classes identified with the NDP, only 16.5% of women expressed such identification (compared with 13.0% and 10.9% of middle-class men and women, respectively).

In short, then, we would propose that the differential attention paid to women and men, and specifically to women's and men's concerns in politics, contributed to divergent patterns of NDP support during the years between female enfranchisement and the development of contemporary feminism. Among respondents who came of age politically through 1950, as well as those residing in union households and identifying themselves as members of the working or lower classes, considerably fewer women than men were NDP supporters. These results, combined with earlier findings concerning NDP partisanship among older women in Western Canada, provide important evidence to the effect that the treatment of women by political organizations constitutes a key factor in determining attitude formation.

CONTEMPORARY PERSPECTIVES ON FEMALE PARTISANSHIP

In the years between 1965 and 1979, important changes occurred in the social, economic, and political status of Canadian women. As described in chapter 1, these changes contributed to the growth of contemporary feminism and, in turn, to the increasingly visible political role of women during the 1970s and following.

The impact of these developments upon partisan attitudes in English Canada is difficult to assess, in part because contemporary feminism remains enmeshed in an older dilemma between conventional partisan-ship, on the one hand, and a more independent route toward political influence, on the other. Despite this tension, however, many feminists who chose to become active partisans in English Canada joined the New Democratic and federal Liberal organizations during the early 1970s and following. We would therefore hypothesize that younger women, whose political experiences included an early and thus impressionable exposure to contemporary feminism, as well as respondents who are committed to

TABLE 2.11
Party identification of Anglophone Canadians, 1979[a]

	Federal level		Provincial level	
	Women	Men	Women	Men
Liberal	37.6	36.9	28.6	24.2
Conservative	42.8	39.3	45.0	38.4
New Democratic	17.4	21.2	18.9	27.9
Social Credit	2.2	2.6	7.5	9.5
(N)	(827)	(730)	(825)	(746)

a Respondents were asked, 'Thinking of *federal* politics, do you usually think of yourself as a Liberal, Conservative, NDP, Social Credit, or what?' Non-identifiers were probed a second time, 'Still thinking of *federal* politics, do you generally think of yourself as being a little closer to one of the parties than to the others?' (If yes) 'Which party is that?' Similar probes, replacing 'federal' with 'provincial,' were employed in order to ascertain provincial party identification.
Source: 1979 Social Change in Canada Study

improved women's rights legislation, would express relatively strong support for the NDP and federal Liberals during the 1970s.

The 1979 Social Change in Canada data offer general support for this proposition, although they also indicate the persistence of gender differences in New Democratic partisanship. As reported in table 2.11, men were 3.8% more likely than women to express NDP identification on the federal level and 9.0% more so on the provincial level (recall that the gender difference on a single measure of party identification in 1965 was 6.5%). This result confirms earlier findings in table 2.3 which show a significant overall gender difference in 1979 using the additive measure of NDP support. In reference to Liberal partisanship, data in table 2.11 also suggest that women were slightly more likely to be Liberal supporters than men at both the federal and provincial levels. In 1979, 37.6% of the female national sample reported Liberal party identification at the federal level, compared with 36.9% of males.

The generational correlates of female party identification in 1979, summarized in table 2.12, show that Liberal and New Democratic support was indeed highest in the youngest birth cohort. That is, women born since 1950, who came of age politically after 1970, were most likely to express preference for the federal Liberals (40.0%) and New Democrats (23.7%); at the same time, Conservative support among both women and men was relatively low in this group. Notably, the gender difference in NDP identification among respondents born after 1950 was less than 1%

TABLE 2.12
Federal party identification of Anglophone Canadians by birth cohorts, 1979[a]

	1950-61		1938-49		1926-37		1914-27		Before 1914	
	Women	Men	Women	Men	Women	Men	Women	Men	Women	Men
Liberal	40.0	43.0	37.8	35.6	35.5	34.6	38.9	34.0	32.4	31.7
Conservative	33.3	31.9	39.0	36.7	50.5	44.3	49.5	47.6	52.7	42.8
New Democratic	23.7	23.3	21.7	25.8	13.6	19.3	9.4	15.8	11.1	18.3
Social Credit	3.0	1.8	1.5	1.9	0.4	1.8	2.2	2.6	3.8	7.2
(N)	(220)	(220)	(223)	(164)	(160)	(127)	(147)	(131)	(74)	(88)

a For exact question wording, see table 2.11.
Source: 1979 Social Change in Canada Study

(0.4%), which represented the lowest sex difference in New Democratic partisanship of any cohort sampled.

What was the relationship between class and unionization factors, on the one hand, and party identification, on the other, in 1979? Data from the Social Change in Canada survey show that as in 1965, gender differences in NDP support among respondents stating that they belonged to the working or lower classes exceeded differences among the middle class. Overall, 36.3% of working-class men and only 24.2% of working-class women stated that they identified provincially with the New Democrats, compared with 24.1% and 15.9% of middle-class men and women.

One plausible explanation of this finding, which follows from lower levels of female unionization in Canada, is that working-class women were less likely to be exposed to partisan – and specifically NDP – stimuli in the workplace than working-class men.[29] If we consider unionized respondents only, however, similar differentials remain, with 38.1% of unionized males and 28.5% of unionized females identifying with the New Democrats provincially, and 36.5% and 22.9% federally. In other words, both subjective social class and unionization appeared to exert a disparate political impact upon women and men in 1979 as well as 1965, perhaps because of a continued masculine bias within trade unions as well as political parties.

Turning in conclusion to the relationship between feminist beliefs and partisanship in 1979, our data (not reported in tabular form) indicate that 26.7% of English-Canadian females who endorsed much more government effort to eliminate discrimination against women identified federally with the New Democrats, while 30.8% did so provincially (comparable figures for men were 27.5% and 28.3%).[30] Given that aggregate levels of NDP support among women (reported in table 2.11) were in the 18% range, these results confirm our expectation that feminist beliefs would be positively associated with New Democratic identification in 1979. In comparison, levels of Liberal partisanship were very similar among respondents endorsing much more government effort as among the sample at large, while Conservative identification was generally lower among those wanting much more effort, relative to the overall sample.

Our two hypotheses regarding contemporary partisanship in English Canada, therefore, are confirmed to some extent by the 1979 survey data. We have reported relatively high levels of New Democratic and Liberal party identification among younger female respondents, as well as a positive relationship between NDP partisanship and feminist attitudes. Overall, these findings suggest that the contemporary feminist movement has helped to shape women's political attitudes in English Canada, particularly in relation to the New Democratic and federal Liberal parties.

CONCLUSIONS

This chapter began by examining the treatment of women in conventional public opinion research, and argued that a number of existing Canadian studies portray women as politically 'traditional' voters whose attitudes result from a general condition of social 'isolation.' Data from the 1965 national election study were introduced in order to evaluate both the direction and correlates of women's attitudes; they confirmed lower female support for the NDP but offered little evidence that this pattern was related to women's religiosity or limited educational attainment.

More importantly, analysis of the 1965 results suggested that patterns of female politicization and partisanship in English Canada are related to enfranchisement-period experiences, including an alliance between suffragist and agrarian / labour interests in Western Canada. Additional figures from 1965 and 1979 also point toward the role of historical influences, since they showed that generational, class, and unionization factors continue to have a differential impact upon men's and women's attitudes through the contemporary period.

Overall, then, we would conclude that the political history of Canadian women holds important implications for public opinion, even though conventional electoral research has tended to overlook this historical dimension.

3

The Higher the Fewer: Women's Participation in Major Party Organizations

She has been working in the trenches of this party for years ... and particularly around the kitchen tables of this party.[1]

Writing in 1950, historian Catherine Cleverdon suggested that a brighter future would await Canadian women who sought to become active in partisan politics. Cleverdon believed there existed 'some evidence that political parties are becoming increasingly aware of the need to offer women something more in the way of political activity than to do party chores and to vote for their candidates (male, of course) on election days.'[2] Cleverdon's hopeful expectations were expressed more than three decades following the federal-level enfranchisement of Canadian women, a struggle which she documented in detail in *The Woman Suffrage Movement in Canada*. In large part, this optimism grew out of a sense that the increasing educational and employment opportunities which were available to women after World War II would serve to enhance future levels of political participation.

Despite these promising trends, however, the political involvement of Canadian women in the post-war years bore close resemblance to that of previous decades. As Rosamonde Boyd (1968) observed in a comparative American-Canadian study, 'women's rise to responsible positions of decision-making and administrative leadership has been slow and sporadic.'[3] The impact of traditional role constraints, combined with what Boyd termed 'an underestimation of their political potential' by North American women generally, thus contributed to an older trend whereby females were less numerous than males in positions of visible political influence.[4] As legislators, cabinet ministers, and party leaders, women were simply few and far between.

A growing recognition of this weak numerical representation in North American political elites helped to fuel the feminist movement of the late 1960s and following. As we have argued in chapter 1, feminists responded to their lack of representation in diverse ways, including through the fielding of independent candidates in federal elections, as well as by the establishment of increasingly assertive women's groups within major party organizations. Overall, the objective of such activities was fairly consistent across time and across party ideologies: namely, to elevate both the numerical and substantive (i.e., policy) impact of women in Canadian politics.

The general approach which was adopted in order to achieve this goal frequently began with an examination of the problem of political candidacy. Following early research in the field of Canadian women and politics by Jill McCalla Vickers and Janine Brodie, partisan and independent feminist activists questioned how the numbers of female candidates in winnable ridings could be increased and, concomitantly, how the overall policy priority accorded to so-called women's issues could be improved.[5]

On the level of research, one of the major difficulties with this approach has been its failure to situate women's participation within the broader context of party life at all levels. While political candidacy remains an important and highly visible form of elite-level involvement, it hardly captures the diverse and oftentimes less visible activities which generate, and regenerate, party organization in a modern democracy.[6] Local constituency-level work, campaign activity other than candidacy for public office, participation in party women's groups, internal party office-holding, delegation to party conventions, and many other types of party involvement have generally been overlooked in Canada because of an overriding concern with female candidacy.

In this chapter, we begin to redress the imbalance in research on women's participation in Canadian politics by examining four major types of party work which have been neglected in the literature thus far. They concern the following: first, local constituency activity; second, delegation to party conventions; third, party office-holding on the provincial and federal levels; and fourth, campaign management. We then introduce data on women's political candidacies, legislative office-holding, and cabinet appointments in order to update existing research in this area and to compare the problem of female candidacy with the constraints facing women at other levels of party activity. This discussion forms the empirical background for our more speculative examination in chapter 4 of female representation on elite levels, where we explore efforts by women to institute internal party affirmative action programs and to achieve positions of major party leadership in English Canada.

Our main purpose in this chapter is to expand the study of women's political participation in Canada beyond the question of candidacy for public office and, in this manner, to situate female political involvement in the broader context of party life at all levels. In so doing, we illuminate some of the constraints which continue to shape female party work at these various levels, and also illustrate the extent to which women in English Canada have been, and are, active and valuable partisans despite their numerical absence as elected legislators. In the words of former Liberal MP Judy LaMarsh, 'All political parties in Canada operate by and through women. Look into any committee room and you will find perhaps a man or two but dozens of women ... My own nomination was secured because, as well as the group of men active in the party's inner circles, I gathered about me a group of women who had done the real donkey work in past elections.'[7]

Like the Conservative activist referred to in the epigraph to this chapter, Liberal and New Democratic women have also laboured long and hard in the 'trenches' of their parties. Although relatively few have advanced beyond the point of routine 'trench warfare,' it is important to recognize their contributions at each level of party activity. In this way, we are able to document from a Canadian perspective the phenomenon which Robert Putnam (1976) refers to as 'the law of increasing disproportion' – that is, the higher one goes in party elites, the fewer women are to be found.[8] As summarized in figure 2, this law is clearly applicable to political party activity by women in Canada, where the percentage of female participants declines from a peak of approximately 70%, in the case of local constit uency association recording secretaries, to a low of 0%, in the case of major party leaders. As a corollary to Putnam's argument, we suggest in the following sections that the more competitive the political position of any given provincial or federal party, and thus the higher the power stakes within that organization, the fewer women are to be found.

We shall begin this study by examining patterns of local constituency activity.

LOCAL CONSTITUENCY ACTIVITY

Local riding associations form a key political groundwork for major pro-vincial- and federal-level parties in English Canada. Although many exist on paper only between elections, their mere presence at the constituency

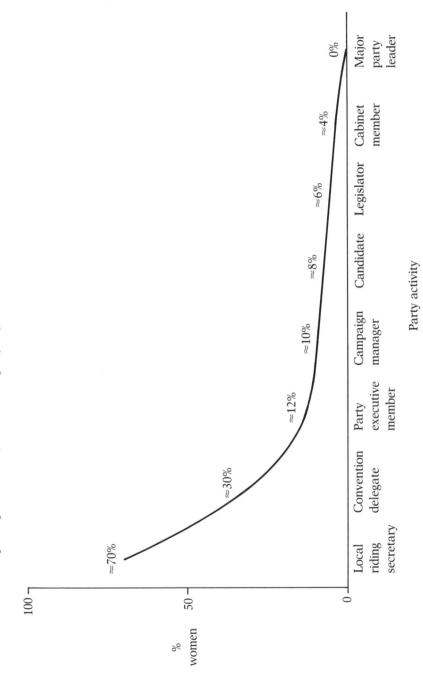

FIGURE 2 Women's participation in major Canadian party organizations

level helps to ensure a credible image of province- or nation-wide organization for the larger party grouping. In addition, by providing a core of
real or potential political activists, and by functioning as a recruitment
and mobilization arm for their parent party, local riding associations
perform a valuable but often neglected role in the party system.

The participation of women in local riding associations is generally
neglected in the Canadian politics literature. One project which does
consider this subject in the context of urban party organizations concludes
that women form a disproportionately small segment of party insider
(intermediate level) and elite (top organizational) strata, at the same time
as they are relatively overrepresented in the party stalwart (routine functionary) category.[9] According to Harold D. Clarke and Allan Kornberg
(1979), the few Canadian women who are involved in urban party activities
tend to work harder than their male colleagues and, at the same time,
expect fewer tangible rewards for their commitment. Clarke and Kornberg
suggest that these females 'are in a very real sense "survivors," ' who
have reconciled themselves to the 'law of increasing disproportion' within
urban party organizations.[10]

What types of activities do women perform in local constituency associations? While data collected by Kornberg, Smith, and Clarke (1979)
suggest that 'relatively similar proportions of men and women were members of their constituency executive committees or held poll captain and
miscellaneous lower level positions,' our own research points toward
considerable gender differences in both the *extent* and *type* of local party
activity in English Canada.[11] More specifically, we suggest that women
perform stereotypically feminine types of party work at the local level in
English Canada. In addition, we propose that the competitive position of
party organizations has a direct impact upon female participation, such
that there are especially few women at the executive level in ridings where
the power stakes are high.

An appropriate place to begin this study of local constituency association activity is the province of Ontario, where approximately 44.8% of
the Anglophone population of Canada reside.[12] With 95 (33.7%) of the
nation's federal ridings, and 125 (18.0%) of its provincial seats, Ontario
remains the longstanding centre of political, as well as economic and
social, gravity for most of Canada.

Figures on local riding participation at the provincial level in Ontario,
presented in table 3.1, document women's involvement in 125 provincial
constituency associations in each of the three major parties. In terms of
riding executive positions, our data indicate that, as expected, women in

TABLE 3.1
Riding-level participation of women in Ontario, by provincial party and year[a]

Riding position	Party and year					
	Liberal	New Democratic		Progressive Conservative		
	1981	1973	1981	1977	1981	
President	20.0 (25)	8.5 (10)	28.8 (36)	9.6 (12)	14.4 (18)	
Treasurer / CFO	29.6 (37)	–	41.6 (52)	5.6 (7)	12.0 (15)	
Recording secretary	76.8 (96)	–	67.2 (84)	62.4 (78)	66.4 (83)	
Membership secretary / memb. chair	–	–	53.6 (67)	–	69.6 (87)	

a Cell entries represent the percentage of riding positions held by women in the years and parties indicated. Figures in parentheses represent the actual number of women holding these positions. Note that percentages for 1977 and 1981 are calculated on a base N of 125 ridings, while those for 1973 are on a base of 117 ridings.
Source: Cell entries for 1981 are drawn from party records made available to the author, while 1973 and 1977 figures are from internal party studies. A dash indicates that information was not available.

all three provincial parties are considerably less likely to serve as local riding presidents than men. In 1981, women comprised 14.4% of Conservative riding presidents ($N = 18$), 20.0% of Liberal riding presidents (25), and 28.8% of NDP riding presidents (36), so that overall in Ontario there were 79 female riding presidents out of a possible 375 in the three provincial parties, or 21.1%. The level of female representation in riding treasurerships was similar, except in the NDP, where male-female parity was approached (41.6%).

Comparing riding secretary and membership secretary data with these figures points toward the existence of a 'pink-collar' sector in local constituency organizations in Ontario. In 1981, between two-thirds and three-quarters of riding secretaries in the three parties were female (notably, 76.8% in the provincial Liberal organization), and membership secretary positions seemed to be held disproportionately by women as well. Therefore, it would appear that the same types of executive and financial positions usually held by men in the Canadian labour force generally are also held by them in the Ontario provincial ridings. At the same time, the more clerical and generally less prestigious positions in which women are clustered in the work force are also those where they seem to be ghettoized in Ontario riding associations. It should be noted, however, that this clustering is least pronounced in the NDP riding associations, where women are better represented as presidents and particularly as financial officers than in the Liberal and Conservative organizations, and are also less likely to serve as membership secretaries than in the Conservative ridings.[13]

What other conclusions can be drawn from these riding-level data? First, in reference to their decision-making implications, the figures would initially suggest that few women wield effective power in local party organizations. However, upon closer inspection of internal riding activity in all three cases, we would propose that large numbers of women perform critical human relations, and especially communications, functions at the local level. As secretaries and membership chairs, they help to ensure organizational continuity by keeping local riding minutes, recruiting new members, and maintaining older memberships. In cases where the riding president or treasurer is not active, these women would also appear to provide the only visible evidence of their party's presence in the riding. Therefore, while it is important to recognize the implicit and often indirect nature of 'pink-collar' power in the Ontario ridings, the importance of women's contributions should not be overlooked.

Second, and parallel with this first point, our research suggests that many Ontario women who have broken out of the 'pink collar' ghetto have done so in ridings where their party is generally inactive and has little chance of electoral success. That is, a considerable number of female riding presidents in all three parties seem to hold symbolic power only, since they have little opportunity to elect members to their legislative caucus and thus cannot attract resources from the central provincial organization – which, in turn, helps to propel party activity on the local level. For example, our research shows that female NDP riding presidents in 1981 were clustered in rural Liberal and suburban Conservative-held seats, while Liberal women were frequently elected in strong Tory and New Democratic areas. In short, then, the number of women holding formal positions of power on the riding level may be less significant than the competitive position of their respective parties – a factor which seems to suggest that there is little real political power in many of the constituencies where women hold prominent executive positions.

A third conclusion which may be drawn from data in table 3.1 concerns longitudinal or cross-time change in female riding involvement. While few longitudinal figures are available, those which are suggest a significant increase in women's participation during the past decade, which corresponds with the growth of feminist activism in Ontario, and in Canada

TABLE 3.2
Riding-level participation of women in major Manitoba provincial parties, 1982[a]

Position	New Democratic		Progressive Conservative	
President	14.3	(8)	12.7	(7)
Vice-president	16.1	(9)	15.1	(8)
Treasurer	41.1	(23)	43.6	(24)
Recording secretary	69.6	(39)	–	
Membership sec'y	40.0	(12/30)	69.8	(37)
(N) of women	(91)		(76)	

a Cell entries represent the percentage of riding positions held by women in the parties
  indicated. Figures in parentheses represent the actual number of women holding these
  positions. Note that Progressive Conservative entries are calculated on a base N of
  53-55 ridings, and NDP entries on a base N of 56 (some of the province's 57 ridings
  had no executive).
Source: Party records made available to the author

generally. In the provincial NDP, for example, only 10 women held riding
presidencies in 1973, compared with 36 in 1981. This change represents
an increase of more than threefold over an eight-year period. Data from
Conservative ridings suggest increased involvement as well, since 19 women
were presidents or treasurers in 1977, and 33 held these same positions
in 1981. However, during this same four-year period women also became
more numerous as Conservative riding secretaries (from 78 to 83), indi-
cating that women continue to fill 'pink-collar' positions in many Ontario
riding associations.

Comparable participation data from Manitoba, presented in table 3.2,
indicate that fairly similar patterns obtain in a two-party provincial political system. In 1982, women comprised less than 15% of NDP and
Conservative riding presidents, with figures for riding association vice-
presidents only slightly higher. As in the case of Ontario, female office-
holding at these levels was greater in the New Democratic than the
Conservative party, but only marginally so. Once again the heavy clustering of women in 'pink-collar' or clerical riding work was pronounced,
with females comprising 69.6% of NDP secretaries and 69.8% of PC membership secretaries at the constituency level.[14]

Overall, the proportions of women who held non-clerical positions in
the main Manitoba provincial parties were generally lower than comparable proportions from the Ontario provincial organizations, a finding
which suggests that contemporary feminism may exert a more profound
partisan influence in the relatively urbanized and industrialized areas of

central Canada. Moreover, the fact that Manitoba would appear to have a more competitive provincial party system than that of Ontario – given the alternation in governing parties during recent decades – may mean that women are more likely to be 'frozen out' of prominent riding-level office in the former than in the latter.

Since much political activity in English Canada occurs outside of local riding associations, particularly at party conventions and in provincial-level and campaign organizations, we shall now turn our attention to these other participatory arenas.

PATTERNS OF CONVENTION DELEGATION

Conventions of the major Canadian political parties provide an important setting for both formal and informal decision-making. Whether organized as leadership or policy forums, conventions are designed to bring together diverse regional, ideological, and ethnic delegations, in an effort to obtain a representative hearing from each segment of the party base.[15]

Despite common assumptions regarding the socially representative character of Canadian party conventions, especially leadership conventions, data on the proportion of female delegates to these meetings point toward a continuing pattern of underrepresentation.[16] In fact, the few studies which consider female involvement generally employ figures from the late 1960s to compare levels of male and female delegation to major party conventions in North America.[17] The extent of women's under-representation during these years, however, and the subsequent growth in their convention delegation from less than 20% in the United States and Canada in 1968 to more than double that figure at the present time, have elicited barely a nod from Canadian political scientists.[18] It is for this reason that we now turn our attention to levels of convention delegation in both Canada and the United States.

In historical terms, the participation of women in Canadian party conventions has been generally viewed as slight, or at best episodic. One source notes that at least two women, including social feminist Nellie McClung, attended the 1914 Manitoba Liberal convention which endorsed woman suffrage.[19] Cleverdon's (1950, 1974) history also points out that the pressure which was applied subsequently by suffragists in British Columbia and Quebec helped to ensure the adoption of pro-enfranchisement platforms – and, ultimately, the successful sponsorship of suffrage legislation – by both provincial Liberal parties. Overall, however, women are more frequently viewed as the perennial spouses of male convention

TABLE 3.3
Women delegates at major American and Canadian party conventions, 1952-83

Party	Year	Women delegates (%)
Democratic	1952	12.5
Republican	1952	10.5
Democratic[a]	1964	25
Republican[a]	1964	27
Federal Progressive Conservative	1967	19
Federal Liberal	1968	18
Democratic	1968	12.9
Republican	1968	16.7
Democratic	1972	39.9
Republican	1972	30.1
Democratic[a]	1976	50
Republican[a]	1976	39
Democratic	1980	50
Republican	1980	N/A
Federal New Democratic	1981	34.7
Federal Progressive Conservative	1981	33.0
Ontario Liberal	1982	39.2
Ontario New Democratic	1982	40.0
Federal Liberal	1982	37.6
Federal Progressive Conservative	1983 (Winnipeg)	41.4
Federal Progressive Conservative[b]	1983 (Ottawa)	28.0

a Denotes Michigan delegates only.
b Alternates to the 1983 Conservative leadership convention included 36% women.
Sources: Carl Baar and Ellen Baar, 'Party and Convention Organization and Leadership Selection in Canada and the United States,' in Donald R. Matthews, ed., *Perspectives on Presidential Selection* (Washington, DC: Brookings, 1973); John C. Courtney, *The Selection of National Party Leaders in Canada* (Toronto: Macmillan, 1973); M. Kent Jennings and Norman Thomas, 'Men and Women in Party Elites,' *Midwest Journal of Political Science* 12 (1968); M. Kent Jennings and Barbara G. Farah, 'Social Roles and Political Resources,' *American Journal of Political Science* 25 (1981); *Congressional Quarterly Weekly Report*, 16 August 1980; and party records.

delegates and as alternates or observers who play only marginal political roles at major party meetings.

This impression is generally confirmed by data from the early 1950s through the late 1960s, presented in table 3.3. In the United States in 1952, for example, women comprised less than 13% of delegates to the two major presidential conventions, while in 1968 the percentage of female delegates at the Republican convention rose to approximately 17%. The comparable figure for the Democratic party in 1968 was 12.9%, only marginally higher than the 12.5% level established nearly fifteen years earlier.

The percentage of women delegates to major Canadian party conventions in this period was slightly higher than in the American case. For example, comparing 1967 Progressive Conservative with 1968 Republican figures in table 3.3, we find that the level of female delegation to the former was 2.3% higher than to the latter, while comparing Liberal with Democratic delegation during this same period, we obtain a difference of 5.1%.

However, this edge in Canadian party delegation was eliminated by American party reforms of the 1970s, most notably the equal representation or affirmative action terms adopted at the 1972 U.S. Democratic convention (see chapter 4, below). As female delegation reached the 50% target in the Democratic case in 1976, women's involvement in comparable Canadian parties remained close to older pre-affirmative action levels in the United States. Perhaps most notably, the percentage of female party delegates to the 1982 Ontario Liberal and NDP conventions resembled closely the figures for Democratic presidential conventions held ten years earlier (see table 3.3). Similarly, federal-level convention delegation in Canada has generally remained in the 33% to 41% range which, while constituting an important improvement over earlier results in the under 20% range, remains similar to the older 1972 Democratic level of about 40%.

The absence of formal affirmative action provisions in most major Canadian political parties may help to account for a continuing under-representation of women as party delegates. Alongside this explanation, however, it is important to recognize that most ex-officio and, in the case of the NDP, union-affiliated delegates to party meetings are men. That is, party officials, elected legislators, unsuccessful legislative candidates, senators, and similarly delegated party dignitaries are overwhelmingly male and comprise a considerable proportion of voting members at any given convention. Therefore, parties which pursue increased female representation on the riding level could find that their efforts are diluted in the convention as a whole because of the presence of ex-officio delegates.

This problem is clearly illustrated in data on delegation to the 1981 federal NDP convention, summarized in table 3.4. Even though women comprised 40% of youth and 41% of riding delegates, their overall presence at the convention was reduced to a level of 34.7% because of weak rep-

TABLE 3.4
Women delegates to 1981 federal NDP convention

Category	Women delegates (%)
Riding delegates	41
Youth delegates	40
Federal council (ex-officio)	30
Affiliated trade unions	11
Federal caucus (ex-officio)	8
Overall delegates	34.7

Source: Party records made available to the author

resentation in the federal caucus (8%), affiliated trade union (11%), and federal council (30%) delegations.

In short, therefore, the limited representation of women within elected party elites holds important implications for their involvement at other levels, including as convention delegates. We shall now turn our attention to this question of party office-holding by women.

PARTY OFFICE-HOLDING

Most important decision-making within Canadian party organizations, both between and during election campaigns, occurs among official and unofficial party elites at the provincial and federal levels. Whether these elites gather at specifically designated executive meetings or in informal backroom settings, their discussions frequently determine party campaign strategies, leadership politics, and the overall deployment of human and financial resources within the larger party organization.

In a recent study of urban activists, Kornberg, Smith, and Clarke (1979) characterize party elites as primarily male, middle-aged, politicized, and well-educated members of the Canadian middle class.[20] In proportional terms, the authors of *Citizen Politicians* acknowledge that few decision-makers are female, particularly after those women who automatically hold provincial- or federal-level party office by virtue of their position in affiliated women's associations are removed from consideration.

Aside from the study by Kornberg, Smith, and Clarke, little systematic data have been assembled to document the dimensions of female under-representation within Canadian party elites. One factor which helps to account for this absence is a general lack of interest in women and politics among Canadian social scientists. In addition, the disparate structures which exist in Canadian political parties discourage such research, since the names and functions of official decision-making bodies vary widely across parties. Moreover, the role of these organizations frequently changes over time within a single party, given that election planning groups, for example, may pre-empt party executives or councils during the period of an election campaign. To complicate matters further, data on female representation in party officialdom may offer a distorted view of actual participation and influence, since 'token' women on figurehead boards or committees are unlikely to provide meaningful input into party decision-making.

Bearing in mind these problems, we can begin to evaluate the extent of formal representation in party elites using data from the Ontario (three-party) and Manitoba (two-party) provincial systems. Briefly, the constitutionally recognized structures of the three Ontario parties are as follows: the Ontario Liberal (OLP) and Progressive Conservative (PC) organizations are both governed by table officers and additional party representatives who form a party executive; this group is responsible for calling meetings and administering party finances and routine operations. In the case of the OLP, representatives of four Ontario regions (three per region) hold seats on the executive committee.[21]

The provincial organization of the Ontario NDP is somewhat more complex. The party is formally administered by nine provincial officers who, in conjunction with fifteen members-at-large, two delegates to the NDP Federal Council, two youth delegates, and one female delegate to the Participation of Women (POW) Committee on the Federal Council, form the provincial executive. However, the party constitution states that 'the Provincial Council shall be the governing body between conventions.'[22] This council meets at least three times annually, and its membership includes the provincial executive, two provincial and two federal caucus members, plus approximately 150 riding delegates, whose numbers are apportioned on the basis of riding membership (with at least one council delegate from each NDP riding executive in Ontario). The provincial council and executive are each empowered to appoint committees to look after administration, fund-raising, and various policy areas.

In light of these differing constitutional arrangements in the three Ontario political parties, what generalizations can be made about provincial-level participation? Data in table 3.5 indicate that it is in the relatively complex and decentralized NDP organization that women are most numerous on the provincial level. A comparison of 1981 executive officers in all three parties shows that females comprise 12.8% of the Liberal provincial leadership, 16.7% of the Conservative, and 39.3% of the New Democratic.

TABLE 3.5
Provincial-level participation of women in Ontario by party, 1981

Party	Organization	Position	% women (proportion)
Liberal	OLP Executive Committee	Table officers	12.5 (1/8)
		Regional rep.	8.3 (1/12)
New Democratic	ONDP Provincial Council	Riding delegates	27.9 (41/147)
	ONDP Provincial Executive	Officers and members	39.3 (11/28)
	ONDP Provincial Committees	Members, 1981, average[a]	27.6
Progressive Conservative	Ontario Progressive Conservative Association Executive	Table officers	16.7 (3/18)

a The ONDP provincial committees which were included in the calculation of this average were as follows: Administrative, Budget, Campaign Techniques Review, Constitution, Education, Election Planning, Electoral District Agents, Ethnic Liaison, Franco-
Ontarian, Fund-raising, Media Advisory, Policy and Resolutions, Policy Review,
Tripartite, and Youth Steering. The Women's Committee Executive is made up of all
women and was excluded from this calculation as it would tend to distort the results.
Source: Party records made available to the author

Informal efforts to produce gender parity on NDP executive slates prior
to the 1982 internal affirmative action resolution would seem to have
contributed to this pattern. The composition of NDP council delegations
(27.9% female) and provincial committees (27.6% female, on average) also
indicates relatively high levels of participation by women, while their
limited representation as regional directors in the OLP (8.3%) suggests
that the absence of a women's organization on the provincial level (see
chapter 5, below) has produced particularly weak patterns of involvement.

Turning to data on provincial elites in Manitoba, presented in table
3.6, we find that the structures of the two major parties parallel closely
their counterparts in Ontario. That is, the mandate of executive committee
table officers in the Manitoba PC organization, and of provincial council
and executive members in the Manitoba NDP, is virtually identical to the
constitutional responsibilities assigned to comparable elites in Ontario.

However, cross-party differences in Manitoba bear little similarity to
those in Ontario. Executive officers in both the provincial NDP and PC

TABLE 3.6
Provincial-level participation of women in Manitoba by party, 1982

Party	Organization	Position	% women (proportion)
New Democractic	Provincial Council	Riding delegates	17.5 (10/57)
	Provincial Executive	Officers and members	42.9 (6/14)
	Provincial committees	Members, 1981 average[a]	25.7
Progressive Conservative	Executive Committee	Table officers	40.0 (4/10)

a Manitoba NDP committees which were included in the calculation of this average were as follows: Agriculture, Constitution, Convention Planning, Editorial Board, Finance, Labour Support, Ethnic Liaison, Organization, Municipal, Policy, and Political Education.
Source: Party records made available to the author

organizations were approximately 40% female in 1982, at the same time as riding delegates to the NDP provincial Council were composed of less than 20% women in that year (see table 3.6). In Manitoba, therefore, the smaller PC executive had a considerably higher proportion of women than in the larger Ontario case (40.0% versus 16.7%), while the smaller NDP provincial council had a substantially lower percentage of women than the Ontario party council (17.5% versus 27.9%). In speculating on possible reasons for these results, we would suggest that the governing position of the Manitoba NDP and Ontario PC organizations, in contrast to the Opposition role of the Ontario NDP and Manitoba PCs, may have created a relatively competitive internal environment which was not conducive to elevated levels of female involvement. By way of comparison, the Opposition status of their provincial counterparts could generate a less competitive atmosphere where levels of female participation were somewhat higher.

Data from 1983 on federal party office-holding, presented in table 3.7, also indicate that women constituted proportionately fewer of the national party elites in the more powerful Liberal and Conservative parties than in the NDP. At a time when the Conservatives ranked particularly high in public opinion polls, relative to both the Liberals and New Democrats, the percentage of females in the Tory national executive was only 23.8%, or approximately 20% less than the 43.3% level which obtained in the Liberal organization. It is notable, however, that within the federal Liberal

TABLE 3.7
Federal party office-holding by women in Canada, 1983

Party	Organization	% women (proportion)
Liberal	National Executive	43.3 (13/30)
	Policy Committee	28.6 (6/21)
New Democratic	Federal Executive	50.0 (6/12)
	Federal Council	60.0 (12/20)
Progressive Conservative	National Executive	23.8 (35/147)

Source: Party records made available to the author

elite, women were not as well-represented in at least one crucial area of party decision-making, namely the Standing Committee on Policy. Although the position of policy chair has been held by women since 1978 (Celine Hervieux-Payette, followed in 1980 by Lorna Marsden), members of the committee overall include 26.8% females, compared with 43.3% in the national executive.

In the third federal party, the NDP, an affirmative action resolution which was adopted and implemented in 1983 (see chapter 4) ensured that female representation in elite bodies would be at or above parity. As reported in table 3.7, women constituted 60.0% of federal council members in 1983 and 50.0% of federal executive members.

The impact of competitive party position on women's representation at elite levels is also reflected in the experience of backroom political strategists. Although this type of party involvement is generally shielded from public view, and thus remains difficult to assess directly, the few women who have held backroom positions in major party organizations tend to agree that their underrepresentation is most pronounced in competitive (usually governing) party organizations. While participation may drop to zero or possibly one in ten in such cases, it is important to note that women's involvement in opposition backrooms is generally low as well. As one informant, a former participant in backroom politics on the federal level, observed, 'We were clearly the third party in national politics, yet the circle around the federal leader remained a real male network ... It was extremely difficult to break through that network and, above all, I found that once inside it, people would raise their eyebrows if I pushed issues – and particularly what they viewed as "women's issues," too hard.'

This account by a New Democratic partisan is confirmed by women in the other major federal parties, and by female backroom participants in a number of provincial party organizations.[23] In general, their experiences offer support for our argument that women remain numerically under-represented in positions (whether formal or informal) of major party responsibility, particularly where such positions are synonymous with political or governmental power.

Ultimately, the focus of activity for most party elites is provincial or federal election day. It is to women's involvement as campaign managers and candidates that we now turn our attention.

CAMPAIGN MANAGEMENT

Although the operation and administration of local election campaigns is generally overlooked in studies of Canadian political parties, experience as a campaign manager would seem to offer valuable organizational training and visibility for aspiring activists. In particular, partisans who aim toward future involvement as candidates on their own behalf may 'learn the ropes' regarding nomination and campaign organization in their role as campaign managers. In the case of female managers, this experience could provide a useful basis from which to cultivate media, party, and external fund-raising contacts.

The extent of women's involvement as campaign managers in English Canada, summarized in table 3.8, has varied widely across time, region, and party. For example, longitudinal data from Ontario suggest that female participation generally increased between 1971 and 1981, reaching as high as 34.7% in the case of NDP managers for the 1980 federal campaign. By way of comparison, there were 22.4% female managers in the provincial Liberal and 12.8% in the provincial Conservative organizations in 1981. These data represent some improvement over figures from the 1970s, since only 19 women (or 16.2%) were NDP managers in the 1971 campaign (versus 41 or 32.8% in 1981), and only 9 (or 7.2%) were Conservative managers in the 1977 election (versus 16 or 12.8% in 1981). Contemporary data from Manitoba, Nova Scotia, and Saskatchewan, also presented in table 3.8, indicate that women's involvement as campaign managers is somewhat lower outside of Ontario, in both federal and provincial campaign organizations.

Although it is difficult to generalize on the basis of these figures, we would suggest that female campaign managers may constitute an important pool of future legislative candidates. That is, women may become more numerous as political candidates if the campaign management route

TABLE 3.8
Campaign management by women in English Canada for various parties and elections

Ontario Liberal		Ontario New Democratic			Ontario Progressive Conservative	
1980 fed.	1981 prov.	1971 prov.	1980 fed.	1981 prov.	1977 prov.	1981 prov.
26.3	22.4	16.2	34.7	32.8	7.2	12.8
(25)	(28)	(19)	(33)	(41)	(9)	(16)

	Manitoba New Democratic 1981 prov.		Manitoba Progressive Conservative 1981 prov.	
	15.8 (9)		8.8 (5)	

Nova Scotia Liberal		Yukon New Democratic		Saskatchewan New Democratic	
1980 fed.	1981 prov.	1980 fed.	1982 terr.	1980 fed.	1982 prov.
–	23.1	–	37.5	–	28.1
(0)	(12)	(0)	(6)	(0)	(18)

Source: Party records made available to the author

to political candidacy is exploited successfully by experienced female managers. However, as is the case with riding-level activism and candidacy itself, it is important to consider the viability of party organization in a specific locale in order to determine just how valuable women's campaign management may be to their political mobility. If female campaign managers become clustered in marginal seats, and later win nomination in these same ridings, then it is unlikely that the basic pattern of 'the higher the fewer,' and 'the more competitive the fewer,' will be altered.

We shall now consider the question of female political candidacies in English Canada.

CANDIDACY FOR PUBLIC OFFICE

Much of the existing research on women's participation in Canadian politics has focused on the troubling question of election to public office. Contemporary studies by Janine Brodie and Jill McCalla Vickers, as well as older work by Catherine Cleverdon, have considered the dynamics of political nomination, candidacy, and election.[24] Most have concluded that gender role socialization, a lack of time and money among qualified women, discrimination within political organizations, and the more general identification of politics as a public and therefore masculine activity militate against female involvement in the Canadian campaign process. Furthermore, these same factors have been linked with the proliferation of women candidates in no-win or long-shot constituencies in Canada.

The extensive documentation of female candidacies by Brodie and Vickers, most notably in the Brodie dissertation, points toward two major empirical generalizations. First, women candidates and office-holders are dispro-portionately involved at the municipal level of government. According to Vickers (1979), this pattern is attributable to the relatively slight financial and personal costs which are incurred by local activists, and to 'the rel-atively low level of power and influence which has the effect of reducing competition [and of weakening] structures such as political parties,' which tend to limit access to recruitment channels.[25] Second, on the basis of this finding and data which show a concentration of women candidates in weak or marginal seats, Brodie and Vickers (1981) suggest that party control over elite recruitment constitutes a critical barrier to increased participation by women in Canadian politics.[26]

While the absence of women in elected legislative office in Canada helps to support this view, the repeated occurrence of 'dirty tricks' within party nomination proceedings provides more direct evidence of gender bias at the level of public candidacy. According to Brodie (1981), 50% of female candidates in competitive ridings experienced 'at least one negative party incident,' compared with 32% among the overall sample of women candidates.[27] Materials gathered by this author during interviews with legislators and candidates also indicate that 'dirty tricks' continue to occur at the riding level, particularly in constituencies where the female nominee has a reasonable chance of winning election. Otherwise, as one candidate in a very weak seat observed, 'the riding executive begs you to run, welcomes you with open arms,.and implicitly recognizes that no man with similar qualifications would consider such a "nomination." '

Since previous studies of female candidacy for public office in Canada address the period prior to 1975, our main purpose in this section is to present contemporary data which update the existing literature. In par-ticular, we consider two specific questions concerning partisan candidacy on the provincial and federal levels: First, to what extent were women underrepresented as candidates during recent election campaigns; and second, how is this pattern of underrepresentation related to competitive party positions in English Canada?

In response to our first point, data in tables 3.9, 3.10, and 3.11 indicate quite clearly that although they are increasingly numerous as legislative

TABLE 3.9
Female candidacies for provincial office in English Canada, 1979-83

Province	Date	Liberal	NDP	PC[a]
Alberta	1979	27.8 (22/79)	13.9 (11/79)	6.3 (5/79)
	1982	16.7 (5/30)	15.2 (12/79)	7.6 (6/79)
British Columbia	1983	18.5 (10/54)	29.8 (17/57)	8.8 (5/57)
Manitoba	1981	15.4 (6/39)	21.1 (12/57)	8.8 (5/57)
Newfoundland	1979	3.8 (2/52)	21.1 (11/52)	3.8 (2/52)
New Brunswick	1982	5.2 (3/58)	17.2 (10/58)	15.5 (9/58)
Nova Scotia	1981	15.4 (8/52)	23.1 (12/52)	1.9 (1/52)
Ontario	1981	6.4 (8/125)	19.2 (24/125)	10.4 (13/125)
PEI	1982	6.2 (2/32)	–	6.2 (2/32)
Saskatchewan	1982	18.7 (12/64)	6.2 (4/64)	6.2 (4/64)

a In British Columbia, Social Credit.
Source: Provincial election returns reported in the *Globe and Mail*, 1979-83

nominees, women continue to be underrepresented on both the federal and provincial levels. On the latter level, for example, the extent of women's participation as candidates has rarely approached 30%, and reached as low as 1.9% in the case of Conservative candidates in the 1981 Nova Scotia provincial election. Overall, our data would seem to confirm arguments presented earlier by Brodie and Vickers, to the effect that there are relatively few female candidates for partisan public office in Canada.

When we turn to the relationship between female candidacies and competitive party position, however, it becomes necessary to refine at least one aspect of the existing literature. More specifically, our data indicate that while female candidates are indeed clustered within parties that hold only a weak or marginal possibility of assuming power, they are not necessarily least numerous in more promising party organizations. As reported in tables 3.9, 3.10, and 3.11, women run fairly often as candidates for perennial third parties, including the Liberals in Alberta and

TABLE 3.10
Female candidacies for House of Commons, 1974-84

Election	Liberal	New Democratic	Progressive Conservative
1974	7.6	15.5	4.2
	(20)	(41)	(11)
1979	7.4	16.7	5.0
	(21)	(47)	(14)
1980	8.2	11.7	5.0
	(23)	(33)	(14)
1984	16.0	22.7	8.2
	(45)	(64)	(23)
Total candidacies	(109)	(185)	(62)

Source: Official Canada Election Returns

TABLE 3.11
Female candidacies for legislative office in Ontario, 1971-84

Election	Liberal	New Democratic	Progressive Conservative
1971 provincial	3.4 (4)	6.0 (7)	5.1 (6)
1974 federal	9.1 (8)	20.4 (18)	4.5 (4)
1975 provincial	14.4 (18)	10.4 (13)	6.4 (8)
1977 provincial	12.0 (15)	15.2 (19)	8.0 (10)
1979 federal	8.4 (8)	16.8 (16)	7.4 (7)
1980 federal	7.4 (7)	10.5 (10)	8.4 (8)
1981 provincial	6.4 (8)	19.2 (24)	10.4 (13)
1984 federal	11.6 (11)	17.9 (17)	5.3 (5)

Source: Official Canada and Ontario Election Returns

Saskatchewan, and the New Democrats in Ontario, Nova Scotia, New Brunswick, and on the federal level.

However, it is important to recognize that the logical corollary to this pattern – that is, parties in a competitive position run few women – is not uniformly the case in English Canada. Although powerful Conservative (and, in British Columbia, Social Credit) parties at the provincial and federal levels consistently nominate relatively few women, this same pattern does not obtain in at least two cases where the NDP holds or approaches a position of governmental responsibility. As reported in table 3.9, New Democratic parties in both British Columbia and Manitoba nominated between 21% and 30% female candidates in recent provincial elections, thus exceeding the proportion of such candidates on both third-party Liberal slates. Party ideology combined with a feminist consciousness inside the party organization, therefore, may constitute an important and widely neglected influence upon patterns of female candidacy, thus complicating an otherwise straightforward relationship between candidacy and competitive party position. A similar conclusion may be drawn from the nomination and election to the federal House of Commons of six Liberal women from Quebec in 1980.

We shall now consider the problem of legislative office-holding among women in English Canada.

LEGISLATIVE OFFICE-HOLDING

The paucity of women as elected legislators in Canada has long been a source of frustration and challenge to observers both inside and outside the chambers of government. In the more than six decades since the election of Louise McKinney and Roberta Macadams as the first female provincial lawmakers (in Alberta) in 1917, and of Agnes Macphail as the first federal MP in 1921, approximately 100 women have held elected legislative office in Canada. Clearly, this record would dismay even the optimistic Macphail, whose biographers describe her initial entrance to the House of Commons as follows: 'She thought of the women who would surely walk this corridor too. "I could almost hear them coming," she said later. Her ear must have been tuned to a still remote time, for in the next quarter century only four other Canadian women were elected to the federal House of Commons.'[28] In light of our discussion of female candidacies, it is not difficult to understand the direct political causes of this situation. As predominantly marginal candidates in federal and provincial elections, women are unlikely to win election, and thus few hold legislative office.[29]

On a deeper level, a wide variety of structural and psychological explanations have been proposed in order to account for the absence of women in elected legislative office, in both Canada and other Western democracies.[30] Perhaps the most compelling reason is one which follows from the interplay of gender role socialization and organizational processes within party politics; that is, the practice and / or expectation of masculine assertiveness, combined with the practice and / or expectation of feminine docility, have served to produce (and reproduce) a predominantly male party elite structure and a predominantly female party support base. Because they are essentially organizations of volunteers, with some careerists in their higher echelons, political parties are very dependent upon the initiative of individual activists – generally men – who until recently had little reason to seek out or encourage women elites. These organizational factors, combined with the impact of gender role socialization, have dealt an especially hard blow to efforts toward increasing female representation within Canadian legislatures.

Many of the women who succeeded Agnes Macphail in the House of Commons shared important personal characteristics and political experiences with her: as a group, female legislators have tended to be unmarried, and childless or else the mothers of grown children. Like Macphail, as well, many have represented Ontario ridings; worked as teachers, journalists, or social workers (unlike their male colleagues who have legal and business backgrounds); and had pre-election political backgrounds.[31] While the specific experiences of these women within the House of Commons have varied, it seems fair to say that all confronted a predominantly masculine environment upon their entrance to Parliament. In the words of Liane Langevin (1977), 'Legislatures are often compared to a men's club in that their membership is predominantly male and consequently, so are their traditions and atmosphere. A woman who enters a legislature as a member is an anomaly, a deviant in the sense that she is defying traditional limits on acceptable feminine behaviour.'[32]

The degree of gender role defiance implied by women's legislative participation has declined, though, with the passage of time. Since the fourteen-year tenure of Agnes Macphail as the sole female MP, and the subsequent election of at least seven women who inherited federal seats from their husbands, the social limitations upon independent political involvement by Canadian women have generally subsided.[33] One important barometre of change has been the appointment of females to federal cabinet positions, beginning in 1957 with the nomination of Hamilton accountant Ellen Fairclough to the secretary of state portfolio (see below).

Despite these notable advances, however, women continue to be vastly underrepresented in both federal and provincial legislatures in Canada.

TABLE 3.12
Female representation in Canadian federal and provincial legislatures, 1982-4

Legislature	Year	% women	(N)
House of Commons	1983	5.7	(16)
House of Commons	1984	9.6	(27)
Provinces overall	1982	6.2	(43)

Sources: Canadian Parliamentary Guide, 1983; *Chatelaine* series on Women in Provincial Politics, 1982; federal election returns reported in the *Globe and Mail*, 6 September 1984

As reported in table 3.12, the percentage of females holding elective parliamentary office in the 1980s remains less than 10%, with an overall provincial figure of 6.2% in 1982 and a federal figure of 9.6% in 1984. The record numbers of women legislators at both levels of government in the contemporary period thus represent a small handful relative to the proportion of women in the Canadian population generally.

Data on female participation in Canadian party caucuses, presented in table 3.13, point toward fairly broad variation in levels of legislative involvement. Governing Conservative parties in Nova Scotia and Ontario, together with the PQ in Quebec, Social Credit in British Columbia, and Liberals federally, tend to have relatively low percentages of women caucus members, as do most Opposition and third parties with the exception of the federal, British Columbia, and Nova Scotia New Democrats, and the Manitoba Conservatives. The highest percentage of female representation in a governing caucus obtains in the Manitoba NDP (14.7%), where a systematic effort was made by party women to secure nomination in winnable ridings prior to the 1981 provincial elections.[34] Similarly, the largest proportion in an Opposition caucus occurs in the British Columbia NDP (15.4%), a finding which may reflect the impact of feminist initiatives by MLA Rosemary Brown and others (see chapter 4).

The appointment of women legislators to provincial and federal cabinets has not necessarily followed from their active caucus participation, however. We shall now conclude this chapter with a brief examination of cabinet-level involvement.

CABINET APPOINTMENTS

The relative absence of Canadian women in competitive, elite-level party roles is most obvious at the pinnacle of political responsibility, where we find no females as either government or major Opposition party leaders.

TABLE 3.13
Female representation in Canadian legislative caucuses, 1982-3

Jurisdiction	Governing party	% women (N)	Official opposition	% women (N)	Third party	% women (N)
Alberta	Conservative	8.1 (6)	Social Credit	0 (0)	NDP	0 (0)
British Columbia	Social Credit	6.4 (2)	NDP	15.4 (4)	–	–
Canada	Liberal	6.8 (10)	Conservative	2.9 (3)	NDP	9.1 (3)
Manitoba	NDP	14.7 (5)	Conservative	8.7 (2)	–	–
Newfoundland	Conservative	9.1 (3)	Liberal	0 (0)	–	–
New Brunswick	Conservative	10.0 (3)	Liberal	3.6 (1)	–	–
Nova Scotia	Conservative	0 (0)	Liberal	0 (0)	NDP[p]	100 (1)
Ontario	Conservative	5.7 (4)	Liberal	3.0 (1)	NDP	4.5 (1)
PEI	Conservative	9.5 (2)	Liberal	0 (0)	–	–
Quebec	Parti quebecois	6.2 (5)	Liberal	7.1 (3)	–	–
Saskatchewan	Conservative	8.8 (5)	NDP	0 (0)	–	–
Territorial governments	Yukon	18.7 (3)	Northwest Territories	9.1 (2)	–	–

Source: Election returns reported in the *Globe and Mail*, 1979-83

In the notch nearest to the top, which is reserved for cabinet-level appointees and prominent Opposition critics (the proverbial 'shadow cabinet'), there are extremely few women, particularly in areas outside of health, education, and status of women portfolios. In fact, females who have assumed cabinet or major Opposition critic roles are often clustered in stereotypically feminine policy areas, generally of a social welfare or cultural nature, or in secondary administrative portfolios which, as in the American case, exploit women's legislative orientation as 'problem-solvers.'[35]

The experiences of the first female cabinet ministers on the federal level in Canada provide a useful illustration of both patterns. Appointed initially to the secretary of state portfolio in 1957, Ellen Fairclough served most of her term in the Diefenbaker cabinet as Minister of Citizenship and Immigration (1958-62) and subsequently as Postmaster General (1962-3). Fairclough describes her appointment and problem-solving orientation toward cabinet responsibilites as follows:

I hadn't expected the Secretary of State portfolio, but rather Labour, but it often happens that the ministerial assignment differs from the earlier shadow cabinet responsibility. Anyway, I was appointed to Citizenship and Immigration shortly thereafter, which proved to be very challenging because I had two citizenship branches plus the one immigration branch under me. I was also superintendant of Indian Affairs, and had a deputy minister in that area. I also had four agencies under me, headed by the Dominion Archivist, and the heads of the National Library, the National Gallery, and the National Film Board ... I worked from dawn to dusk, often on administrative and technical matters which had to do with the establishment of a citizenship courts system, and the coordination of various agencies and ministerial branches under Citizenship and Immigration. People recognized that administration was my strong point, and I imagine this robbed me of some colour.[36]

Fairclough's experiences in cabinet thus indicate fairly early appointment to an adminstratively complex portfolio, which challenged her problem-solving abilities but made little direct impact upon the broader policy directions of the Conservative government.

If Fairclough's appointments and administrative orientation 'robbed some colour' from her cabinet career, then the subsequent nomination of Judy LaMarsh to the Pearson cabinet quickly reversed this trend. LaMarsh entered the Liberal cabinet in 1963 as Minister of National Health and Welfare, a portfolio later assumed by Monique Bégin; subsequently, she became Secretary of State and organized the Canadian centennial celebrations of 1967. During this five-year career in cabinet, LaMarsh was freqently embroiled in conflicts over a new Canada Pension Plan, revisions to the Canada Broadcasting Act, and, probably most important, the establishment of a royal commission on the status of women. Her perceptions of discrimination within the Pearson cabinet and party politics more generally were deep-seated, as reflected in her 1969 autobiography, *Memoirs of a Bird in a Gilded Cage*: 'Throughout my years in the Liberal Party, I never saw evidence that any real attention was paid to seeking out and grooming women as part of the party machinery, or as parliamentary material, except in one area and that was the importuning of fresh widows of MP's to seek their husbands' unexpired terms.'[37]

LaMarsh's belief that gender tended to limit the political roles of female legislators was generally confirmed by later developments. Although Flora MacDonald assumed the external affairs portfolio in the 1979 Clark government, and while Jeanne Sauvé became Speaker of the House of Commons following 1980, many female elites continue to hold conventional health, education, human resource, and social development portfolios, as well as newer status of women responsibilities.[38] The clustering of female cabinet and shadow cabinet members in these areas thus remains intact, at the same time as men's specialization in the more prestigious fields of finance, justice, treasury, and industry and trade is further entrenched – and provides renewed evidence of our thesis that the higher and more competitive echelons of political responsibility in English Canada contain extremely few women.

CONCLUSIONS

This discussion has considered data on provincial and federal party activity, including at the constituency association executive, convention delegate, party official, and campaign manager levels. Combined with our review of patterns of political candidacy, legislative office-holding, and cabinet appointment, these figures offer strong evidence that higher, more powerful, and more competitive political positions in English Canada remain overwhelmingly in the hands of men.

Despite contemporary efforts to increase female involvement in many phases of party activity, therefore, our initial generalizations regarding 'the higher the fewer' and 'the more competitive the fewer' are empirically confirmed through the early 1980s. We shall now consider these attempts to improve female political representation in greater detail.

4

Increasing Representation on Elite Levels: Affirmative Action and the Pursuit of Party Leadership

Canada could benefit from the contribution of many more women than are now involved in the political process.[1]

Existing patterns of female participation in mainstream party politics in English Canada, examined in detail in chapter 3, have led to numerous efforts toward increasing women's involvement on elite levels. In particular, data presented in the 1970 *Report* of the Royal Commission (one conclusion of which is quoted above), and more recently in internal party reports and task forces, served to generate extensive discussion and debate concerning a response to these patterns.

On a theoretical level, the main focus of many such discussions has been the issue of representation. In general, the representativeness of key political institutions, including political parties, is regarded as a sine qua non of democratic government. As Hannah Pitkin argues in a major study of this subject, much of modern democratic thought and practice begins with assumptions regarding a demographic similarity between mass and elite (which she terms descriptive or 'standing for' representation), as well as a substantive or policy-based linkage between the citizenry and political leadership (termed 'acting for' representation).[2]

Canadian party activists and political scientists make frequent reference to the representative character of existing political institutions and processes. Contemporary discussions of party leadership conventions, for example, maintain that the selection of elite personnel within the major party organizations is responsive to and hence representative of a broad variety of social interests. According to one well-known Liberal senator, these conventions are 'designed to obtain "the fullest possible representation of party views." '[3] Similarly, in the words of Donald Smiley, Canada has successfully amalgamated American and British influences, such that it 'is the only country in the British parliamentary tradition which chooses its party leaders through representative party conventions called for that purpose.'[4]

Despite its seeming importance as a subject of social and political analysis, however, the representativeness of Canadian party institutions, including conventions, has received relatively little academic attention. From the perspective of women and politics, this neglect is particularly apparent, since neither the descriptive (i.e., numerical) nor policy-based representation of women in party organizations has been accorded systematic treatment. Overall, the numerical facts of female involvement, as well as recent efforts to increase women's political participation, have both been ignored by Canadian political researchers.[5]

It is for this reason that the present chapter focuses upon responses to the problem of representation or, more accurately, underrepresentation at elite levels of party activity in English Canada. In the following sections, we examine two types of efforts to increase female party involvement in the contemporary period, namely internal affirmative action programs and the election of female party leaders. Our discussion gives particular attention to these subjects in the context of provincial-level politics in Ontario and, more specifically, in light of developments at two 1982 party leadership conventions in the province.

In political terms, Ontario is widely identified as a one-party dominant system on the provincial level, since the Progressive Conservatives have governed without interruption since 1943.[6] Following 1981 provincial elections, the Conservatives held a clear majority of 70 seats in the 125-member provincial legislature. The two main opposition parties during the post-war period have been the Liberals (OLP) and New Democrats (NDP), both of which held conventions in 1982 for the purpose of selecting new leaders and generally renewing themselves in the face of yet another Conservative electoral victory in 1981.

In a number of different ways, the 1982 Ontario provincial leadership conventions are particularly well-suited to the study of responses to female underrepresentation. First, the NDP meeting included one of the early Canadian debates over an explicit internal affirmative action policy, presented by the party's Women's Committee. While generally neglected by media and academic analysts, this debate represents an important event in the political history of women in Canada. Second, the OLP convention was marked by the first campaign of a woman, Sheila Copps, for the leadership of a major Ontario provincial party. It is notable that only a small handful of Canadian women had previously contested major party leadership at either the federal or provincial levels, and that in none of these cases was the candidacy systematically evaluated in relation to female political involvement.[7]

While both of these events, the NDP affirmative action debate and Copps's leadership candidacy, provide an important focus for research on women and politics, the following discussion is not meant to imply that experiences in the Ontario opposition parties in 1982 were necessarily typical of those in other Canadian political organizations, whether at the local, provincial, or federal level. Rather, given the continuing neglect of this area, we shall use both case studies to inform a general set of concerns regarding efforts to increase women's representation in Canadian party politics.

RESPONSES TO UNDERREPRESENTATION

In order to understand the background to recent Canadian efforts toward increasing female representation on elite levels, it is useful to review briefly the dimensions and impact of structural reforms that were introduced during the 1970s in U.S. party organizations. As early as the 1920s, the American Democratic and Republican parties adopted rules which established numerically equal representation of men and women on national party committees. Both parties also urged their state and local committees to adopt similar by-laws, so that by 1947, 39 or 81.3% of Democratic state committees had adopted some form of equal representation, as had 30 or 62.5% of Republican state committees.[8] One problem with these by-laws, however, was that female representation in American party organizations was often limited to designated co-chair or vice-chair positions which, according to Frank Sorauf (1976), 'long confirmed their separate but unequal status.'[9]

It was not until 1972 that equal representation was established for national party conventions in the United States. At the 1968 Democratic convention, criticism of traditional party structures, including the delegate selection process, spilled over into the formation of a Commission on Party Structures and Delegate Selection, popularly referred to as the McGovern-Fraser Commission. Perhaps the best-known guideline introduced by this commission was the 'affirmative action' provision, which required 'all states to "overcome the effects of past discrimination by affirmative steps to encourage representation on the national convention delegation of young people ... and women in reasonable relationship to their presence in the population." An identical requirement applied to blacks and other minorities."[10] This particular initiative, which was adopted informally by Republicans as well in 1972, helped to increase female convention representation from 12.9% to 39.9% between 1968 and 1972 in the Democratic case, and from 16.7% to 30.1% over this same period in the Republican case.[11] As reported above in table 3.3, the percentage of women convention delegates has subsequently increased in both major parties, reaching as high as 50% in the case of the 1980 Democratic presidential convention.

Aside from its obvious numerical impact, one of the major consequences of affirmative action in the American context was its effect upon party recruitment and policy. As indicated in research by Kirkpatrick (1976) and Jennings and Farah (1981), the Republican and especially the Democratic parties were compelled to locate new female activists during the 1970s, many of whom turned out to be youthful, well-educated, employed and, not incidentally, feminist in their social and political orientations.[12] These new recruits helped to change the face of female party participation in the United States, since they argued for the inclusion of significant 'women's issue' statements in party platforms and also contested increasingly powerful and visible positions within their organizations. As Sorauf (1976) reflected in the wake of American party reforms, 'the more activist women want a role in the regular party organizations, or else they prefer to become active in nonparty organizations (such as the National Women's Political Caucus).'[13]

Affirmative action in the United States also held important implications for Canadian politics, and especially for female partisans who believed that women's status could be improved by working within existing political structures. Figures presented in the 1970 *Report* of the Royal Commission on the Status of Women, as well as internal party studies and research by Brodie, Vickers, and other writers, indicated that Canadian women were poorly represented in all major federal and provincial political parties, in all regions, and at virtually all levels of party activity; furthermore, very few women were nominated outside of marginal ridings and only a small handful attained public office.[14] Comparisons between Canadian figures and data from other Western industrialized nations indicated the following: First, the numerical representation of women in Canadian legislatures was particularly weak;[15] and second, as shown above in table 3.3, the slightly higher percentage of female delegates to Canadian party conventions in the late 1960s was eliminated by American party reforms of the 1970s. Perhaps most notably, the percentage of female party delegates to the 1982 Ontario leadership conventions resembled closely the figures for Democratic presidential conventions held ten years earlier.

In light of the extent of women's underrepresentation in legislatures and extra-parliamentary party organizations, activists in the major Canadian parties pursued two general strategies during the mid-1970s and following. One approach, which was employed primarily by women in the New Democratic party, involved the introduction of structural reforms modelled on earlier rule changes in the U.S. Democratic party. In adopting this route, Canadian women sought to obtain numerically equal representation across the board, including on party committees and convention delegations, as well as increased recognition as candidates in winnable ridings. The 1982 ONDP resolution on affirmative action, discussed in the following sections, offers an important example of this approach.[16]

A second strategy, pursued to some extent in all three major Canadian parties, used less formal methods to elevate the position of women who already belonged to the parties and, at the same time, to recruit new female partisans. Among these relatively informal means were campaigns for party leadership by prominent women activists; conferences, caucuses, and training sessions designed to attract and prepare new activists; campaign literature and speakers' notes which devoted attention to female employment and day-care issues; and personal out-reach or 'networking' activities by party women.[17]

Common to both strategies was an expectation that, in the near future, more women would join political parties, become active in them, and, ultimately, contest positions of organizational leadership – thereby offering females greater collective voice and policy input within Canadian politics. Increased numerical representation, it was thus assumed, would produce greater substantive representation in major party organizations.

The impact of these various initiatives remains open to question, however, largely because their recent introduction within a Canadian context makes it difficult to evaluate the effectiveness of such efforts. On a speculative level, we suggest in the conclusion to this chapter that despite a growing recognition of women's underrepresentation within major party organizations, there are political sanctions which continue to restrict the attention paid to 'women's issues' by female elites. As a result, the conversion from descriptive (or numerical) to substantive representation by women in the major Canadian parties – which is assumed within both the affirmative action and party leadership responses to underrepresentation – may be blocked for some time to come.

We now turn our attention to the background and terms of the NDP affirmative action resolution.

BACKGROUND TO THE RESOLUTION

At the time of its establishment in 1973, the Women's Committee of the ONDP was constituted as an essentially feminist committee of the party's provincial council. The primary goals of this committee included the following: 1) increasing 'the participation of women in the Party at all levels'; 2) educating 'women in the NDP in all aspects of political activity'; 3) participating 'with women outside the Party in areas of mutual interest'; and 4) '[encouraging] these women to join the Party and work with the Party.'[18]

In the years between 1973 and 1980, the Women's Committee organized a series of policy conferences, presented resolutions on various 'women's issues' at provincial council meetings and party conventions, and monitored the participation of women within the party overall.[19] This general approach culminated in the adoption of a comprehensive 'Policies for Equality' resolution at the 1980 Women's Committee conference, which was in turn approved at the provincial council and by delegates to a subsequent party convention in the same year. This lengthy policy document, which addressed such issues as economic rights for women, pensions, health, day care, housing, and education, was designed to replace existing and often outdated party policy on women's issues. It was also viewed as a resolutions package which would elevate the external feminist profile of the ONDP, as well as the status of women within the organization.[20]

Contrary to the expectations of many party activists, including some in the Women's Committee, 'Policies for Equality' encountered little serious opposition on the floor of the 1980 convention. In fact, the passage of these and a number of related resolutions led to the subsequent hiring of a women's organizer at the provincial party headquarters and of a women's co-ordinator at the NDP legislative caucus. Overall, it appeared as if the goal of the Women's Committee to obtain greater organizational and policy voice for females in the party was within reach.

A number of developments during the period of the 1981 provincial election campaign, however, suggested that the commitment of the mainstream party organization to female participation and feminist policy directions remained limited. First, the very low visibility of the women's organizer, women's co-ordinator, and 'Policies for Equality' document during the campaign was notable, since both of the former were assigned to routine inside responsibilities for the duration of the election, while a much-awaited women's issue focus was barely in evidence.[21] This low visibility may be attributed to an apparent decision by campaign strategists to eliminate all unnecessary risks – including the women's issue electoral focus mandated by 'Policies for Equality' – in light of the weakness of the provincial leader and party as a whole in 1981.[22] As well, one cannot discount the uneasiness and occasional antagonism which greets public discussion of feminist issues in many contemporary political parties.[23]

Second, monitoring of internal party participation during this period suggested that while more women were involved in the NDP than in 1973, females remained substantially underrepresented in most parts of the organization.[24] This conclusion follows from data presented above in chapter 3, which show that although there were higher percentages of women in decision-making positions in the New Democratic than in the other two provincial parties in Ontario, a clear majority of 1981 NDP riding presidents, riding treasurers, provincial officers, provincial candidates, and provincial campaign managers were male. One notable exception to this trend of lower female involvement can be found in figures on riding recording secretaries and membership secretaries (table 3.1), where women form more than 50% of local office-holders in all three parties. It would therefore seem that outside of a clerical or 'pink-collar' sector in local constituency associations, women were considerably less numerous than men in the ONDP in 1981.[25]

A third factor which encouraged the Women's Committee to revise its approach was the advent of a party leadership campaign. While no woman entered the leadership race, all three male candidates focused upon party renewal, which provided the Women's Committee with a useful opportunity to raise the question of women's status in the party and to present possible remedies to underrepresentation. In addition, the leadership convention was viewed as a large, prestigious, and relatively captive forum for debate on these issues.

THE AFFIRMATIVE ACTION RESOLUTION

During the summer of 1981, members of the Women's Committee executive reached consensus on the need for a formalized response to what they increasingly identified as a problem of systemic discrimination within the party organization.[26] An affirmative action draft resolution, approved by the committee executive in October 1981, established four major objectives: 1) to broaden the female electoral base of the ONDP by emphasizing policies of particular relevance to women both between and during election campaigns; 2) to encourage equal ('at least 50%') representation of women in riding executives, and to require this in provincial council delegations, the provincial executive, and party committees; 3) to develop a leadership training program for women; and 4) to recruit female candidates in strong ridings, and to assist with the child-care and household management expenses of all candidates.[27]

Taken together, this program represented a very significant, and probably the most systematic and formalized attempt thus far to increase female involvement in a Canadian political party. By way of comparison, earlier initiatives in the federal NDP and Liberal parties were less comprehensive in scope and promoted voluntary co-operation as opposed to specified quotas for increased female participation. In the case of the federal NDP resolution, adopted at the 1981 Vancouver convention, constituent party sections were encouraged to recruit women candidates and to assist with child-care costs; to seek out women for party office and to provide leadership training for such women; and to study women's participation and the impact of voluntary affirmative action.[28] This strategy was later formalized at the 1983 Regina convention, where an official party nominating committee was, in the words of its chairman, 'under constitutional obligation to implement affirmative action.'[29] Ultimately, twelve women (including an associate president and treasurer) were nominated and elected to the new twenty-member NDP federal council, and resolutions which would ensure gender parity in the future on federal councils and executives were adopted. While numerical representation was thus achieved among elected federal elites in 1983, constituent New Democratic parties continue to be urged or encouraged to implement similar procedures.[30]

Efforts which were undertaken during the winter of 1982 and following in the Liberal Party of Canada (LPC) were also less comprehensive, and more voluntary in nature than the Ontario NDP program. In January 1982, the LPC established an Ad Hoc Committee on Affirmative Action and charged this body with gathering data on the participation of women, assessing party recruitment procedures as they affect women, and establishing short- and long-range goals 'to achieve the objective of parity between men and women.'[31] The introduction of specified targets or quotas for female involvement was rejected by the committee, which has pursued data collection activities as well as consultation with various branches of the federal party organization.

RESPONSES TO AFFIRMATIVE ACTION

A draft version of the Ontario NDP affirmative action resolution was presented at the November 1981 conference of the party's Women's

Committee, where each of the three provincial leadership candidates was invited to comment. All three expressed support for the proposal and, following a series of workshops devoted to discussion of the policy, it was endorsed unanimously by conference participants. However, at ONDP riding association meetings held between November and February, a number of convention delegates expressed opposition to the 'at least 50%' terms of the resolution, particularly when applied to local party executives. In light of these objections, the Women's Committee prepared a two-page 'fact sheet' for the convention; it offered contemporary statistics on female participation and emphasized that ridings were 'urged' rather than required to adopt equal representation.

At the February party convention, debate on affirmative action was scheduled between two important items, namely elections to the party executive and nomination of leadership candidates. The floor debate, which lasted approximately thirty minutes, covered a number of issues which have been raised in other – primarily American – discussions of affirmative action. Notably, speakers in favour of the resolution emphasized three main points:

1 In light of experiences in political parties and the labour force, voluntary 'targets' do not provide sufficient means to achieve numerically equal representation.[32]
2 The Ontario NDP organization as a whole would benefit from adoption of internal affirmative action, since this resolution will make party policy on women's issues more credible.[33]
3 The resolution as presented provides a 'minimum' for women, since it only urges ridings to act. Waiting for a more comprehensive study of underrepresentation, and possibly for a series of constitutional amendments in this area (see below), simply 'delays effective action' on the problem, to the detriment of both women and the provincial party.[34]

Delegates who spoke in opposition to the resolution included three younger women from Metropolitan Toronto ridings. Their major criticisms, which also echoed older American arguments, were as follows:

1 The terms of 'at least 50%' representation, especially on the riding level, imply that gender will take precedence over merit, ability, and experience. According to one speaker, 'I would always want to be elected because I was good, not because I was a woman.'[35]
2 Affirmative action is unnecessary in the ONDP, because individual women are already equal participants. In the words of one opponent, 'I have never in this party been denied the right to run for an executive position or to be a candidate. In fact, I have been encouraged to do so.'[36]

3 Insufficient attention has been given to the implementation of the resolution, and therefore it should be referred to a committee for further
study.[37] (This referral motion was defeated.)

On a standing vote following the eleventh speaker, the resolution carried.
Notably, post-convention tabulations showed that 40% of the voting delegates had been women and 60% men. In addition, results of a questionnaire survey conducted at the convention indicated that approximately
62% of NDP respondents approved of the resolution as presented, with
25.3% of male and 32.4% of female delegates expressing strong approval.[38]
In light of these results, we would conclude that affirmative action was
probably supported by a majority of voting delegates on the convention
floor, and opposed by a relatively small but vocal minority.

To what extent can affirmative action within the Ontario NDP be expected to achieve the goals of the Women's Committee? On the level of
numerical representation, it seems likely that more females will obtain
formal positions of decision-making responsibility, if only because the
terms of the resolution are explicit and binding upon most party opera-
tives. However, in reference to substantive or policy-making influence,
the prospects are less certain, since the relative importance accorded to
women's issues remains dependent upon the party leader and his advisers,
who can claim to be accountable not only to feminist interests, but also
to party interests which are defined more broadly.

It is to the issue of women's representation at the level of party leadership that we now turn our attention.

WOMEN AND MAJOR PARTY LEADERSHIP

When Sheila Copps announced her candidacy for the provincial Liberal
leadership in November 1981, she joined a handful of Canadian women
who had previously contested major party leadership, including Rosemary
Brown (federal NDP, 1975), Flora MacDonald (federal PC, 1976), and
Muriel Smith (Manitoba NDP, 1979). While Copps's own background and
experience were distinctive, many of her experiences as a leadership contender resembled those of earlier female candidates – not only because
she was unsuccessful in her bid for political leadership, but also because
much of the response to her candidacy reflected a fundamental unease
with the prospect of a female party leader. Three specific questions which
were raised by both media commentators and partisans tended to weaken
Copps's and others' chances of winning major party leadership during the
contemporary period; in this manner, they militated against increased

female representation within party elites. The three questions are as follows: First, would a women make a suitable political party leader? Second, what is the personal style or image of this particular female candidate? And third, is she a 'token women's' or a 'real' candidate?

Although the attention paid to these points has varied across political parties and leadership campaigns, it has generally obscured a more salient question, namely 'Would this individual make a good party leader?' Moreover, in suggesting that female candidates may represent only other women or other feminist women, observers have imposed a major constraint upon the practical conversion from numerical to substantive representation by female elites. That is, by labelling women candidates as 'women's candidates,' political commentators and partisans have tended to marginalize significant policy issues raised by these participants.

One way of approaching contemporary leadership campaigns by Canadian women is to review briefly the candidacies of Brown, Smith, and MacDonald, which provide a useful background to Copps's 1982 candidacy. Before beginning this summary, it is important to note that in the NDP campaigns of Rosemary Brown and Muriel Smith, the question of female suitability to political leadership was rarely raised directly. Because the NDP has long been committed ideologically to gender equality, any overt challenge to this position would probably not have been well received. Therefore, much of the questioning of a woman as party leader, especially during Rosemary Brown's federal campaign, was relatively subtle or oblique. It generally focused upon two points: first, the candidate's personal style, and second, her 'token' candidacy.

During the 1975 federal NDP leadership campaign, Rosemary Brown was frequently described in the press as an elegant, eloquent, well-dressed black woman who resided with her American-born psychiatrist husband in the wealthy Point Grey neighbourhood of Vancouver. In addition, Brown was reported to hold an extensive portfolio of private stocks as well as real estate on the Gulf Islands.[39] Since comparable data on the other three (male) candidates for NDP leadership was not provided in journalists' accounts, it would seem that personal background factors played a disproportionately large role in the media portrayal of Brown, as they did in accounts of Flora MacDonald, Sheila Copps, and the female municipal candidates examined in Archibald et al. (1980).[40] While it may be argued that media images are irrelevant within a decentralized, grass-roots organization such as the NDP, the type of personal style suggested by many accounts of Brown was hardly conducive to her acceptance in a socialist milieu.

The Brown campaign was also weakened by allegations regarding a 'token' candidacy. It was particularly vulnerable in this area because of an identifiably pro-feminist orientation, which was reflected in campaign literature encouraging delegates to 'Celebrate International Women's Year by Nominating Rosemary Brown as Leader.'[41] This explicit policy emphasis upon issues of particular concern to women, including affirmative action, day care, and abortion, produced mixed results. On the one hand, Brown was dismissed initially by journalists as well as party insiders, who viewed her as a marginal candidate with limited legislative experience.[42] On the other hand, however, Brown's unexpected strength at the convention led a number of reporters and Broadbent supporters to speculate that she was simply a 'token' candidate who would attract 'first ballot support to show there is no prejudice against blacks or women.'[43] In the words of former party leader T.C. Douglas (who endorsed Broadbent), this support for Brown constituted 'a sort of prejudice in reverse.'[44]

Nevertheless, despite allegations of tokenism, Brown retained a strong second-place position through four rounds of voting. As well, her statements and literature at the convention attempted to link feminism with a broader socialist policy platform:

Indeed to suggest that to be a feminist is a liability to a leadership candidate, surely is to fail to understand that feminism is a revolt against decaying capitalism, surely is to lack the vision to see that feminism, like socialism, calls for a new human community. The question then must be – is it possible for a leader of a socialist party not to be committed to feminism, not to see as one of her or his priorities the examination of the position of women in Canadian society, and the eradication of their oppression. The answer to this question must surely be 'NO.'[45]

A similar effort to synthesize feminism with more global socialist concerns was evident in Muriel Smith's 1979 campaign, which resulted in a respectable second-place finish on the first (and only) ballot for Manitoba provincial leadership.[46]

Concerns about female suitability to party leadership, personal style, and 'tokenism' were probably most apparent during Flora MacDonald's 1976 campaign for federal PC leadership. In terms of suitability, the willingness of Conservative partisans to question explicitly the acceptability of a woman leader indicated that gender constituted an important criterion for a fair number of PC delegates.[47] In addition, MacDonald's attempts to raise much of her campaign money among women (including well-known feminists) who were not Conservative partisans suggest that she lacked solid support within important sectors of the party organization.[48]

Issues of personal style were also raised throughout MacDonald's campaign. Notably, the candidate was consistently referred to as 'Flora,' the red-haired 'girl Friday' 'spinster' who was raised in a large Scottish family in Cape Breton, and who seemed to have no existence outside of politics in her adult life.[49] Captions in one press account reflect the prominence accorded to these personal factors: 'I can barely boil an egg. My job is my life – yes! My constituency is my family.'[50] Compared with treatments of the other (male) contenders for PC leadership, it would appear that accounts of MacDonald were distinctively style- or image-oriented. However, since MacDonald's campaign was itself geared in a populist direction, the candidate was especially vulnerable to these types of characterizations.

Probably most damaging to MacDonald and subsequent female leadership contenders were strong allegations regarding a 'token' political candidacy. MacDonald travelled widely to gauge delegate support before declaring her formal intentions; as she stated in an interview at the time, 'I'm not going to be stampeded into a decision I'm not ready for; I've seen too many women used as sacrificial lambs.'[51] Apparently, the response which MacDonald received during these travels convinced her that a serious leadership candidacy was possible. She therefore organized a campaign oriented toward some 'Red Tory' issues, including the removal of abortion from the Criminal Code and the elimination of capital punishment, as well as toward fiscal conservatism, particularly in the area of social spending.

During the campaign, MacDonald was frequently asked about the relationship between her policy positions, especially on women's rights issues, and her gender. Aware of the 'women's candidate' image which she was developing, [52] MacDonald began to refer to herself as 'a politician who happens to be a woman, not a woman politician.'[53] Furthermore, she tried to refute this image by arguing that so-called women's issues were in fact 'society's issues,'[54] and by suggesting that her gender was an asset to the Conservative party. This last point was emphasized in MacDonald's main address to the leadership convention: 'I am not a candidate because I am a woman. But I say to you quite frankly that because I am a woman my candidacy helps our party. It shows that in the Conservative Party there are no barriers to anyone who has demonstrated serious intentions and earned the right to be heard. It proves that the leadership of this great party is not for sale to any alliance of the powerful and the few.'[55]

Despite MacDonald's hopeful expectations, however, her delegate support failed to materialize and she finished in a disappointing sixth place on the first ballot. This weak showing, termed 'the Flora syndrome,' offered credence to allegations regarding token female candidacies and thus overshadowed very credible leadership campaigns by Rosemary Brown, Muriel Smith, and others.

THE COPPS CANDIDACY

In common with Canadian women who had previously contested major party leadership, Sheila Copps was relatively unknown politically when she declared her candidacy; in November 1981, Copps was a Liberal backbencher who had represented the constituency of Hamilton Centre for less than one year. Furthermore, Copps shared a somewhat anti-establishment reputation with such earlier candidates as Brown and MacDonald, since she had adopted a number of independent positions during legislative debates and had written publicly about the patronizing and sexist treatment which she received as a new MPP.[56]

There were at least three important features of Copps's candidacy, however, which distinguished it from previous campaigns by women for major party leadership in Canada. First, Copps was an exceptionally young candidate; at the age of 28, she was approximately twenty years younger than candidates Flora MacDonald and Muriel Smith, and about fourteen years younger than Rosemary Brown. In generational terms, Copps was part of a birth cohort which came of age politically when the contemporary women's movement was already well established. This demographic background may help to explain Copps's expectation that she would be treated as an equal in the Legislature, and the surprise and anger which greeted her recognition of a lingering 'men's-club mentality' at Queen's Park.[57]

Second, Copps brought valuable 'insider' connections to the provincial leadership race. As the daughter of a long-time Hamilton mayor and federal Liberal leadership candidate, her surname was recognized in the party, particularly in the Hamilton area. Similarly, Copps's experience as a constituency assistant and protégée of retiring party leader Stuart Smith conferred important legitimacy on her candidacy.[58]

Third, Copps's campaign was distinctive because of its conscious orientation *away* from feminism and a 'women's issue' policy focus. On the explicit advice of one supporter who was active in the federal-level Women's Liberal Commission in Ontario, Copps worked to avoid the image of a 'women's candidate,' since it was believed that she would already draw support from many feminists in the OLP, and since 'women's issue' priorities might alienate important interests within the party, especially farmers. Copps's speeches and campaign literature were thus notable for their focus upon economic recovery, party reorganization, and improved social services, and for their consistent inattention to such questions as equal pay, day care, and affirmative action.[59]

Given her age, 'insider' connections, and careful avoidance of a 'women's candidate' image, the fairly stereotypic response to Copps's candidacy during 1981-2 is particularly notable. As had occurred during the campaign of Flora MacDonald, Copps was confronted directly with questions about female suitability to political leadership. For example, party delegates asked, 'Are we ready for a woman leader?' Or, 'Will Ontario vote for a woman,' '... a 29-year-old woman,' or '... a 29-year-old single woman?' One prominent newspaper columnist posed the suitability issue as follows: 'The question facing the delegates of the OLP leadership convention when they gather here next February is simple. Will the voters of Ontario in 1985 choose a government led by a 32-year-old woman, albeit an attractive, intelligent one?'[60]

This same journalist went on to describe the personal style of the candidate whom he referred to as 'Sheila' as 'brash, gutsy, impudent, even impatient.'[61] As might have been expected, readers were not provided with an assessment of personality traits among the other four (male) leadership contenders, although it seems likely that these same characteristics would have been deemed acceptable, and even advantageous, in a male candidate. Similarly, Copps was described by other commentators as a 'vivacious brunette,' the candidate 'with a fallen marriage six years behind her' and, in one especially biased treatment, as 'some jumped-up combination of Jayne Mansfield and Joan of Arc. Jayne of Arc?'[62]

Questions about a token candidacy were also raised during the Copps campaign. A number of discussions referred explicitly to the 'Flora syndrome'; for example, one *Globe and Mail* columnist noted that ' "Sheila" even sounds a bit like "Flora." '[63] Copps vehemently, and apparently correctly, rejected this possibility, since she made a strong and credible second-place showing on both convention ballots – and this despite a concerted 'Stop Copps' effort by the party establishment on the last day of the convention.[64]

These results helped to elevate Copps's individual political profile as well as the issues which she had highlighted during the campaign, since after the convention she was appointed the Opposition health critic and given charge of a travelling health-care task force. It was thus clear to the newly elected party leader, David Peterson, and others that Copps was a serious contender for party leadership in the future, and that, in the meantime, her sizable constituency within the party would require immediate appeasement.

From Copps's own perspective, the leadership candidacy was a very fruitful exercise, since it provided personal visibility in the media and Liberal organization, offered a clear alternative in policy terms to the party front-runner, and paved the way to a front-seat assignment on the Opposition benches. In addition, by seeking the leadership, Copps gained important political and organizational expertise, which could be used in the future in the OLP or in the federal Liberal party.

We would conclude, however, that Copps's experiences as a candidate and the policy orientation of her campaign provided an unusual juxta-position. On the one hand, her leadership candidacy was greeted with stereotypic concerns about the suitability of women leaders, their personal style or image, and 'token' female candidacies. On the other hand, by refusing to focus upon feminism and 'women's issues,' Copps's campaign strategy reflected a conscious effort to avoid precisely this same 'women's candidate' imagery. Overall, Copps's ability to transcend gender was thus limited by the same types of constraints which had affected previous female leadership candidates, even though her political connections, family back-ground, and campaign strategy might have been expected to minimize or possibly eliminate such difficulties.

CONCLUSIONS

This discussion of two contemporary responses to female underrepresen-tation in Canadian party elites, namely affirmative action and the pursuit of party leadership, points toward a variety of conclusions. In terms of numerical representation, it suggests that the numbers of women who are active on the elite level will probably increase over time, particularly in parties which introduce formal or informal affirmative action policies. Our examination of the Ontario NDP resolution indicated that many party women were dissatisfied with their continuing underrepresentation in decision-making positions in local constituency associations and on the provincial level, as well as with the party's practice of fielding female candidates in marginal ridings. Supporters of this resolution, along with other similar initiatives in the federal New Democratic, Liberal, and PC parties, could therefore include women who aspire to hold elite positions within major party organizations, as well as men who are prepared to share political responsibility more equitably with women.

At the level of party leadership, Sheila Copps's credible showing as a provincial Liberal candidate may also encourage greater numbers of women to consider seriously a career in party politics. In particular, younger women like Copps – who came of age politically during the early 1970s period of social and especially feminist activism – are more likely than older women to possess the self-confidence and personal support networks necessary for elite-level participation. As well, newer cohorts may be less constrained by conventional gender role norms and family responsibilities, including child-rearing, which have limited female party involvement in the past.[65]

The background to affirmative action in the Ontario NDP, and the response to campaigns for major party leadership by Copps and others, however, demonstrate that there remain important psychological and structural barriers to increased female representation in Canadian party politics. In the case of the provincial NDP, the treatment of 'women's issues' and of specially appointed female staff members during the 1981 provincial election campaign indicated that party planners were unwilling to implement a fairly direct policy mandate from the 1980 convention, which concerned the inclusion of a feminist issue orientation in the party's electoral strategy. As well, the vocal opposition to affirmative action on the floor of the 1982 convention reflected a strong belief among some party activists that a formal response to underrepresentation was unnecessary, and that lower female participation was simply a result of limited political aspirations among party women.

While advocates of affirmative action argued successfully against both of these points and employed the treatment of 'women's issues' during 1981 as evidence in their favour, obstacles to the increased numerical and substantive representation of women in the Ontario NDP continue. Since the party is frequently split along right / left, establishment / anti-establishment lines, feminist issues are often obscured by broader political conflicts. In addition, this division has meant that female recruits are sometimes wedged in political terms by the many interests which are caught up in internal party controversies. In short, numerical and policy-based representation within the mainstream party organization continues to be an elusive goal for women in the Ontario NDP, even after the passage of a formal internal affirmative action resolution in 1982.

Evidence of considerable barriers to increased representation on elite levels can also be identified in women's experiences as party leadership candidates. Questions regarding their suitability to party leadership, personal style or image, and the possibility of a 'token' candidacy were raised during a number of bids for major party leadership. Even though Sheila Copps's individual ties with the Liberal party through her father and the retiring party leader were close, and her 1982 campaign strategy consciously excluded 'women's issues' and a 'women's candidate' focus, these same types of concerns were evident in the uneasy response to her leadership campaign.

One obvious question which follows from this experience is: Can females run for party leadership without being labelled as 'women's candidates' and 'tokens'? In light of Copps's candidacy and those of other Canadian women, we would conclude that it remains extremely difficult for female elites to avoid this imagery. More importantly, the possibility that a female leadership candidate could highlight feminist policy directions, and then win major party leadership, remains especially remote.

Additional research on women and politics in Canada and elsewhere is required, however, in order to document this relationship between numerical and substantive representation in party organizations. To what extent have targets and quotas for female political involvement contributed to increased feminist policy initiatives? How has the media and partisan treatment of female leadership contenders compared with the response to legislative nominees and candidates? Are the constraints upon 'women's issue' representation by female elites greater in parliamentary than in congressional systems, given the degree of party discipline and presumed policy coherence which characterizes the former? These and other questions demand careful attention from political researchers, in order that contemporary responses to underrepresentation in party organizations begin to receive the serious consideration which they deserve.

We shall now turn our attention to the complex question of women's organizations within the Canadian parties.

5

Women's Organizations in the Major Parties

Most parties hold together as an entity only because women's groups meet regularly, year in and year out; although they rarely concern themselves with the issues of the day, they are the muscle of all political parties.
Judy LaMarsh, *Memoirs of a Bird in a Gilded Cage* (1969)[1]

We believe that the public life of Canada would benefit from the full participation of women and that women should be accorded full access to political affairs through the party structure. Therefore, *we recommend that women's associations within the political parties of Canada be amalgamated with the main bodies of these parties.*
Report of the Royal Commission (1970)[2]

During the period of suffragist activism in English Canada, and for the next fifty years approximately, women's associations provided among the only evidence of sustained female involvement in either the Liberal or Conservative parties. These associations, commonly referred to as women's clubs or auxiliaries, were instrumental in helping to channel female energies into local, provincial, and national party activities, in some cases before enfranchisement was formally obtained. Notably, in Toronto, Vancouver, and Charlottetown, women's Liberal associations were founded prior to the passage of provincial suffrage legislation, in 1913, 1915, and 1922, respectively.[3]

Many activities engaged in by separate Liberal and Conservative women's associations, and by a variety of standing committees of the main party organization in the CCF and NDP, were reflective of a 'ladies' aid' approach to volunteer party work. As providers of support services to the mainstream party organizations, women's associations frequently raised money through banquets, luncheons, bazaars, cookbook sales, and other similar projects. Their members also performed valuable clerical, social, and fund-raising tasks within riding associations, particularly during election campaigns, and staffed registration, credentials, and arrangements committees for various party meetings and conventions. In general, as MP Judy LaMarsh observed in her memoirs (quoted above), these contributions were taken for granted by the mainstream or parent party organizations, even though the latter would have been hard-pressed to operate without them.[4]

The constitutionally recognized status of women's affiliates in both the Liberal and Conservative parties, where separate membership dues, leadership structures, and internal regulations were established, meant that some prominent female activists were appointed to mainstream party executive and, in a few cases, Senate seats by virtue of their group involvement (see chapter 1). Such appointments, however, rarely signified that women's associations or their leaders exerted substantive influence within the Canadian political system. Rather, their lack of tangible policy impact, combined with the minimal attention devoted to problems of numerical representation by party women's associations, contributed to a major re-evaluation of their goals and purposes during the late 1960s and following. As reflected in one recommendation of the Royal Commission on the Status of Women (quoted above), it was increasingly believed that these associations impeded full political participation by Canadian women. A majority of royal commissioners thus recommended 'that women's associations within the political parties of Canada be amalgamated with the main bodies of these parties.'[5]

The concept of amalgamation received a favourable response in many quarters, including among feminists and male party strategists who viewed traditional associations as politically ineffective and unattractive to younger recruits.[6] Despite consistent opposition by the older groups, both the national Liberal and Progressive Conservative women's associations were dissolved and replaced by the new Women's Liberal Commission (established in 1973) and the National Progressive Conservative Women's Caucus (established in 1981). Both of the latter, which were formally committed to improving the status of women within the parties rather than to providing support services for the mainstream organization, were viewed as more appropriate to the changing socio-economic and political roles of Canadian women than their predecessors.

The dissolution of older women's groups and the establishment of more contemporary commissions and caucuses, however, has brought to light important conflicts regarding female participation in the major English-Canadian parties. In the Liberal and Conservative cases, one continued source of contention has been the treatment of older associations and especially their participants, many of whom have felt betrayed by both the party hierarchies and younger female activists. According to this view, the latter eliminated legitimate women's groups in order to 'impose' a feminist direction upon contemporary organizations.

A second problem, which affects the two established parties as well as the NDP (where a separate women's association never existed at the national level), concerns the relationship between contemporary associations of party women, on the one hand, and the broader party organization and feminist movement, on the other. Most notably, the expectation that newer caucuses and commissions would function as a conduit for feminist policy initiatives and for ascendant female activists has proved difficult to achieve in all three major parties – even though the mandate for such groups rests precisely in this area of numerical and substantive representation.

In the following sections, we begin to explore the history and contemporary status of women's organizations in the three major English-Canadian political parties. While the study of both older and newer associations is complex and essential for an understanding of wider changes in the party system, it has thus far attracted little systematic attention from political researchers. It is in light of this longstanding neglect that we open our discussion with a survey of older women's associations in the Liberal and Conservative parties.

EARLY WOMEN'S LIBERAL ASSOCIATIONS

In the years prior to the awarding of the provincial franchise in Ontario, British Columbia, and Prince Edward Island, associations of Liberal women were organized both to pressure for suffrage and social reform legislation, and to contribute to the activities of existing Liberal parties. The earliest of these groups was the Toronto Women's Liberal Association (TWLA), established in 1913 and presided over at its inception by Mrs Newton Wesley Rowell, wife of the pro-suffrage Liberal Opposition leader in the Ontario legislature. The first constitution of the TWLA, drafted with the assistance of Newton Rowell and Sir Wilfrid Laurier, helped the group to acquire a provincial charter in June 1918. This charter specified three main objectives, namely improving the welfare of women and children in Ontario, establishing a Liberal government in the province, and striving for a united Canada. According to one internal history, members of the TWLA held fund-raising socials, worked in election campaigns, and developed policy resolutions concerning social welfare issues (including pensions, equal pay, and health care) during the early decades of this century.[7] In addition, at least one prominent activist in the organization, Mrs Wesley Bundy (who served as president from 1918 to 1920), ran as a candidate in the 1921 general elections.

During this same period, the Ontario Women's Liberal Association (OWLA) was also founded. Established in 1914, with Mrs Rowell again as first president, the OWLA began as an attempt to impart central direction to the growing number of Liberal clubs in the province. With the encouragement of both Lady Aberdeen, wife of the former governor-general, and Prime Minister Mackenzie King, the OWLA set out to organize more women's clubs, to offer program materials to these groups, and, in general, to promote Liberal principles.[8] In the years between 1914 and 1928, the OWLA established 47 clubs which were organized into 10 districts, each of which was responsible to a district vice-president. During the subsequent decade, the OWLA grew rapidly to embrace a total of 105 clubs and, at its twenty-fifth-year anniversary celebration in 1939, it boasted an active membership of some 4, 000 Liberal women.[9] This organizational strength weakened with the advent of World War II, however, so that by the mid-1940s, the OWLA included only 56 active affiliates.

Although the origins of early women's Liberal associations in British Columbia and Prince Edward Island are more difficult to document, it would appear that both were established with essentially the same aims as the Toronto and Ontario groups. According to accounts in Cleverdon (1974), MacGill (1980), and Crossley (1980), both the Women's Liberal Association of Vancouver and the Women's Liberal Club of Charlottetown lobbied extensively for the provincial franchise, as well as for social reform legislation during the 1920s.[10] In the case of the Vancouver Women's Liberal Association, close ties developed with the provincial Liberal caucus, particularly following the appointment of one of the association's founders, Mary Ellen Smith, to the provincial cabinet in 1921. In addition to Smith, a number of other prominent suffragists and social feminists – including Helen Gregory MacGill and Evlyn Farris (founder of the University Women's Club of Vancouver) – assumed major roles in the establishment of the BC Women's Liberal Association in 1915.

THE NATIONAL FEDERATION OF LIBERAL WOMEN

Many of these same activists were also instrumental in the founding of the National Federation of Liberal Women of Canada (NFLW). The first assembly of the federation, held in Ottawa in April 1928, attracted some 500 women and was organized by Cairine Wilson, an Ontario Liberal who later served as NFLW president and as the first female member of the Canadian Senate. Reports presented at the first meeting covered the activities of both the Toronto and the Ontario associations; for its new executive, the federation elected British Columbian Mary Ellen Smith to serve as first national president.

According to a recent historical study of the federation by Patricia Myers (1980), the early years of the organization were generally inactive ones, since the work of the Liberal party overall was interrupted by both the Great Depression and World War II.[11] Following a formal end to hostilities, however, the federation established a network of one hundred constituent clubs, published a *Liberal Woman* newsletter, and maintained an extensive list of French- and English-speaking members. In fact, Myers's research indicates that by 1967, the NFLW included some 450 affiliated clubs with a combined membership of approximately 31,000 women.

The relationship between the Women's Federation and the larger National Liberal Federation reflected an auxiliary-mainstream linkage throughout most of this period. Since the NFLW served as a federation of local women's clubs, it developed as a less centralized and less policy-oriented organization than the parent party grouping. As Myers demonstrates, the Women's Federation newsletter was frequently a gossip sheet which reported on individual club activities, while federation conventions were festive social occasions graced by tours, teas, receptions, and banquets with the federal leader as keynote speaker.[12]

Policy issues which were broached in the context of NFLW meetings generally concerned such questions as family life; social welfare; and the appointment of women to boards, commissions, and the Senate. The attention accorded these resolutions was limited by a number of important factors, including the marginal position of the Women's Federation in the broader Liberal party and the secondary role of policy concerns among organized women themselves. As Myers reports, it was not until the late 1960s that NFLW members as a group began to evaluate the partisan effectiveness of their organization, and to challenge its financial and political dependence upon the mainstream Liberal party. In the interim, the campaign and convention labours of federation activists became increasingly important to the larger party organization and, in the words of Mackenzie King, continued 'a noble effort' on behalf of Canadian Liberalism.[13]

The post-war activities of other Liberal women's associations also reflected a growing, albeit unstated reliance upon their contributions. Within the Toronto Women's Liberal Association, for example, a group of 'new university women graduates' formed a Tuesday Luncheon Club in 1948. According to a statement marking its twenty-fifth anniversary in 1973, 'The club is a Women's Liberal Organization which provides a forum for visiting speakers to discuss topics of general interest. Members of the Senate, Cabinet, Commons, Legislative Assembly and the academic and business worlds are frequent speakers at the regular luncheon meeting on the first Tuesday of the month from October to May.'[14] As of 1983, the club remained in existence with a membership of some ninety women.[15]

The establishment of the Tuesday Luncheon Club in Toronto, combined with the aggressive recruitment activities of the Ontario Women's Liberal Association during the post-war years (notably, constituent clubs at its fiftieth anniversary meeting in 1964 numbered 110, with 275 delegates in attendance), suggest that the mainstream party organization became increasingly dependent upon the varied services which its female support structures could provide. As relatively well-educated and well-motivated party workers, Liberal women fulfilled such crucial duties as poll captain, canvasser, volunteer publicist, coffee party hostess, election day driver, and convention registrar. Their associations in the post-war years thus grew to be closely identified with basic social, fund-raising, and clerical maintenance functions. In the words of one OWLA historian, recounting experiences during the 1963 federal election, 'The Liberal Women threw all their know-how and energy into the campaign, knocking on doors for the candidates, licking stamps and stuffing envelopes and pouring coffee at social functions to "meet the candidate." They spoke at Liberal rallies and on television and radio. They tacked up candidate placards along the roads and highways. Nothing was too difficult or too trivial to perform.'[16] In the following year, many OWLA members also attended an Ontario provincial leadership convention where, in the words of a group historian, they were 'convention hostesses, wearing their carnation corsages and pouring tea at the receptions.'[17]

The conventional role of pouring tea at party meetings, however, became a source of concern and distaste to some Liberal women during the 1960s. In reflecting upon a year as OWLA president prior to her by-election victory in 1960, Judy LaMarsh concluded that 'women did the donkey work' in party organizations.[18] While publicly appreciative of the important contributions made by women's associations and their members, including in her own campaigns, LaMarsh endorsed a growing, largely non-partisan effort toward changing the position of women in Canadian party politics.

Before examining these attempts at reform, we shall first review the development of older women's organizations in the Conservative and CCF / NDP organizations.

CONSERVATIVE WOMEN'S ASSOCIATIONS

Early records of Conservative women's groups are somewhat less detailed than those which exist in the Liberal party. One internal history of Tory women, published in 1966 by the Progressive Conservative Women's Association of Canada, suggests that isolated clubs existed in Vancouver as early as 1917 (the old Vancouver Women's Conservative Club), in Quebec City in 1918 (a district association encompassing four urban federal ridings), and in Montreal as early as 1920 (L'Association des Femmes Conservatives de Montréal).[19] According to this same account, 'in 1938, the first attempt at a national organization was made by the Honourable R.B. Bennett asking Mrs. Hugh MacKay of Rothesay to come to Ottawa. This meeting led to one at Port Hope where a national organization began to take shape and the decisions made there were formally confirmed at the Winnipeg Convention in 1942.'[20] Since World War II interrupted the organizational development of this group, it was not until 1946 that the 'Women's Committee within the Progressive Conservative Association of Canada' became active, under the leadership of Hilda Hesson.[21]

As a full-time party organizer and president of the Committee, Hesson devoted her considerable energies to publishing a women's newsletter (which appeared in both English and French) and to establishing new or expanded associations in Nova Scotia, Newfoundland, New Brunswick, Prince Edward Island, Alberta, Manitoba, Quebec, and Ontario. By 1950, the PC Women's *News Letter* reached a mailing list of approximately 10,000 readers, compared with only 1,500 at its inception in 1946. This communication ceased publication, however, following Hesson's retirement in 1956.

The exact size of the PC Women's Association during this early period is difficult to estimate, in part because constituent local and provincial groups expanded and disbanded with some frequency. For example, a biographical summary of leading Conservative women refers to the establishment in 1938 of a PC Women's Association of New Brunswick, which was founded by Katie MacKay upon her return from the Ottawa meeting with R.B. Bennett.[22] Later in this same report, a quotation from Lucy Sansom (who was elected president of the national association in 1954) suggests that the New Brunswick organization had grown moribund through the war years: 'When I came to New Brunswick after World War II, I found no Women's Associations, although a few women had gone to meetings and tried to hold things together. I organized Women's Associations in the cities, towns, and villages and as the men of the province gave us no financial help, I had membership cards printed and sold. For membership we charged $1.00 – of which 50 cents went to the Provincial Women's Association.'[23]

A similar pattern of wax and wane occurred in many other regions of Canada where Conservative women's associations were organized, only to become inactive due to the pressures of wartime work or an absence of local activists. Figures which are available indicate that PC activists in Fredericton attracted 'over one hundred women' to meetings held in 1948,[24] while the Victoria Women's Association 'had a membership of one hundred names' in this same period.[25]

In practical terms, the activities engaged in by Conservative women through the 1960s generally resembled those organized by their counterparts in the Liberal party. In campaign organizations, for example, Conservative women frequently fulfilled stereotypically feminine types of tasks, as the president of the Alberta PC Women's Association observed following the 1962 federal elections. According to Eva MacLean, Tory women 'should be the best cooks in the world after the thousands of cookies, donuts and sandwiches they made for "meet-the-candidate" receptions.'[26]

The element of personal and collective ferment which developed in response to these tasks within the Conservative party, however, surfaced somewhat later than in the Liberal case. It is notable that a 1966 Progressive Conservative Women's Association report concluded that organized Tory women should 'oust the Liberal government' and defend Conservative philosophy.[27] The view that PC women should coalesce for the purpose of improving their own status in the party and broader political process did not take shape organizationally until 1981, approximately eight years after the establishment of newer women's groups in both the Liberal and New Democratic parties. In the interim, Conservative women provided valuable support services to the parent organization and, as in the Liberal case, made important contributions to the election of female legislative candidates, including federal MPs Margaret Aitken[28] and Sybil Bennett.[29]

WOMEN IN THE CO-OPERATIVE COMMONWEALTH FEDERATION

The role and history of women's organizations in the CCF / NDP is more complex than in either the Liberal or Conservative cases, in part because separate, constitutionally recognized women's associations were never established on a national scale. As stated in the 1970 *Report* of the Royal Commission, the NDP 'has never had a separate women's organization. It has had federal and provincial women's committees which were, in effect, standing committees. Women, as well as men, are full members of the constituency, provincial and federal associations.'[30] The egalitarian ideology of the CCF and NDP, combined with the challenge involved in founding a new national organization, thus impeded the formation of the same types of auxiliary support structures which evolved in the two older parties.

Although this institutional background suggests that from the outset, CCF women were full and equal participants with men, recent research points toward a somewhat different conclusion. According to historical studies by Manley (1980) and Beeby (1982), as well as personal interviews and documentary research conducted by the author, females as a group were generally fewer in number, less politically influential, and more likely to fulfil conventional feminine (e.g., clerical, fund-raising, and social) tasks in the party than males.[31] While this pattern would seem to follow from the fact that traditional gender role socialization cuts across class and ideological lines, the existence of conflict within the CCF over female participation is notable, and frequently overlooked in standard accounts of party development.[32]

Early materials on involvement in the CCF suggest that from the party's inception in 1932, the difficult task of building a new national organization demanded sustained commitment from all members, whether male or female. By itself, the human energy which was required in order to establish a unified, grass-roots social movement, and to dislodge the entrenched two-party system, was formidable.[33] Women were thus encouraged and expected to 'pitch in,' which many did in such diverse capacities as legislator (federal MP and later Ontario MPP Agnes Macphail, as well as BC MLA Dorothy Steeves are notable examples from the early years), party propagandist (Grace MacInnis, later an MP, co-authored at least three publications during the 1930s), provincial functionary (both the Saskatchewan and Manitoba parties had women as provincial secretaries or directors during the 1930s), and general purpose volunteer. Clearly, this last category embraced many CCF women who were active as riding-level and especially campaign workers. In the words of one early activist, 'we were always trying to branch out, so whenever we found people, male or female, who would contribute, we put them to work. It was such a struggle to keep the party alive at all.'[34]

Probably the most significant dispute regarding female participation in the CCF during these early decades concerned separate versus integrated approaches to involvement – an issue which continues to draw attention in the NDP as well as the two older parties through the 1980s. In the province of Ontario in particular, CCF members frequently differed over such questions as the following: First, were women equal participants in the mainstream CCF organization and, if not, might the establishment of an affiliated women's committee remedy this situation? Second, should the party develop a distinctive electoral strategy to attract women voters and new female activists? And third, would the development and implementation of such a strategy be controlled by a formally constituted women's group in the party? These three questions, while deceptively simple, involved complex issues related to organizational cohesion, the power of central party bureaucrats, and, particularly in the case of the early CCF, the role of 'united front' alliances with non-party, and especially Communist party, women.

Some disputes involving the role of women and women's organizations in the Ontario CCF came to the fore during the mid-1930s, when a group known as the Toronto CCF Women's Joint Committee attempted to establish what John Manley (1980) refers to as 'an autonomous agency of sexual and political struggle.'[35] Briefly, the Women's Joint Committee grew out of 'united front' activities by a number of left-wing CCF women in Toronto. For approximately six months during 1936, veterans of the Canadian League against War and Fascism (a Communist party front group) worked together in this committee 'to promote female activity on the widest possible basis.'[36] As critics of 'the standard party clubs [which] failed to provide their women members with adequate opportunities' in public speaking and political leadership, Joint Committee activists set out to establish an affiliated but independently directed women's organization.[37]

Their success in challenging the status of women in the CCF was limited by frequent charges of 'united front' collusion. In a period when the CCF was increasingly concerned with electoral respectability, party functionaries carefully avoided involvement in any activities which might be perceived as Communist-inspired or otherwise politically 'tainted.' The willingness of the Women's Joint Committee to violate official party doctrine on this point led to the eventual expulsion of many of its key activists, including Jean Laing and Elizabeth Morton. Those who remained within the CCF often became resigned to their traditional fate. As Caroline Riley (who later led the first Ontario CCF Women's Committee) observed in 1938, the electoral success of the party meant 'we must come back to the old business of women's organizations, for the present, that of financial aid. Little as some of us like that, we shall probably have to put on teas, bridges, raffles, etc., to fill the treasury.'[38]

Throughout the Depression and the period of World War II, many CCF women indeed contributed valuable time and effort toward this end – as did their counterparts in the two older political parties. Therefore, although the ideological climate of the former was more egalitarian, and while a fair number of CCF women ascended to positions of political responsibility during this period (including Alice Loeb, a Joint Committee activist who became head of the Ontario CCF Literature Committee), the overall position of party women remained a source of concern to some members through the war years.

CCF WOMEN IN THE POST-WAR PERIOD

Conflicts concerning the role of affiliated women's groups, as well as an appropriate electoral approach to female voters, were particularly apparent in the Ontario CCF after World War II. Since these same issues continue to attract attention in all three major federal parties during the contemporary period, the early Ontario debates warrant close consideration.

One source of contention in the post-war CCF involved the basic need for a women's organization within the party. According to a historical study by Dean Beeby (1982), as well as documentary and interview materials gathered by the author, opinions regarding a women's organization were fairly clear cut along pro versus con lines.[39] On the affirmative side, such prominent CCF'ers as Marjorie Mann, Peggy Brewin, and Alice Katool were convinced that, in order to achieve electoral success, the party needed to recruit more female activists and voters. In 1942, therefore, the Ontario party council established a women's committee and, three years later, delegates to a CCF convention endorsed a resolution which committed the party to 'draft a clear statement of CCF policy toward women.'[40]

Although a 1949 equal pay bill was one of the only policy initiatives to follow from this resolution (notably, it constituted one of the first efforts to introduce equal pay legislation in Canada), the organizational impact of the Women's Committee was substantial. As Beeby (1982) reports, 'The Ontario CCF Women's Committee ... was the first partisan female organization to be established as something other than an auxiliary to the main party structure. Whereas the Conservatives and Liberals had kept their women's groups organizationally separate, the CCF Women's Committee was established as a standing committee of the main party council and thus entitled to a continuing voice in CCF affairs.'[41] The central problem with this new committee was how it might go about influencing party activities. Would a separate network of local CCF women's groups provide the organizational base for the larger provincial committee? Many party members, both male and female, were uncomfortable with the idea of such a network, since it ran contrary to the basic CCF philosophy of integrated and unified party work.

A number of opponents of the committee held major organizational responsibilities within the Ontario party, or were close confidantes of party functionaries. Their perceptions, frequently grounded in a daily struggle for additional funds, members, and electoral respectability, began with a view that there was little need for a separate women's section. According to this perspective, men or women who sought to become active in the CCF had abundant opportunities to do so, given that the party was in continual need of new volunteers.[42] Women who were active in the main-stream organization were particularly hesitant about the committee; in the words of one Ontario respondent, 'We didn't believe in separate associations because we didn't want to be set aside and apart. Marjorie Mann and Peggy Brewin felt that a Women's Committee could attract some of the non-political women, but we political women felt that the separate Committee would demote all of us within the larger organization.'[43]

The organizational strategy of the CCF Women's Committee was also of concern to party insiders, who questioned the ability of the group to recruit new members through women-oriented issue campaigns. These campaigns, which occasionally ran the risk of accustions of 'united front' collusion, attempted to draw housewives into the CCF through such activities as consumer price monitoring, cookbook projects, and rummage sales. As stereotypically feminine activities, these projects were opposed by some CCF members who disagreed with the view that 'you should appeal to women where they were rather than where you thought they should be.'[44] Furthermore, the broader issue focus of the committee drew strong criticism on tactical grounds. According to one respondent who worked as a CCF organizer during the post-war years,

The Committee would do things that I thought were tactically wrong, like making women's issues separate, and letting them get hived off from the policy mainstream, whereas I wanted to see them integrated. I recall one resolution on day care which they brought to a provincial Council meeting during the 1950s. I was definitely sympathetic until they read a section calling for day care to be free. They were so ahead of their times – just think about day care in the 1950s, let alone making it free, and here we were, fighting against all those claims that the CCF was full of crazy spendthrifts. I successfully argued tactics against the free section, so it read something about day care being free only for poor women ... Now looking back, I can see that they were trying to popularize issues and make an impact.[45]

Ultimately, these conflicts with party insiders, combined with internal strains between feminist activists and more traditional Women's Committee members, meant that by the late 1940s, the group had become a relatively weak structure which 'engaged in activities reminiscent of a ladies' auxiliary.'[46] The very existence of such a committee, however, provided important evidence that the question of female status in party organizations was significant as early as the World War II period. Furthermore, as a standing committee of the main party council, the Ontario Committee provided a useful model for subsequent feminist activists in the NDP and elsewhere – at the same time as it foreshadowed the important organizational problems which continue to confront party women's groups.

EFFORTS TOWARD REORGANIZATION IN THE NDP

A number of developments during the early 1960s and following helped to renew interest in the question of women's party participation in English Canada and, more specifically, in the issue of women's organizations within the parties. One factor which helped to draw attention to this subject was the establishment in 1961 of the New Democratic Party (known initially as the New Party), formal successor to the CCF. In October 1961, Eva Latham was appointed to the newly created position of Director of Women's Activities in the federal NDP, a post which reported to the federal executive. During this same period, older CCF women's councils and groups were renamed women's committees of the NDP, and a federal women's committee was established to advise the Director of Women's Activities. According to its initial statement of structure and purpose (dated August 1962), the national NDP Women's Committee was to include three members appointed by the federal council, as well as two members appointed from each constituent provincial council.

Notably, this federal committee viewed its mandate in terms which were similar to those of the earlier Ontario CCF Women's Committee of the 1940s, namely as part of a recognition 'that women in general, and housewives in particular, have specific interests, needs and problems.'[47] The committee sought to mobilize, for partisan purposes, non-political women who were affiliated with 'trade union ladies' auxiliaries' or 'who are able to work for the party in special money raising or social events.'[48] By 1963, approximately 135 constituency-level women's committees had been established in the federal NDP, along with five provincial committees. Furthermore, through the mid-1960s, a number of women's conferences were held in Ontario and British Columbia, and substantial monies were raised 'through the sale of cookbooks, earrings, and Christmas cards.'[49]

This relatively traditional type of committee activity became increasingly outdated by the late 1960s, however. As Eva Latham, the director of women's activities, observed in her report to a 1967 federal party council meeting, 'younger women were seeking answers to personal and community problems and were not just interested in fund-raising and social activities.'[50] Furthermore, she explained that traditional committee activities drew limited interest because as a group, 'women were eager to improve their own financial, educational and career status.'[51] Latham's report was followed in 1968 by a federal executive decision to eliminate her position and, in 1969, by a constitutional amendment which created a new Participation of Women (POW) Committee at the federal level. This new group, as a standing committee appointed by the federal council, was 'to assist and encourage women's participation in all forms of political activity.'[52]

The fulfilment of this new mandate proved difficult to implement within the federal NDP, in part because of major organizational and ideological problems. On an organizational level, the appointment of a federal women's organizer, the relationship between this organizer and the POW Committee, and the method by which POW members would be selected remained contentious issues through the late 1970s. Although delegates to a 1971 federal convention endorsed a resolution calling for the appointment of a women's organizer, this position was not filled on a continuous basis until 1977, when Judy Wasylycia-Leis was hired by the federal executive. Prior to that year, a succession of hirings, dismissals, and disputes between the federal executive and the POW Committee over the role of the women's organizer rendered the position largely inoperative.[53]

During this same period, conflict also developed around the selection of POW members. While proposals were offered as early as 1975 that committee members be elected by provincial women's groups, it was not until 1977 that a federal constitutional amendment (article 8, section 1e) established POW representatives as specially designated delegates to the federal council, who were to be elected at their respective provincial conventions. Once again, the implementation of this change was delayed until 1980, when all constituent provincial and territorial New Democratic parties chose designated POW delegates.

These organizational problems within the NDP were frequently related to the ideologically conflictual atmosphere of the party during the late 1960s and following. More specifically, the growth of a renewed women's movement, especially within the extra-parliamentary left of this period, held important consequences for NDP women, as did the development of a radical Waffle wing within the party. As reflected in a 1968 NDP brief to the Royal Commission on the Status of Women, two surveys of party women conducted in fifty-six communities across Canada showed growing identification with the grievances and ideals of a nascent feminist movement: 'Women expressed the view that they were conditioned, by tradition, to regard their role in public life as the quiet worker behind the scenes, the organizer for the more aggressive male ... It is quite within the scope of this attitude that a woman would well find herself a recording secretary for a constituency association, but seldom its president.'[54] Ironically, this identification of a potential for discriminatory attitudes within the NDP was expressed in the same year as the federal party executive eliminated the Director of Women's Activities position. In retrospect, it seems that this post might have provided an appropriate vehicle for addressing grass-roots concerns regarding female participation, as raised in the NDP brief to the RCSW.

Major factional splits between right and left, establishment and anti-establishment, also developed within the NDP during this period. In particular, the organizational and ideological challenge presented by the radical Waffle group in the years 1970-2 included a demand that women's status within the party, as well as 'women's issue' policy concerns, receive increased attention.[55] A Waffle women's committee within the Ontario NDP was especially active during these years, and helped to organize a new ONDP women's committee following 1972.[56]

One apparent influence of the Waffle upon women's activities in the NDP, which continued long after the group's expulsion in June 1972, was a fear among some party insiders concerning the political loyalty and malleability of feminist activists. In the view of such elites, newer women's caucuses, women's committees, and demands for greater policy emphasis upon 'women's issues' were tainted by their association with the Waffle, and thus constituted a potential threat to organizational unity. Moreover, the increasingly assertive position adopted by feminist women within the NDP – notably in the Rosemary Brown campaign for federal leadership in 1975 – meant that the distinction between pro- and non-feminist party activists grew more clear with the passage of time.

Over the longer term, though, it would appear that the federal POW Committee, provincial women's committees, and federal women's organizers accomplished some meaningful gains for women in the NDP. The recruitment of greater numbers of females for party and public office (see chapter 3), the development of policy initiatives on equal pay and other 'women's issues,' and the adoption of internal party affirmative action programs (see chapter 4) evidence the role of NDP women's groups in improving the status of females inside the party organization, and within the political process more generally. Although these achievements fall considerably short of the egalitarian ideals set forth by the NDP, they provide continuing evidence of the valuable contributions made by women and women's groups to the development of the Canadian left.

We shall now turn our attention to contemporary women's organizations in the Liberal and Conservative parties.

AMALGAMATION IN THE LIBERAL PARTY

Just as the Liberal party in Ontario was the first to establish separate women's organizations during the suffragist period (notably, the Toronto and Ontario Women's Liberal Associations, formed in 1913 and 1914, respectively), so it also initiated the movement toward amalgamating these older groups. In 1969, the Ontario Women's Liberal Association (OWLA) disbanded as part of an effort to increase female integration within the mainstream party organization. According to minutes of a final OWLA executive meeting, the group was to integrate with the larger Liberal Party of Ontario (LPO) 'subject to the following provisions: (a) The Annual Meeting of the LPO on March 29, 1969, approve in their new constitution the guarantee of a minimum of two women on the Executive Committee of LPO.'[57]

While the vote to amalgamate carried in 1969, its consequences for

Liberal women remain somewhat problematical. First, a number of older activists who had long identified with OWLA became convinced that their organization was unjustly dissolved and, as evidence of their lingering dissatisfaction, could be seen wearing OWLA pins at Liberal party functions as recently as 1983. Furthermore, as discussed below, OWLA veterans maintained that the ability of Liberal women to become delegates to party meetings was impaired by efforts to integrate (and, in their view, destroy) older groups.

Second, in simple organizational terms, amalgamation was complicated by the division of LPO into separate federal (Liberal Party of Canada, Ontario or LPC[O]) and provincial (Ontario Liberal Party or OLP) wings following 1975. One important effect of this division was that Liberal feminists who supported integration generally became more involved with the federal than the provincial wing, so that although new national and Ontario Women's Liberal commissions were established, in 1973 and 1981, respectively, the provincial-level OLP was left without any women's affiliate. In short, therefore, the dissolution of OWLA in 1969, followed by a federal-provincial party split in the mid-1970s, meant that many older women's association activists grew disenchanted with the mainstream Liberal organization at the same time as younger status of women partisans directed the bulk of their energies toward party work at the federal level.

The formation of a national Women's Liberal Commission in 1973 provided the locus for much of this activity. According to Joseph Wearing (1981), 'Women at the national level first balked at the idea of integration, allegedly because the elderly members were afraid of losing their right to attend national meetings as women's delegates. In a final paternalistic coup de grace, the national executive cut off their funding and in 1973 the women at last accepted the wisdom of disbanding the organization.'[58] An older Women's Liberal Federation was thus replaced in 1973 by the Women's Liberal Commission (WLC), whose membership encompassed all female members of all Liberal Party of Canada (LPC) organizations, including older women's clubs.

The commission differed from its predecessor in a number of important ways. Perhaps most notably, the executive of the WLC was to be elected by and responsible to a caucus of all Liberal women, who would gather at each LPC Convention to elect a national president and five regional representatives.[59] Unlike the older federation, which was constituted as a separate but affiliated support organization within the LPC, the newer WLC was thus established as an integrated part of the larger party organization. Its statement of purpose reflected clearly the broader objectives behind amalgamation: 'The purpose of this organization shall be to represent and promote the interests of women within the Liberal Party of Canada and to encourage the active participation of women at all levels of the Party.'[60] As in the NDP, therefore, integrating more women within the mainstream party organization was established as a key priority of the new Women's Liberal Commission.

Implementing this mandate has also proved difficult inside the LPC, however. In terms of paid staff, the commission has frequently been without a full-time liaison person in party headquarters. Furthermore, while the WLC has succeeded in publicizing internally the status of Liberal women, particularly through its affirmative action plan (see chapter 4) and an effective series of flyers and fact sheets,[61] the group remains an uneasy alliance between older auxiliary and newer feminist elements. In the words of one early member of the WLC executive, 'I realized soon after my election that these women from across the country were *not* feminists – although eventually more feminists became involved.' The gap between auxiliary and feminist perspectives was also identified by a more recent regional representative to the WLC executive, who remarked that 'the Commission embraces women at very different stages of political development. At one extreme you find those ... who are very integrated in the federal mainstream, while at the other you find groups of farm women, for example, who retain something of an auxiliary mentality.'

Reconciling older supportive with newer assertive notions regarding the role of party women's groups has also challenged constituent bodies of the LPC, including the federal Liberal organization in Ontario (LPC[O]). As a result of the dissolution of OWLA in 1969, and the subsequent federal-provincial division of its parent party following 1975, women's clubs in the newly created federal wing in Ontario lost their right to elect delegates to party conventions. This loss remained a source of resentment among OWLA activists, who noted that older groups of Liberal women in New Brunswick and elsewhere had retained their constitutional right to delegate through the contemporary period.

In an effort to reinstate women's delegates, and thus increase numerical representation at party conventions, members of a Standing Committee on Women in the LPC(O) recommended in 1981 that each recognized women's club or association in the province be allowed to send two voting delegates to every convention. This constitutional amendment permitting women's delegates was passed in November 1981, along with a number of modifications which created the Ontario Women's Liberal Commission.[62]

Older and newer perspectives toward the role of Liberal women have thus converged somewhat in recent years, as the need for province- or nation-wide organization and for increased numbers of female convention delegates became clearer to holders of both points of view. It remains to be seen, however, whether newer women's commissions can enhance female involvement in mainstream party politics at the same time as they actively encourage participation in (and convention delegation through) separate clubs or associations at the local level.

We shall now consider the emergence of a similar dilemma within the Progressive Conservative Party of Canada.

WOMEN'S ORGANIZATIONS IN THE CONSERVATIVE PARTY

Unlike the New Democratic and Liberal parties, which reorganized or amalgamated their federal women's organizations during the early 1970s, the federal Conservative party retained its older Women's Association through 1980. In fact, one summary of party involvement among Canadian women reports that as recently as 1967, the PC Women's Association had a membership of approximately 75,000.[63]

Attempts to reform this older association grew out of discussions both within the group itself, as well as within the national executive of the parent PC party. According to a number of accounts, the last seven years of the association's existence (from 1973 to 1980) were marked by frequent internal questioning of the reasons for its existence. In the words of one respondent, 'The Association met during that period for about two hours at each national convention, asking itself whether or not to exist. Then, those in attendance went to lunch with the wife of the federal party leader. It simply grew into a blue-rinse set ... They were a small group who were busy re-electing each other.'

Concern over the viability and direction of the PC Women's Association was also expressed in the national executive. By the summer of 1980, party elites began to question why they should continue funding an increasingly moribund organization. Similarly, at this same time, a number of Association activists recognized the imminent demise of the older group and proposed to the executive a major reorganization along the lines of the National Women's Political Caucus in the United States. The purpose of a new women's group, in the view of PC caucus advocates, would be to recruit more female activists for involvement in the party mainstream; in fact, the theme which was proposed for a new PC Women's Caucus was 'Into the Mainstream.'[64]

The method by which party women were to be thus integrated, however, has proved as contentious within the Conservative organization as it has in the New Democratic and Liberal parties. On the level of organization, the National PC Women's Caucus, which grew out of a name-change meeting of the older association in February 1981, has frequently been confused both with the latter and with new local caucuses established by the Women's Bureau at national headquarters. Notably, the National Caucus differs from its predecessor in that 'every woman who is a member in good standing of any Association of the Progressive Conservative Party of Canada, Provincially or Territorially,' is a Caucus member.[65] The National Caucus, like the Women's Liberal Commission, is thus composed of all female party members, with voting membership open to all female delegates to party conventions. The National Caucus executive, elected at each convention, includes a president; the director of the Women's Bureau; ten provincial vice-presidents, each of whom presides over a provincial women's association; and ten provincial representatives.[66]

One additional source of confusion within the PC organization involves the relationship between the National Caucus, on the one hand, and local women's caucuses and riding associations, on the other. Following the contribution of more than $30,000 by former Ottawa MP Jean Pigott, the federal Conservatives established a three-member Women's Bureau within their national headquarters in January 1981.[67] The first director of the Women's Bureau, Barbara Ford, worked to establish a network of city or regional women's caucuses in urban areas with a population of more than 100,000.[68] While Ford's initiative began as an attempt to provide female partisans with an adjunct or alternative route to political mobility through riding associations, some of which remain inactive between elections and may be less than receptive to new female (and especially younger feminist) recruits, it tended to blur an important distinction between the national and city caucus organizations. That is, the local or regional caucuses – generally referred to as Federal PC Women's Caucuses – were designed as relatively small-scale skills training groups, in contrast to the National Caucus, which was established as an advisory and lobby organization at the national level.[69] Moreover, the Federal Caucuses were perceived in some quarters to be competing with established constituency associations, even though their original mandate was to operate as specialized recruitment vehicles for the eventual benefit of local ridings.

On a more ideological plane, both types of PC caucuses received an uneasy reception among supporters of older party women's groups. In Nova Scotia and Ontario, in particular, traditional women's associations continued to operate even after the dissolution of the National Association, so that friction between older and newer groups persists. As one National Caucus activist reflected in light of her experiences between 1980 and 1982, 'It's been a long two years trying to address these people who feel threatened.'

Probably the most vocal opposition to reorganization in the Conservative party has come from the Ontario Progressive Conservative Association of Women (OPCAW), a provincially based group which was established in 1973. OPCAW is composed primarily of older Conservative women who, although extremely active as party workers, remain loyal to an essentially supportive or auxiliary role within the mainstream PC organization.[70] This purpose is reflected in an official statement of principles: 'OPCAW exists to strengthen the capability of women to be of service to the Party, to share information of importance with its membership and to draw the matters of concern of its membership to the attention of the Party and the Government.'[71] The Ontario group has considered and rejected amalgamation, notably at a 1976 meeting where provincial MPP and cabinet minister Dr Bette Stephenson stated that women's associations are 'dangerously close to being irrelevant.'[72] This allegation was denied by a core of OPCAW activists, who continue to maintain that PC success in Ontario is largely dependent upon the existence of parallel female support structures at both the riding and provincial levels.[73]

Internal conflicts between older association and newer caucus approaches to the organization of Conservative women were clearly evidenced at a June 1982 meeting of OPCAW in Toronto. Given that no executive positions in OPCAW were contested, the president of the National PC Women's Caucus, Elizabeth Willcock, was invited to address the group. Willcock began her speech by acknowledging the dedicated work of OPCAW activists, but followed these comments with a reference to the 'anachronistic' nature of women's associations in the party. Her description of the National Caucus, Women's Bureau, and city caucuses concluded with a statement that younger women in particular desire 'fuller participation in the political process ... and input into all issue areas. Canadian women must walk into the twenty-first century with full equality in all spheres of our society.'[74]

Willcock's address was followed by a question-and-answer session, during which a number of OPCAW delegates expressed their confusion regarding the relationship among older associations, the National PC Women's Caucus, city caucuses, and riding associations. More importantly, some participants challenged Willcock to explain why, in establishing a new national caucus in 1981, PC women on the federal level forfeited their right to recognize independently local women's associations, which could in turn send delegates to party conventions.[75] This issue of delegation to conventions, combined with a general sense that the federally based caucuses were overly assertive and feminist, contributed to the defeat of an OPCAW constitutional amendment which would have formally recognized the National PC Women's Caucus. In the words of one strong opponent of the amendment, 'By recognizing this new National Women's Caucus, we automatically unrecognize existing federal women's associations in Ontario, which I don't think any of us in OPCAW would want to do.'

The integration of women within the Conservative mainstream, and the amalgamation of older women's groups at the federal level, have thus been complicated by major organizational and ideological difficulties. As in the Liberal and New Democratic cases, it remains unclear whether newer PC women's groups can challenge successfully the traditional division of party labour by gender, at the same time as they attempt to organize political women within distinctive – albeit 'integrated' – national and local caucuses.

CONCLUSIONS

This chapter has traced the historical development of women's associations in the Liberal, Conservative, and CCF / NDP organizations from the early suffrage period through the present. Overall, it suggests that despite continuing tensions within party organizations, older auxiliary-type attitudes and women's groups are gradually being replaced by more explicitly pro-feminist ones. Unlike traditional associations, which frequently functioned as support structures for mainstream parties, the latter generally give priority to increasing female representation in party activities, especially policy-making.

We shall now turn to a cross-cultural examination of women and party politics, one portion of which considers the development of party women's groups in comparative perspective.

6

Comparative Perspectives on Women and Party Politics

One hundred years hence, what a change will be made
In politics, morals, religion, and trade,
In statesmen who wrangle or ride on the fence
These things will be altered a hundred years hence.[1]
Frances Dana Gage, 'A Hundred Years Hence' (1852)

The formal entrance of women to many political systems of North America and Western Europe was accompanied by widespread expectations of rapid moral improvement, particularly in the corrupt domain of party politics. As one American women's rights advocate, Frances Dana Gage, predicted in a song composed in 1852, enfranchised females would generate sweeping changes 'in politics, morals, religion, and trade.'[2]

During the contemporary period, the extent of female political influence has, in popular terms, been associated with the success of such women as Golda Meir, Indira Gandhi, and Margaret Thatcher in gaining positions of major party leadership, followed by prime-ministerial responsibility. The national and international profiles of these leaders have suggested to some observers, including a number of Canadian writers, that women's political experiences are no longer defined by their suffragist beginnings, traditional patterns of gender role socialization, or discriminatory treatment within political institutions.[3] Rather, the achievements of female notables in the 1970s and 1980s are viewed as 'proof' that historical and social constraints upon women in politics have disappeared.

This chapter adopts a somewhat different perspective in its comparative examination of women and party politics. Rather than beginning with the careers of a handful of exceptional cases, notably Thatcher, Gandhi, and Meir, and questioning why Canada has thus far failed to elect a similarly exceptional female prime minister, we suggest that the experiences of most women in comparable Western party systems resemble closely the patterns described above in chapters 1 through 5. For example, we argue that the political wedging of early feminism and suffragism in English Canada was paralleled in other North American and Western European cultures, where broader demands for social reform as well as the events of World Wars I and II frequently combined to obscure basic women's rights concerns. Furthermore, we suggest that contemporary patterns of public opinion and party participation in these same systems reflect the distinctive experiences of females within established party institutions. In this manner, we maintain that women's involvement in British party politics generally – to take one obvious example – bears closer resemblance to the trend toward underrepresentation outlined above in our discussion of English Canada than it does to the popularly cited 'exceptional case' of Prime Minister Thatcher.

In exploring these comparative dimensions of women and party politics, we rely upon a variety of studies (including dissertation research by the author) which address political history, attitudes, and participation in Quebec, the United States, Western Europe, and Australia.[4] Our discussion opens first with a brief review of the historical context of enfranchisement in areas outside English Canada, using Evans' (1977) distinction between Catholic and Protestant cultures as a useful starting point.[5] Second, we consider the relationship between this historical background and patterns of public opinion, highlighting the cases of France, Quebec, and the United States. The third major section of the chapter explores patterns of party involvement, including local constituency-level, campaign, and legislative participation. As in chapter 4, we consider efforts to increase female representation on elite levels and, as in chapter 5, evaluate the role and effectiveness of women's organizations within other major North American and Western European political parties.

Although this chapter presents only the barest foundations for a longer and much-needed comparative study of women and party politics, it does provide important cross-cultural perspectives on the political status of women in English Canada. Moreover, in examining the Canadian case in light of newer comparative materials, it points toward a number of possible directions for future research on women and politics, both in English Canada and elsewhere.

THE HISTORICAL DIMENSION

In his comparative study of feminist history in Western democracies, Richard Evans (1977) suggests a useful distinction between women's political experiences in Catholic and Protestant cultures.[6] More specifically, Evans compares women's development in predominantly Catholic societies (such as those of France and Quebec), where traditional values regarding women's roles were deeply entrenched and where feminists faced strong clerical as well as political opposition in their pursuit of political rights, with that in Protestant systems (such as those of the United States, Great Britain, and English Canada), where women's roles were less strictly circumscribed and where feminist activists had somewhat less difficulty in pursuing legal reforms.

Because traditional norms regarding 'woman's sphere' were better established and thus more vigorously defended in Catholic than in Protestant cultures, Evans suggests that attempts by nineteenth- and early twentieth-century feminists to alter conventional gender roles were more successful (and occurred at an earlier date) in the latter than in the former. The ability of suffragists in major Anglo-American cultures to obtain the vote during the period of World War I, compared with delays which restricted enfranchisement until the World War II period in such Catholic cases as Quebec, France, and Italy, provides one important illustration of Evans's argument regarding the resistance to, as well as timing of, legal reforms in Protestant as opposed to Catholic cultures.

A similar argument concerning the cultural bases of women's political development has been presented more recently by Margaret Inglehart (1981).[7] In an analysis of contemporary patterns of political interest in Western Europe, Inglehart argues that 'the historical experience of a given nation (whether Catholic or Protestant) has left an imprint on the relative politicization of the respective sexes in that society as a whole.'[8]

Although studies by Evans and Inglehart help to explain substantial gender differences in levels of political interest and awareness within Catholic cultures, as well as differences between women in Protestant and Catholic systems (see below), they also point toward at least two common threads which connect women's early political experiences in both types of cultural environments. First, these historical discussions suggest that an important alliance linked early feminist and suffragist activism, on the one hand, and broader social reform movements, on the other. Whether defined in terms of radical secularism and anti-clericalism, as in the French case, or urban improvement, temperance, and child welfare, as in the American and English-Canadian contexts, early feminism maintained a clear connection with wider reformist activities, particularly in those political systems where a divisive struggle over enfranchisement ensued. In 'frontier societies' of the American West, Australia, and New

Zealand, such alliances and prolonged debates were rarely necessary, in part because of widespread assumptions that female voters would 'civilize' politics in rough frontier areas.[9]

Second, existing historical materials indicate that despite their alliances with broader reform movements, early feminists frequently found their key legislative concerns were wedged outside the main political agenda of the day. In France, Quebec, and other Catholic cultures, female enfranchisement was often opposed by clerical and political authorities for reasons which had to do with the fate of particular social institutions, notably the family, were women to gain increased rights. Feminist arguments thus became wedged in wider systemic disputes involving right and left, clericalism and anti-clericalism, such that women themselves did not necessarily become an independent political force either during these debates or with the formal granting of political rights during the 1940s.[10]

In Protestant, Anglo-American societies, a similar type of wedging occurred as a result of the events of World War I. In the United States, Great Britain, and English Canada, enfranchisement was granted more as a recognition of and reward for women's wartime contributions than as part of a broad social consensus regarding female rights to legal equality. The large bulk of non-suffragist women in Protestant cultures thus gained formal political equality following limited direct public debate over their rights and roles; in fact, their enfranchisement was generally overshadowed by wartime mobilization and by concurrent changes or realignments in the party systems of Great Britain, the United States, and English Canada.[11]

The attitudinal implications of a cross-cultural tie between early feminism and social reform, as well as of a political wedging of suffragism in both Catholic and Protestant contexts, are explored in the following sections.

CHANGING PATTERNS OF FEMALE POLITICIZATION

Our hypothesis that changes in female political status were very strongly opposed in Catholic cultures, where feminist and suffragist movements were frequently wedged by broader societal conflicts, points toward at least two major attitudinal questions. First, to what extent might women's historical experiences in Catholic cultures have contributed to particular patterns of public opinion formation and, more specifically, to a collective hesitancy or ambiguity vis-à-vis politics in the decades immediately following enfranchisement? Second, could this phenomenon of limited female politicization be expected to weaken with the passage of time, and especially with the decline of older cohorts? In this section, we introduce longitudinal data from France on political interest, electoral abstentions, and survey non-response in order to evaluate these questions, and also re-examine parallel data from Francophone Quebec and English Canada which were presented in chapter 2.

The relationship between women's political history during the enfranchisement period, on the one hand, and subsequent patterns of female politicization, on the other, is perhaps best evaluated in reference to the French political system. In France, survey-based electoral research was initiated shortly after General de Gaulle decreed female enfranchisement in 1944; this coincidence permits researchers who employ longitudinal data to examine trends in female political interest, electoral abstention, and survey non-response from a relatively early date. When compared with the more lengthy gap between enfranchisement and the beginnings of electoral research in other Western cultures, including those of Great Britain, Italy, Quebec, English Canada, and the United States, this coincidence of timing in France becomes especially clear. Our main purpose in introducing French data, then, is to illustrate the impact of women's enfranchisement-period experiences upon politicization and to trace subsequent changes in patterns of female politicization.

As summarized in table 6.1, gender differences in levels of political interest in post-war France were generally large, reflecting considerably greater interest among males than females. As might have been expected given the background to woman suffrage in Catholic cultures generally, the largest gender difference in political interest in table 6.1 (32%) appears in 1953, the first year for which data are available, while the highest absolute level of female political interest (59%) is obtained in 1976 and 1978, the most recent years for which figures are reported. While gender differences in interest tend to fluctuate in the 11% to 22% range during the years between 1953 and 1978, it is notable that women's interest increased nearly 20% through this period, at the same time as relatively little change occurred among men. Women therefore became increasingly interested in politics between 1953 and 1978, even though their absolute level of interest in 1978 remained substantially less than that of men.

In light of these figures in table 6.1, it would seem that the growth in female political interest between 1953 and 1978 was fairly systematic. That is, except for 1970 data which show major declines among both men and women, female interest tended to increase by approximately 7% during three periods, namely 1953-8, 1958-65, and 1969-76. By way of com-

TABLE 6.1
Political interest among French women and men, 1953-78[a]

	1953	1958	1965	1969	1970	1976	1978
Women	40	46.8	53	53	31	59.9	59.4
Men	72	69.4	64	66	47	78.4	71.7
Difference, women – men	– 32	– 22.6	– 11	– 13	– 16	– 18.5	– 12.3

a All data are derived from nation-wide samples with the exception of the 1965 figures, which are drawn from a study of Boulogne-Billancourt, a working-class area of Paris. Each entry represents the percentage of respondents professing any level of interest in politics, except for the 1976 and 1978 results which combine the percentage of cases reporting frequent or occasional political discussion.
Sources: 1958 French Election Study; Euro-barometres no. 6 (1976) and no. 10 (1978); Mattei Dogan and Jacques Narbonne, *Les françaises face à la politique* (Paris: A. Colin, 1955); Guy Michelat, 'Attitudes et comportements politiques dans une agglomération de la région parisienne,' in Gérard Adam et al., eds., *L'élection présidentielle des 5 et 19 décembre 1965*, (Paris: A. Colin, 1965); Gisèle Charzat, *Les françaises, sont-elles des citoyennes?* (Paris: Denoël, 1972); Philippe Braud, *Le comportement électoral en France* (Paris: Presses Universitaires de France, 1973); and Janine Mossuz-Lavau and Mariette Sineau, *Les femmes françaises en 1978* (Paris: CORDES, 1980)

parison, male political interest generally declined over the period 1953-70 and peaked in 1976 (78.4%), at the same time as female interest rose quite steadily to a 1976-8 plateau of approximately 59%.

This relatively consistent growth in women's political interest, particularly during specific chronological periods following the end of World War II, may be related to broader historical changes of direct relevance to French females. The years 1953-65, for example, are widely identified by political scientists with recurring constitutional crises of both the Fourth and Fifth Republics.[12] In cultural terms, however, this same period was characterized by the development of an increasingly urban, industrialized, and national society, as access to the mass media, consumer goods, and a modern transportation system widened. Particularly during the years after 1958, the de Gaulle government initiated a series of programs which achieved what Bourricard (1977) has termed 'conservative modernization.'[13] Levels of formal educational attainment rose and, especially among married women, rates of non-agricultural employment grew rapidly.[14]

These changes held potentially important consequences for French politics and, more specifically, for women's political attitudes. In demographic terms, many older women who had tended to be regularly practising

TABLE 6.2
Electoral abstentions among French women and men, 1951-78[a]

Year	1951	1953	1958	1962	1962	1965	1965	1967	1968	1969	1969	1973	1977	1978
Type of election	legis.	munic.	refer.	refer.	legis.	Paris munic.	pres.	legis.	legis.	refer.	pres.	legis.	Paris munic.	Vienne legis.
Female abstentions	24	25	53	27	30	32	18	24	27	23	32	25	31	18.9
Male abstentions	17	13	47	17	18	24	11	17	14	16	34	18	30	16.7
Difference, women – men	7	12	6	10	12	8	7	7	13	7	-2	7	1	2.2

a Cell entries represent the percentage of electoral abstentions, with figures on presidential elections derived from the second round of voting.

Sources: Georges Dupeux, Alain Girard, and Jean Stoetzel, 'Une enquête par sondage auprès des électeurs,' in *Le référendum de septembre et les élections de novembre 1958*, by Mattei Dogan et al. (Paris: A. Colin, 1960); Guy Michelat, 'Attitudes et comportements politiques à l'automne 1962,' in François Goguel, ed., *Le référendum d'octobre et les élections de novembre 1962* (Paris: A. Colin, 1965); Alain Lancelot, *L'abstentionnisme électoral en France* (Paris: A. Colin, 1968); Charzat, *Les françaises*; Albert Brimo, *Les femmes françaises face au pouvoir politique* (Paris: Editions Montchrestien, 1975); Mossuz-Lavau and Sineau, *Les femmes françaises*; and Monica Charlot, 'Women in Politics in France,' in Howard R. Penniman, ed., *The French National Assembly Elections of 1978* (Washington, DC: American Enterprise Institute, 1980)

Catholics passed from the electorate and were replaced by new cohorts whose religious affiliation seems to have been less profound, and whose political socialization thus diverged from that of passing generations. A related demographic change was the process of urbanization, which reduced population in many of the heavily christianized rural areas, and thus provided the basis for an increasingly radical form of urban Catholicism.[15]

As large numbers of women became more and more distant from traditional French Catholicism in the late 1950s and early 1960s, their pre-enfranchisement political experiences also receded into history. These twin processes of modernization and especially female secularization, and the passing of pre-enfranchisement cohorts, likely contributed to the 13% increase in female political interest between 1953 and 1965, reported in table 6.1.

Similarly, in 1968 and following, France experienced social and political conflict on a scale which Ehrmann (1976) and other analysts have termed 'traumatic.'[16] In specific reference to women, however, these same events and processes seem to have had a reverse, distinctively liberating effect, since student and anti-war movements of the 1960s provided a major organizational and ideological base from which contemporary French feminism has developed. As in other Western European and North American societies, women's rights and women's liberationist activities largely grew out of these movements and, as such, they represented an important challenge both to the institutions of the old and new left and to the values and gender role norms of French culture more generally.[17]

The events of 1968 and the subsequent growth of feminism and a revitalized French left (especially the Parti Socialiste) thus exposed younger female cohorts to an increasingly activist, egalitarian, and leftist political milieu. The growth of women's political interest to a level of nearly 60% in 1976, representing approximately a 20% increase over the base figure of 40% reported in 1953, suggests that these broader social processes influenced, and indeed enhanced, the level of female politicization in France through the late 1970s.

Data on electoral abstentions during the period 1951-78, reported in table 6.2, offer somewhat less direct evidence of growing female politicization over time. Comparing figures on non-voting in 1951 and 1973 legislative elections, for example, we find little change in the turnout levels of either men or women, such that the gender differential in both years remained at a level of 7%.

One possible explanation for the relatively consistent pattern of French

TABLE 6.3
Non-response to party identification and party preference items, France, 1958-78[a]

Year	% women (N)	% men (N)
1958	54.5 (606)	40.5 (521)
1968	21.7 (871)	17.7 (837)
1978	21.2 (621)	17.6 (574)

a Cell entries represent the percentage of cases reporting no response to party identification (1958, 1968) and party preference (1978) items.
Sources: 1958 French Election Study; July 1968 IFOP survey reported in David R. Cameron, 'Stability and Change in Patterns of French Partisanship,' *Public Opinion Quarterly*
36:1 (Spring 1972), table 3; and 1978 (no. 10) Euro-barometre study

electoral abstentions since 1951, as compared with changes in political
interest during this same period, is that parallel short-term influences
affected non-voting among both men and women.[18] That is, although
females had lower levels of political interest than males, they were probably encouraged to vote in the 1950s through the 1970s by clerical and
rightist political organizations, at the same time as men received similar
cues from left-wing parties and trade unions. This explanation is supported
by the 1969 entries in table 6.2, which show that in one presidential
election where both the Communists (PCF) and Unified Socialists (PSU)
recommended that their supporters abstain from voting, male abstentions
slightly exceeded female (by 2%). In 1969, therefore, the specific electoral
cue given to men apparently differed from that offered to women, such
that the regular pattern of male-female abstentions shifted somewhat.
Over the longer term, differences were generally in the opposite direction,
with female non-voting slightly higher than that of males.

Figures on 1977 and 1978 abstentions in table 6.2, however, indicate
that even these older gender differences are disappearing. Since Paris
municipal and Vienne legislative non-voting differed by only 1% to 2%, it
would seem that the exit of older female cohorts, combined with the
entrance of younger women who came of age politically after 1968, tended
to reduce remaining disparities. This generational view is confirmed by
results reported in Mossuz-Lavau and Sineau (1978), which show that
the gender difference in municipal non-voting among Parisian respondents
born before 1900 was considerably higher than in the overall sample (14%
versus 1%).[19]

A third measure of female politicization in France is provided by data
on survey response or, more accurately, non-response. The extent of non-
responses among women in post-war surveys was widely noted, including

in one study which claimed that females constituted 63.5% of those who held no opinion about the 1958 Constitution.[20] In fact, the problem of ascertaining women's electoral preferences has provided a major impetus for experimentation with separate ballot urns for men and women in France.[21]

Non-response data from the first wave of the 1958 French Election Study, reported in table 6.3, offer a useful baseline from which to analyse this phenomenon.[22] They show that the proportion of women professing no party identification or stating that they did not know their identification was 54.5%, compared with 40.5% among men. Notably, levels of non-response in 1958 exceeded 64% among rural, university-educated, and younger (under age 29) women.

Comparing these 1958 figures with patterns of non-response in 1968 and 1978, we find that significant changes occurred during the two decades following the establishment of the Fifth Republic. In both the 1968 IFOP and 1978 Euro-barometre (no. 10) surveys, approximately 21% of women reported no party identification, which represented less than one-half the level obtained in 1958 (see table 6.3). Moreover, gender differences in non-response for both 1968 and 1978 were in the 3% to 4% range, as compared with 14% in 1958. These major reductions in both the level of female non-response and the gender differences in non-response indicate that a considerable politicization of French women occurred between 1958 and 1978 and, more specifically, between 1958 and 1968.

Additional 1968 data reported in Cameron (1972) indicate that non-responses among younger respondents in that year were relatively low and did not differ at all by gender.[23] Moreover, comparing women age 21 to 29 in 1958 and 1968 samples, Cameron shows a very considerable drop-off in non-response from 69.0% to only 17.4%, which suggests once again that younger female cohorts in 1968 and following were relatively interested, aware, and as politicized as younger males.

To summarize this discussion of changing patterns of female political interest, abstentions, and non-response in France, we would conclude that substantial shifts occurred over time in all three indicators of politicization. First, in reference to political interest, we have shown that the absolute level of female interest increased considerably during three periods between 1953 and 1978, while the relatively extreme gender differences in interest which existed during the 1950s decreased in these same years. Second, in terms of non-voting, the data indicated that although levels of male and female abstention were relatively similar from 1951 through the 1970s, both 1977 and 1978 figures suggested that even these residual differences were disappearing, probably as a result of the entrance of new cohorts to the female electorate. Third, in analysing patterns of non-response, we demonstrated the magnitude of this phenomenon among women in 1958 and showed that the extent of female non-response as well as gender differences in non-response had both diminished considerably during the decade 1958-68.

Parallel data on political interest and survey non-response among women in Canada, presented above in chapter 2, also suggest that enfranchisement-period experiences may hold important implications for patterns of female politicization. Even though the lag between enfranchisement (in both English Canada and Quebec) and the beginnings of Canadian electoral research is much longer than in the French case, available longitudinal data point toward similar conclusions. First, as summarized in tables 2.5 and 2.6, Anglophone and particularly Quebec Francophone women reported considerably less political interest than comparable men in both 1965 and 1979; and second, as shown in table 2.7, survey non-response among Francophone females was especially high in these same years. Although longitudinal changes are more difficult to measure than in the French case, in part because of divergent question wordings in available Canadian surveys, we would propose that the existence of gender differences in politicization through 1979 suggests the continued impact of women's historical experiences in Canada, and especially in Francophone Quebec.

SOCIAL REFORM AND THE DEVELOPMENT OF WOMEN'S ATTITUDES

Our brief review of women's political development in both Catholic and Protestant cultures also suggested that, in many cases, organized feminism was closely associated with wider social reform activities. In the United States, for example, woman suffrage and other feminist issues were allied with a larger progressive issue agenda, which encompassed pacifist, urban improvement, and general social welfare concerns. Similarly, suffragists in Quebec established a more distinctively partisan alliance following 1938 with the reform-oriented Liberal party. While these early feminist alliances are generally overlooked in existing public opinion research, they may hold important implications for the development of women's attitudes in Western democracies.

The American case is especially relevant in this context because of social feminist efforts to establish non-partisan, reform-oriented organizations on a national scale.[24] Historical research by Lemons (1973) dem-

TABLE 6.4
Opinion differences between American women and men on selected issues, 1978[a]

	% support among opinion holders ($N = 1,270$)			Signif., tau$_c$
	Women	Men	Difference	
Too little money spent on improving and protecting environment	57.4	48.9	8.5.	.001
Too little money spent on solving problems of big cities	44.8	37.4	7.4	.001
Too little money spent on military, armaments	27.4	33.6	−6.2	–
Government should take action to reduce income differences between rich and poor	63.1	52.0	11.1	.001
Favour death penalty for murder	68.8	79.2	−10.4	.001

a In this table, cell entries are based on analysis of white respondents only.
Source: 1978 NORC General Social Survey

onstrates that suffragist victory on the federal level was followed by the creation of a National League of Women Voters, which consistently engaged women in discussions and activities related to progressive social issues, including health care, education, the environment, and urban improvement.[25] As a major volunteer organization of American women through the 1970s, the National League and its local affiliates could be expected to shape the attitudes of females in a pro-social reform direction, especially in issue areas related to the older progressive movement.[26]

As reported in table 6.4, American women in 1978 indeed reflected significantly greater support for environmental, urban improvement, and income redistribution programs than men, at the same time as the former were also less willing to endorse increased military expenditures and the death penalty.[27] These results from a 1978 survey by the National Opinion Research Center resemble older figures reported elsewhere which show that American females have been more supportive than males of federal spending on income maintenance and social services, and less in favour of war, military expenditures, and the death penalty.[28]

While they provide indirect evidence only of an older social feminist influence upon women's attitudes, our data do suggest that historical factors may help to inform contemporary discussions of social opinion. Moreover, in an American context, such linkages could also prove useful in efforts to explain an apparent 'gender gap' in political – including par-

TABLE 6.5
Party identification of Anglophone and Francophone Quebeckers, 1965[a]

	Anglophones		Francophones	
	Women	Men	Women	Men
Liberal	64.9	66.7	64.3	55.9
Conservative	21.1	21.7	13.8	19.4
New Democratic	14.0	8.3	12.2	9.9
Créditiste	–	3.3	8.5	11.7
Union nationale	–	–	1.2	3.1
Total N	(57)	(60)	(319)	(324)

a Respondents were asked, 'Generally speaking, do you think of yourself as Conservative, Liberal, Social Credit, Créditiste, NDP, Union nationale, or what?' Non-identifiers were probed a second time: 'Well, do you generally think of yourself as a little closer to one of the parties than the others?' (If yes) 'Which one?' All missing data have been excluded from this and the following tables.
Source: 1965 Canadian Election Study

tisan – attitudes, since they point toward an older reform-based orientation which could be mobilized by liberal feminists and Democrats.[29]

A second cultural milieu where the attitudinal implications of early feminist alliances may be explored is Francophone Quebec. According to materials in Cleverdon (1950) and Casgrain (1972), women obtained the provincial franchise in Quebec following the 1940 election of a provincial Liberal (PLQ) government, which was strongly encouraged to implement its 1938 party convention resolution regarding suffrage by officials of the governing federal caucus.[30] Since provincial suffrage legislation was therefore attributable in large part to a single political party – the PLQ – and since the federal Liberals appear to have pressured their provincial affiliate in the direction of enfranchisement, then we might expect to find a fairly strong Liberal predisposition among women in Quebec. More specifically, female cohorts who came of age politically during the period of suffragist activism in the 1920s and following might tend to be especially supportive of the PLQ, given that an important feature of their politicization experiences was the Liberal granting of the vote, followed by government-sponsored legislation that enabled women to participate in municipal politics and to practise law in the province.[31]

To what extent have females in Quebec expressed greater support for the Liberals than have males? As reported in table 6.5, Francophone women in 1965 were approximately 8% more likely to identify with the Liberals than were Francophone men, and were about 6% less likely to

TABLE 6.6
Party identification of Francophone Quebeckers by birth cohorts, 1965

	1931-45		1916-30		1901-15		Before 1900	
	Women	Men	Women	Men	Women	Men	Women	Men
Liberal	58.8	48.1	61.1	50.6	80.4	57.1	63.0	65.8
Conservative	9.8	20.8	13.9	14.5	12.5	21.4	14.8	23.7
New Democratic	17.6	15.6	12.5	13.3	3.6	3.6	–	–
Créditiste	10.8	9.0	12.5	16.9	3.5	17.9	18.5	7.9
Union nationale	3.0	6.5	–	4.7	–	–	3.7	2.6
Total N	(102)	(77)	(72)	(83)	(56)	(56)	(27)	(38)

Source: 1965 Canadian Election Study

support the relatively weak Conservative party.[32] By way of comparison, Anglophone women and men in Quebec held relatively similar levels of Liberal and Conservative partisanship in 1965, although Anglophone females were approximately 6% more likely to identify with the New Democrats than Anglophone males. Party identification data from 1979, not presented in tabular form, also indicate that at the federal level, 3.1% more females than males were Liberal identifiers (71.7% versus 68.6%), while on the provincial level, 10.7% more of the former were Liberals (51.5% versus 40.8%).[33]

The relationship between women's history and subsequent patterns of public opinion in Quebec is reflected more directly in cohort breakdowns in table 6.6. According to these data, support for the Liberals was indeed highest (80.4%) among women who came of age politically during the 1920s through late 1930s, when suffragist activism was at or near its peak. Females born between 1901 and 1915 tended to be more Liberal than any male cohort in the 1965 sample (the most Liberal being men born before 1900, who were 65.8% Liberal). Figures in table 6.6 thus indicate that the absolute level of Liberal identification among women in the enfranchisement cohort was exceptionally high, or 17.4% above the next most Liberal female cohort and 14.6% above the most Liberal male cohort. A similar pattern obtains in 1979 survey data, not presented in tabular form.

Following through with a generational thesis, we would propose that other groups of Francophone women, who may have lacked such compelling reasons to support the Liberals, would reflect lower but fairly consistent levels of support for that party. Data in table 6.6 tend to support this proposition, since they show that cohorts outside the enfranchisement group were composed of approximately 60% Liberal identifiers. In other words, patterns of female identification with the Quebec Liberals suggest that an older feminist alliance may have influenced political partisanship, especially among voters who came of age politically during the peak of suffragist activism.

Combined with U.S. data on social reform attitudes presented above, English-Canadian data on partisanship analysed in chapter 2, and French and Canadian patterns of female politicization discussed in the previous section, these Quebec results point toward a number of empirical and theoretical conclusions, each of which may prove useful in future Canadian and comparative political research. First, survey data presented here suggest that the historical experiences of women, and especially their treatment by political organizations and institutions, may provide an important determinant of female attitudes. Our analyses in chapter 2 showed relatively high levels of New Democratic and Liberal support among female enfranchisement cohorts in Western Canada – where suffragism was closely allied with Liberal as well as agrarian and labour organizations (which predated the CCF / NDP in that region). Similarly, related research on France indicates that, in 1958, leftist partisanship was relatively strong among women who resided in regions where Communist and Socialist women's affiliates were active.[34] While this type of empirical evidence remains fragmentary and heuristic, it does offer a very promising basis for future research on the relationship between women's political history and especially the treatment of women by established party institutions, on the one hand, and female public opinion, on the other.

Second, and parallel with this last point, our analysis sheds critical light on older explanations of women's political attitudes. Although relatively little systematic research is available in this area, most conventional studies tend to claim that North American and Western European women have generally been more 'conservative,' 'traditional,' and 'moralistic' than men, owing to the isolated and apolitical existence of females in the private household. Lacking direct ties with the main lines of modern social communication, it is argued that women are more likely than men to be attached to status-quo traditions and institutions.[35]

Our historical approach challenges many tenets of this established view. For example, by proposing that women are indeed affected by and involved in processes of institutional and social change in Western cultures, we reject the conventional argument which attributes female attitudes to a timeless condition of isolation in the domestic household. Similarly, in examining the specific partisan direction of women's views, we take issue with the oftentimes vague, misleading, and disparaging terminology of the older literature. That is, despite the frequent description of female opinion as 'conservative' or 'moralistic,' our study shows that women's views have mainly been centrist or reformist in direction, rather than rightist or reactionary, and that these attitudes tend to reflect the impact of distinctive political and historical influences.

We shall now examine patterns of female party participation in comparative perspective.

PATTERNS OF PARTY INVOLVEMENT

In our discussion of English Canada in chapter 3, we argued that contemporary party participation is generally characterized by an absence of females in upper-echelon elite positions, particularly in organizations which hold or are in a position to challenge the reins of government. We presented empirical support for this view regarding 'the higher the fewer,' as well as for its corollary concerning competitive party environments, using data on local constituency executives, convention delegates, campaign managers, party office-holders, candidates for public office, legislators, and cabinet appointees.[36]

From a cross-cultural perspective, it is difficult to examine each of these individual activities, since delegation to party conventions, for example, may reflect a very different functional role in one system than in another. That is, although U.S. convention delegates are frequently responsible to particular state caucuses or groups of primary election voters and are delegated above all to select a national presidential nominee, British party delegates may be viewed as somewhat more independent policy discussants, whose extra-parliamentary impact on the choice of a national party leader is relatively limited.[37]

Alongside these functional differences, our comparative study of party participation is complicated by the absence of data gathered at a single point in time and by the lack of a unified set of research objectives in the literature.[38] By gathering figures from a variety of existing sources, most of which result from research within a single culture at a single point in time, we attempt in the following sections to provide a concise comparative summary of female party involvement. Functional differences in party roles across cultures and limitations within the existing research, however, suggest that a more extensive book-length treatment of this subject is required.

We shall begin our examination of party involvement by reviewing levels of party membership and local activity, and will then consider pat-

TABLE 6.7
Comparative levels of female party membership, 1979

Country	Party	% female membership
Australia	Labour	25
	Liberal	50
Britain	Labour	40
	Conservative	51
Finland	Social Democratic	35
	Centre	46
	Conservative	50
France	Communist (PCF)	33
	Socialist (PS)	22
	Gaullist (RPR)	41
Italy	Communist (PCI)	24.6
	Christian Democratic (DC)	37.6
Sweden	Communist	34
	Social Democratic	40
	Liberal	45
	Centre	43
	Conservative	50
West Germany	Social Democratic (SPD)	22.4
	Free Democratic (FDP)	23.0
	Christian Democratic (CDU)	20.8

Sources: Marion Simms, 'Australia,' in Joni Lovenduski and Jill Hills, eds., *The Politics of the Second Electorate* (London: Routledge and Kegan Paul, 1981), 83-111; Jill Hills, 'Britain,' in Lovenduski and Hills, 8-32; Elina Haavio-Mannila, 'Finland,' in Lovenduski and Hills, 228-51; Janine Mossuz-Lavau and Mariette Sineau, 'France,' in Lovenduski and Hills, 112-33; Maria Weber, 'Italy,' in Lovenduski and Hills, 182-207; Maud Eduards, 'Sweden,' in Lovenduski and Hills, 208-27; and Jane Hall, 'West Germany,' in Lovenduski and Hills, 153-81

terns of convention delegation, office-holding, political candidacy, and legislative participation.

PARTY MEMBERSHIP AND LOCAL CONSTITUENCY ACTIVITY

Although data on national party membership in Canada are not at present available, fairly extensive comparative results are presented in a series of articles in Lovenduski and Hills (1981).[39] As summarized in table 6.7, female party membership in Australia and five Western European political systems tends to be highest – and, in some cases, approaches parity –

within parties of the centre-right and right, and lowest in parties of the left. One possible explanation for this pattern follows from the traditional mobilization of women by conservative, church-affiliated organizations, especially in Catholic cultures, and from the parallel development of leftist parties in a more masculine, trade union milieu.[40] Notably, in one European system documented in table 6.7, that of West Germany, there appear to be no significant differences in party membership between the rightist CDU (20.8%) and leftist SPD (22.4%).

Overall, data presented in table 6.7 show that the numerical representation of women at the baseline level of party membership is highest in such parties as the Australian Liberal (50%), British Conservative (51%), Finnish Conservative (50%), French Gaullist (RPR, 41%), Italian Christian Democratic (37.6%), and Swedish Conservative (50%). At the same time, these figures indicate that women's membership is generally lower in such parties of the left as the Australian Labour (25%), British Labour (40%), Finnish Social Democratic (35%), French Socialist (22%), Italian Communist (24.6%), and Swedish Communist (34%).

Do patterns of local party activity, however, reflect similar left-right differences? This question is somewhat difficult to address, given that the bulk of research on constituency-level involvement has been conducted in the United States, where ideological variation within the party system is relatively limited. In fact, one set of contemporary American studies suggests that party identification itself is irrelevant in determining patterns of local activity, since in both the Democratic and Republican organizations, women are expected to contribute significant political efforts for very limited political rewards.[41]

The extent to which females are active in local American party work is reflected in articles by Margolis (1981), Porter and Matasar (1974), Boneparth (1977), and Maisel (1975).[42] Although the geographical focus of these studies varies widely, from rural Maine (Maisel) and Connecticut (Margolis) to the city of Chicago (Porter and Matasar), their major empirical conclusions are strikingly similar. First, as Margolis shows in her study of Democratic and Republican town committee interactions, female party activity at the local level is generally less visible, more routine, and more maintenance- (as opposed to decision-) oriented than that of males. Even though time logs submitted by party respondents indicated that women were 'far more active than the men,' a check of local office-holders indicated that males outnumbered females in titled party positions – which enabled the former to obtain visibility and final decision-making authority at the town committee level.[43]

TABLE 6.8
Female office-holding in local Democratic Party committees, State of Maine

Position	% women, 1968	% women, 1972
Chairperson	12.7	19.5
Secretary	76.9	79.4
(N)	(283)	(354)

Source: Louis Maisel, 'Party Reform and Political Participation,' in Louis Maisel and Paul M. Sacks, eds., *The Future of Political Parties* (Beverly Hills: Sage, 1975), table 9

Second, as research on local campaign activity in the United States demonstrates, women have conventionally specialized in such volunteer activities as stuffing and addressing envelopes, licking stamps, telephoning, chauffeuring voters and candidates, canvassing door to door, and hosting coffee parties.[44] Therefore, just as local activity between elections among women appears to be routine and maintenance-oriented, so too do their campaign contributions. Boneparth's (1977) research on Santa Clara County, California, however, suggests that this pattern may be changing as growing numbers of female partisans contest public office, and in turn elevate the status of women in their campaign organizations, and as younger women more generally reject gender-stereotyped roles in the parties.[45]

Third, as reflected in Maisel's data from Maine in table 6.8, municipal party committees in the United States have included disproportionately few female chairs (19.5% in 1972), at the same time as they have relied heavily upon women to serve as local secretaries (79.4% in 1972). This finding parallels closely the 'pink-collar' phenomenon identified above in our discussion of local constituency organizations in English Canada, where women tended to be clustered disproportionately in the position of riding secretary and far less widely represented in the more prestigious and decision-making roles of constituency president, vice-president, and treasurer.

Fourth, Maisel's (1975) study of Democratic activism in Maine also makes reference to the importance of competitive party position as an influence upon local female involvement. During the early 1970s, when women as a group began to elevate their profile in American politics, local Democrats in Maine were less able to accomplish this objective in competitive, as opposed to uncompetitive, party areas. According to Maisel,

Many more women participated in more highly Republican areas, as identified by respondents to the questionnaire. This suggests that the Democratic organizations in these areas were dormant, and women saw an opportunity to participate in a meaningful way. In fact, the Democratic organization in one highly Republican city – and those in many of its towns – was completely taken over by a group of new Democrats who then chose a woman to head the city committee. The corollary of this finding, of course, is that it is harder for new women to participate where strong organizations already exist. That is, party leaders in office, where that office has some potential influence, appear to be less anxious to encourage new participants to try to enter the system.[46]

As is true of women in English Canada, therefore, American women who reside in uncompetitive party areas may find access to local party office – and to public nomination as well – to be far easier than in competitive party areas. Females who obtain elite party positions and campaign roles at the local level may thus remain figureheads in both countries, since their effective control over financial resources and political strategy is dependent upon the competitive character of the constituency in question.

We shall now examine the question of convention delegation in comparative perspective.

PATTERNS OF PARTY DELEGATION

As summarized in chapter 3, Canadian party conventions in the contemporary period have included a somewhat lower percentage of female delegates than their American counterparts. Much of this U.S.-Canadian difference is attributable to the entrenchment of formal quotas regarding female delegation within the Democratic and, to a lesser extent, Republican parties following 1972, as discussed in chapter 4, and to the absence of similar affirmative action guarantees in major Canadian parties during this same period.[47]

What are the more general characteristics of female convention delegation in areas outside of English Canada? One of the only sources of information on this subject is the American literature on state and national convention participation, which suggests that, as in Canada, women delegates have performed primarily clerical and ceremonial functions at party conventions. In addition to assuming roles as credential and registration clerks, American women have escorted speakers to the platform, seconded nominations, and called the roll of the states at presidential conventions.[48]

The method by which women traditionally obtained delegate or, more frequently, alternate status was related to broader assumptions about these activities. As Maisel (1975) quotes from his interview with one urban Democrat in Maine, 'Because of the reforms the entire delegate selection process was more wide-open. In the past this was done solely by the city committee. We would get together and make a list of us and our friends and would choose whoever wanted to be delegates. Usually most of the women were wives. Like a husband would be the delegate and his wife the alternate. It made a nice weekend trip to wherever the convention was held.'[49] Women were thus assumed to be secondary, apolitical companion delegates (or alternates) to American party conventions, while men were perceived to be the primary political actors in a convention context.

More recent studies of American convention delegation suggest that as the confidence, ambition, and feminist consciousness of female partisans increase, there is growing dissatisfaction with traditional role assignments. Longitudinal research by Jennings and Farah (1981) on Michigan national party delegates offers clear evidence to this effect.[50] As the authors conclude,

While the political ambitions of women still lag behind those of men, the advances made by women in social background and political resources between 1964 and 1976 were nonetheless striking. Many of these changes reflected the broader transformation taking place in women's lives during this time period. Pressures from the women's movement, coupled with internal reforms in both political parties, have helped to reduce the disparities between the sexes among party elites. If the ambitions of women continue to climb, it seems likely that these disparities will diminish much more quickly.[51]

Therefore, according to Jennings and Farah, Kirkpatrick (1976), and other analysts, women's increasing numerical representation at American party conventions may help to generate a deepened interest in and commitment to political careers,[52] which in turn could elevate levels of female participation in upper-echelon party elites – including national party office and elective public office.

PARTY OFFICE-HOLDING

Comparative examination of party office-holding by women is complicated by a number of factors, including differences both within and across party systems in the titles and responsibilities attached to an elite position. For example, party secretaries in an American state organization might be responsible for compiling minutes on occasional executive meetings, while in a European socialist or communist grouping, secretaries would wield day-to-day control over a large and complex party bureaucracy.

Furthermore, the appointment or election of token female representatives to party office, frequently as a result of internal arrangements with older women's associations, suggests that it is important to distinguish between substantive and ceremonial office-holding by party women. As Eleanor Roosevelt observed in 1954, the practice of appointing 50% women to American national party committees 'looks better on paper than it has worked out in practice. Too often the vice-chairmen and the committee women are selected by the men, who naturally pick women who will go along with them and not give them any trouble. Thus they are apt to be mere stooges.'[53] More recent research on party office-holding in metropolitan Chicago, Minneapolis, and Seattle offers strong empirical support for Roosevelt's assertion. According to Porter and Matasar (1974) and Clarke and Kornberg (1979), efforts to include a respectable number of females in urban party elites have generally led to the recruitment of token women with limited political ambition, very minimal feminist consciousness, and exceptional commitment to the male party selectorate which recruited them.[54]

One useful way of approaching the question of party office-holding is to use our initial hypothesis regarding the 'law of increasing disproportion' as a basis from which to compare levels of female party membership and office-holding. If we evaluate party office data in table 6.9 in light of membership figures in table 6.7, it would appear that in virtually all six countries considered, women are far less likely to hold office than membership. For example, if we compare female membership in the British Conservative and Italian Christian Democratic parties with office-holding in these same organizations, we find fairly extreme percentage differences, ranging from 51% membership to only 15% policy committee representation in the British case ($\Delta = 36\%$), and 38% membership to only 2% National Council representation in the Italian case ($\Delta = 36\%$).

Among parties of the left, these differences are less extreme, in part because female membership is generally lower in leftist than in rightist parties. Comparing membership and office-holding in the British Labour party, for example, we find a difference of approximately 13% (40% membership minus 27% representation in the Executive Committee), while among the French Socialists, a difference of only 8% obtains (22% membership minus 14% representation on the Executive Bureau).

Within single party organizations, our hypothesis regarding 'the higher

TABLE 6.9

Comparative levels of party office-holding by women

Country	Party	Office	Year	% women
Australia	Labour	National Conference	1979	4.6
		State Conference	1979	11.0
		National Executive	1979	14.3
		State Executive	1979	6.1
	Liberal	NSW State Council	1976	19.0
	Country National	Central Council	1980	41.9
		General Conference	1977	39.5
Britain	Labour	Annual Conference	1971	10.6
		Executive Committee	1972	26.9
	Conservative	Annual Conference	1977	38.0
		Executive Committee	1977	20.0
		General Purpose Cttee	1971	15.0
		Policy Committee	1971	14.8
Finland	Social Democrats	Party Conference	1979	19.0
		Party Council	1979	14.0
	Centre	Party Conference	1979	23.0
		Party Council	1979	25.0
	National Coalition	Party Conference	1979	32.0
		Party Council	1979	16.0
France	Communist (PCF)	Federal Committee	1977	23.3
		Political Bureau	1977	17.3
		Federal Secretariat	1977	11.4
	Socialist (PS)	Executive Bureau	1979	13.7
	Radical (PR)	Political Bureau	1979	23.1
	Gaullist (RPR)	Political Council	1979	13.3
		Central Committee	1979	8.0
Italy	Communist (PCI)	Federal Committees	1976	13.1
	Christian Democratic (DC)	National Council	1976	2.0
Sweden	Communist	National Executive	1979	26.0
	Social Democratic	National Executive	1979	31.0
	Centre	National Executive	1979	24.0
	Conservative	National Executive	1979	37.0

Sources: Jill Hills, 'Britain,' in Joni Lovenduski and Jill Hills, eds., *The Politics of the Second Electorate* (London: Routledge and Kegan Paul, 1981), 8-32; Marion Simms, 'Australia,' in Lovenduski and Hills, 83-111; Janine Mossuz-Lavau and Mariette Sineau, 'France,' in Lovenduski and Hills, 112-33; Maria Weber, 'Italy,' in Lovenduski and Hills, 182-207; Maud Eduards, 'Sweden,' in Lovenduski and Hills, 208-27; Elina Haavio-Mannila, 'Finland,' in Lovenduski and Hills, 228-51; Margaret Stacey and Marion Price, *Women, Power and Politics* (London: Tavistock, 1981), 146; Yann Viens, 'Femmes, Politique, Parti communiste français,' in *La condition féminine* (Paris: Editions sociales, 1978), 357; and Monica Charlot, 'Women in Politics in France,' in Howard R. Penniman, ed., *The French National Assembly Elections of 1978* (Washington, DC: American Enterprise Institute, 1980), 180

the fewer' may also be applied. That is, if we hypothesize that women tend to become increasingly underrepresented as one moves toward positions of higher, and presumably more competitive and powerful party office, then intra-party data from the British Conservative and French Communist (PCF) parties (see table 6.9) are consistent with this approach. At the level of delegation to the Conservative Annual Conference, where special provisions ensure at least one female from each local constituency, women are fairly well represented (38%), but this figure drops sharply in the national Executive Committee of some 200 members (20%), and in the smaller, very influential General Purpose (15%) and Policy committees (14.8%).[55] A similar pattern obtains at the elite level in the PCF, where there is a more than 50% decline in female representation between the relatively large Federal Committee (23%) and the smaller, more powerful Federal Secretariat (11%).[56]

In terms of overall conclusions, our comparative discussion of party office-holding points toward two main findings. First, the thesis that women would be weakly represented at higher levels of party activity was confirmed by comparison of membership and office-holding data, which showed that particularly in European conservative parties, females were far less numerous as party officers than members. Second, intra-party comparisons using British and French materials indicated that very few women held competitive, upper-echelon party offices, such that females were found to be increasingly underrepresented in numerical terms as one moved toward higher and more powerful levels of party office in a single organization.

Both of these conclusions shed valuable light on the question of candidacy for public office, to which we now turn our attention.

LEGISLATIVE RECRUITMENT AND PARTICIPATION

Of all the subfields of women and politics, the area of female legislative participation has probably attracted the greatest amount of empirical interest. Beginning with early monographs by Comstock (1926), Duverger (1955), and Werner (1966, 1968),[57] the literature on public candidacy, election, and legislative tenure has grown to include a sizable number of book-length studies, and an even larger volume of articles, conference papers, and research notes.[58] Since it is impossible in the present section to review each contribution to the comparative literature on legislative recruitment and participation, we have chosen instead to focus upon major theses in this research area. More specifically, our attention is directed toward two key questions which inform much of the legislative literature: First, in simple numerical terms, how many women contest and obtain legislative office? Second, on an explanatory plane, what factors help to account for patterns of female legislative recruitment and election? Examination of these two points, in turn, provides an introduction to contemporary responses to female underrepresentation at elite levels, considered in the following section.

The numbers of women who contest and obtain legislative office in most Western democracies have historically been quite limited. As Kathleen Newland remarks in her cross-cultural study of this phenomenon, 'Most women who participate in party activities are cannon-fodder; they knock on doors, answer telephones, hand out leaflets, and get out the vote – usually in the service of a male candidate.'[59] The extent to which females have been underrepresented as both candidates and legislators, and specifically the failure of many women nominees to win election in Western political systems, is thus related to their more general status within party organizations.

In order to evaluate comparative patterns of national candidature and legislative election, we have assembled longitudinal data from eight countries in table 6.10. Taken as a group, these figures indicate that women have tended to increase their numerical representation both as candidates and legislators over time, such that they comprised as much as 28% of the Swedish national legislature (Riksdag) in 1980. In the Nordic countries overall, females would appear to have comprised approximately one-quarter of national legislators during the late 1970s, while in other Western European countries and the United States, they remained a far less sizable group of between 3.0% (British House of Commons, 1980) and 8.2% (Italian Chamber of Deputies, 1979). Therefore, even though women's involvement as both candidates and legislators has generally increased over time in European and North American political systems, their percentage within national legislatures has – with the exception of the Nordic countries – remained less than 10% through the 1980s.

What factors help to account for this fairly limited legislative representation, particularly in areas outside the Nordic region? Two major sets of explanations have been proposed in the literature on female candidacy and recruitment; one is grounded in structural or systemic evaluations of this problem, while the second emphasizes social psychological factors. On the level of political structures, writers have frequently observed that women's legislative participation is considerably higher in countries with proportional representation electoral systems than in those with single-

TABLE 6.10
Comparative patterns of female candidacy and legislative office-holding, national level

Country	Year	% candidates	Year	% legislators
Britain	1918	1.2	1929	2.3
	1929	3.9	1975	4.4
	1979	8.2	1980	3.0
Denmark	1979	21.8	1945	5.4
			1970	11.8
			1979	23.0
Finland	1948	12.1	1907	9.5
	1970	17.3	1948	12.0
	1979	26.0	1970	21.5
			1979	26.0
France	1968	3.3	1945[a]	5.5
	1973	6.7	1981[a]	5.9
	1978	15.9	1981[b]	2.3
Italy	n/a		1948	7.8
			1968	2.8
			1979	8.2
Norway	1945	13.2	1969	9.3
	1957	18.0	1975	16.1
	1969	19.7	1979	23.9
Sweden	n/a		1971	14.0
			1977	22.9
			1980	27.8
United States	1979[c]	5.3	1975[d]	4.4
			1979[d]	3.7
			1983[d]	5.0

a Represents National Assembly members only.
b Represents Senate members only.
c Represents major party candidates only for House of Representatives.
d Represents House of Representatives members only. Notably, state legislatures in the United States included 4.0% women members in 1969, 9.0% in 1978, and 13.3% in 1983. U.S. Senate representation in 1983 was 2.0%.

Sources: Jill Hills, 'Britain,' in Joni Lovenduski and Jill Hills, eds., *The Politics of the Second Electorate* (London: Routledge and Kegan Paul, 1981), 8-32; Janine Mossuz-Lavau and Mariette Sineau, 'France,' in Lovenduski and Hills, 112-33; Maria Weber, 'Italy,' in Lovenduski and Hills, 182-207; Maud Eduards, 'Sweden,' in Lovenduski and Hills, 208-27; Elina Haavio-Mannila, 'Finland,' in Lovenduski and Hills, 228-51; Walter S.G. Kohn, *Women in National Legislatures* (New York: Praeger, 1980); Ingunn Norderval Means, 'Political Recruitment of Women in Norway,' *Western Political Quarterly* 25:3 (1972), 491-521; Margaret Stacey and Marion Price, *Women, Power, and Politics* (London: Tavistock, 1981), Appendix; Monica Charlot, 'Women in Politics in France,' in Howard R. Penniman, ed., *The French National Assembly Elections of 1978* (Washington: American Enterprise Institute, 1980); Gisbert H. Flanz, *Comparative Women's Rights and Political Participation in Europe* (Dobbs Ferry, NY: Transnational, 1983); Center for the American Woman and Politics, *Women in Public Office* (Metuchen, NJ: Scarecrow Press, 1978); Bella Abzug, with Mim Kelber, *Gender Gap* (Boston: Houghton Mifflin, 1984)

member plurality arrangements. Figures on representation in the Swedish Riksdag (see table 6.10), which has been a unicameral legislature elected through proportional representation since 1970, provide useful support for this view, as does the tendency for female Bundestag members in West Germany to be elected through Land lists rather than through single-member constituency seats.[60]

Structural analysts have also looked beyond the simple issue of electoral arrangements, in order to question the political viability of female candidacies within single-member plurality systems. In the United States, Great Britain, and France, a series of studies report that women candidates are disproportionately clustered on the electoral slates of weak parties and in the marginal constituencies of strong ones. In reference to the former, writers caution that the recent growth in female candidature in Great Britain and France is related to the increased number of minor parties in both systems, which in turn have afforded women access to many uncompetitive, essentially protest nominations. Whether one considers the British Liberal, Scottish National, French Ecologist, or French Feminist (Choisir) cases, it becomes clear that 'the increase in the *number* of women candidates in recent years reflects a more general increase in the number of candidates fielded by minor parties.'[61] Moreover, as Stacey and Price (1981) point out, any improvement in the electoral viability of minor parties produces increased competition for nominations, such that women are frequently eased out of candidates' lists once the minor party ceases to be 'simply a quixotic venture.'[62]

As nominees in the weaker seats of major parties, women confront similarly depressing prospects. Many are referred to as 'sacrifice candidates,' since their role as loyal party standard-bearers takes precedence over any reasonable hope of electoral victory. In an American context, studies by Deber (1982), Tolchin and Tolchin (1974), Van Hightower (1976), and others argue that one of the major characteristics of female legislative candidates has been their nomination in 'throwaway districts,' where prospects for electoral success are extremely limited.[63] Western European research by Stacey and Price (1981), Stobaugh (1978), Vallance (1979), Currell (1974), Charlot (1980), and Means (1972) confirms this finding, showing that women in proportional representation systems are infrequently placed at the top of their party lists, while those in single-member plurality systems rarely secure nomination in viable seats.[64] According to Currell (1974), therefore, one major distinction between female legislators and unsuccessful women candidates is simply the safeness of their local constituencies.[65]

Parallel with these findings concerning minor party and marginal seat nominations, researchers report that uncompetitive political environments are characterized by comparatively high levels of female participation. That is, American states which have small populations, large legislatures, and, as a result, fairly limited competition for legislative seats, include relatively high numbers of women in elective office.[66] Similarly, British, Australian, and American constituencies which were previously held by men have on occasion been contested and won by the widows of these deceased incumbents, so that temporary conditions of diminished political competition in such seats have permitted a pattern of 'widows' succession' to develop.[67]

In contrast with these structural or systemic explanations of female candidacy, researchers have also identified important social psychological influences upon legislative recruitment and office-holding. In its simplest terms, the social psychological view maintains that a major source of political underrepresentation rests in the roles, attitudes, and perceptions of women themselves. More specifically, conventional patterns of gender role socialization teach females to be submissive, deferential, private beings and also define elite-level political participation as masculine and thus inappropriate for women. As a group, therefore, women are not encouraged to develop the self-esteem, confidence, and other personal resources (including advanced education and professional careers) which are necessary for upward mobility in party organizations.[68]

The influence of role and attitudinal constraints has been demonstrated in a number of comparative empirical studies of women and politics. Beginning with a pioneering study of American state legislators by Jeane Kirkpatrick (1974), this literature has evidenced the continued impact of traditional role norms (particularly a problem of role incompatibility for younger women with children),[69] personal resource poverty (including lower income and education than male partisans),[70] and relatively low levels of political ambition upon female partisans.[71] The tendency for women activists to be motivated by expressive, as opposed to instrumental, factors has been a common concern of social psychological studies, many of which maintain that the human service orientation of females toward political work provides a major reason for their limited mobility within party organizations.[72]

One additional focus of social psychological research has been the argument that few women obtain elective public office because of biases or discriminatory attitudes which are held by voters at large. The question of public receptivity to female elites has thus become a prominent concern of public opinion analysts, who generally conclude that Western European and North American voters do *not* discriminate against women candidates. That is, despite widely held assumptions within party elites that female candidates lose elections because of popular resistance to their gender, relevant empirical research which is based upon election simulations, mass surveys, and longitudinal analysis of actual election returns offers little evidence in support of this view.[73]

We shall now consider party women's organizations in comparative perspective.

PARTY WOMEN'S ORGANIZATIONS

In comparative terms, the establishment of traditional party women's associations, and their evolution toward increasingly assertive feminist organizations within the parties, have generally paralleled the English-Canadian developments which were discussed in chapter 5. First, the service-oriented rationale behind the formation of separate organizations is reflected in American as well as Western European studies, which illustrate how older auxiliaries had the ultimate effect of isolating the bulk of their constituents from channels of mainstream party influence. Ingunn Means (1972) provides a succinct review of this problem in her article 'Political Recruitment of Women in Norway'; according to Means, auxiliaries were established initially as 'an aid to greater political influence for women. Women's alleged lack of political sophistication, it has been argued, necessitated separate clubs where they could acquire political training, and where they would not be inhibited by the presence of "superior" males, but could feel free to speak and develop their political talents. Further, through united efforts in their own clubs, women would be able to exert pressure for increased representation.'[74] This notion of remedial or catch-up organizations for political women was thus entrenched in many Western party systems during the turn-of-the-century period; for example, the Conservative Women's Council was formed in Britain in 1885, while a Women's Organization of the (British) Labour party (the Women's Labour League) was founded in 1906.[75]

As Means (1972) and others demonstrate, however, the philosophical intentions and actual impact of these early groups differed widely. That is, the initial goal of providing a springboard or training ground through which newly enfranchised female partisans could enter mainstream politics was soon replaced by a far different purpose, namely the provision of volunteer social, fund-raising, and clerical services by women for the mainstream party. Means (1972) summarizes a series of interviews with

Norwegian legislators as follows: 'They tended to see the women's clubs as more humanitarian and social organizations than political ones, and providing not political schooling, but the comfortable, cozy, and undemanding atmosphere of the coffee-klatch; a poor preparation for the rough-and-tumble of political life.'[76]

This general conclusion is echoed in much of the comparative literature on older party women's groups. Whether one considers the Democratic Women's Clubs chartered by American state committees, or the National Federation of Republican Women (established in 1938), Sorauf's (1976) view that these organizations have played a 'docile, subordinate role' throughout most of their history would seem to be confirmed.[77] Moreover, Sapiro's (1981) evaluation of these same party women's sections in the United States suggests that while they perform important symbolic functions by offering women the image of political influence and mobility, they frequently segregate females and thus 'are designed very much for appeasement or cooptive purposes.'[78]

A similar set of perspectives flows from research on Italian party participation by David Kertzer (1980, 1982).[79] As in the Culley (1981) study of British Labour party women's sections, Kertzer suggests that while a modicum of political education work may have been provided by the Communist (PCI)-affiliated Unione Donne Italiane (UDI), a far more frequent focus of the latter at the local level was the organization of dinners for the elderly, children's puppet shows, and the like.[80] Kertzer thus concludes that the UDI reinforced rather than challenged conventional gender role norms in the PCI, such that 'the primary sphere of women's activities in party affairs, indeed, comprises none other than the traditional women's chores: preparing food for the annual party *feste* and preparing snacks and meals for party pollwatchers on election day.'[81] Notably, Kertzer's findings are supported by at least one other contemporary study of Italian party involvement, which argues that 'the UDI plays only a subordinate role in PCI strategy and has only limited mobilization capacity.'[82]

Second, comparative studies of party women's organizations indicate that as in English Canada, newer feminist movements have challenged older associations on the level of style, purpose, and basic raison d'être. This challenge has been especially clear within European parties of the left, where contemporary women's movements had a relatively early and direct impact upon both women and men. Lorraine Culley (1981), for example, describes this influence in terms of

an increasing militancy of women in the [British] Labour Movement which has arisen in the context of the disillusionment of many women with the effects of the

'Equality Legislation' and the performance of recent Labour governments, the explicit attacks on women by the present Tory government and the general debate concerning democratization of the Party. This militancy has been expressed in the formation of two new groups in recent months ... [which] are concerned with campaigning for changes in the Party in order to increase the representation of women.[83]

Recent studies of a parallel radicalization among women in the French Communist party (PCF) by Jane Jenson (1980), and in the German Social Democratic party (SPD) by Gerard Braunthal (1983) also point toward a cross-cultural trend whereby leftist and feminist commitments are fused within an activist core of party women, who then seek (often unsuccessfully) to ensure increased numerical and policy representation in the larger political organization.[84]

Contemporary feminism has held important implications for women's organizations in contexts other than European socialist and communist parties, however. As our Canadian discussion illustrated, criticisms of increasingly weak, outdated, and politically segregated auxiliaries have been voiced in liberal as well as conservative settings, such that non-socialist women's groups have also changed during the past decade. Perhaps the clearest reflection of these shifts may be found in the American party system, where as Sorauf (1976) comments, older party women's associations risk extinction in the face of a demand for power and political integration by younger females. In Sorauf's words, the latter 'more activist women want a role in the regular party organizations, or else they prefer to become active in non-party organizations (such as the National Women's Political Caucus). Certainly they do not have in mind the docile, subordinate role that the auxiliaries traditionally had.'[85] As in English Canada, the consequent searching for 'a new and proper role' among American female partisans has led to a modernization of existing national women's divisions, which increasingly work toward improved leadership training programs and candidate recruitment among Republican and especially Democratic women; and to the development of newer, more assertive women's groups which will presumably hasten female integration within mainstream party organizations.[86]

The question of continuing women's organizations in any guise has also been a subject of considerable controversy in the United States and Western Europe. As Sapiro (1981) points out, it is important to examine 'formalization of the women's interest in terms of strategies of segregation and integration. Special offices within parties or governments have important symbolic meaning and they are generally, although not always, staffed by activists and specialists in women's problems. At the same time, however, segregation can "ghettoize" the problems; it can segregate the issues both from other related problems and from experts and leaders in other fields.'[87]

Few contemporary political organizations have been exempt from these debates over amalgamation or integration as opposed to separate status, including such groupings as the West German Social Democratic party (SPD), which did not have a history of separate associations. According to Braunthal (1983), feminists in the SPD pressured for the establishment of a constituent association (the Arbeitsgemeinschaft für Sozialdemokratische Frauen, or ASF) in 1971, and by 1977 had established a base of some 16,000 activists.[88] Despite this growth, though, the ASF has largely been unsuccessful in its attempts to increase elite-level representation in the SPD and, according to Braunthal, the group 'has felt isolated and without decisive influence within the party. Many of its most perceptive members became apathetic or quit the party altogether.'[89]

RESPONSES TO UNDERREPRESENTATION

In the absence of any clear answers to the organizational dilemma over integration versus separate status, party women in both North America and Western Europe have focused increasingly on the introduction of rule changes which would guarantee a specific level of numerical representation, as one straightforward route toward increased participation. Following the affirmative action guidelines which were introduced in the U.S. Democratic party in 1972, and which guarantee numerically equal representation of men and women at presidential nominating conventions,[90] feminists in a variety of Western European socialist parties sought to obtain similar commitments.

Few have pursued this strategy, however, as effectively as the American Democrats. As Culley (1981), Charlot (1981), and Hills (1981) point out in the case of the British Labour party (where the Women's Action Committee of the democratization movement has pressured for 50% representation in the party executive and parliamentary short lists), women's status remains congealed at the point of a 1918 constitutional guarantee.[91] The terms of this well-worn statute are as follows: A special women's section, composed of five members, is reserved on the Labour National Executive Committee. All five reserved positions are elected by delegates to the Annual Labour Party Conference – who are disproportionately made up of male trade unionists – rather than by delegates to the yearly National Conference of Labour Women.[92]

A numerically based response to underrepresentation has also been pursued by feminists in the French Socialist Party (PS). Under the leadership of writer and later cabinet minister Yvette Roudy, PS activists secured an important constitutional amendment in July 1977:[93] 'Article 6 was changed to institute a minimum female quota of ten per cent at all levels of the party from the Executive Committee to the grass roots, the quota to be revised at each party conference so as to take into account the proportion of women in the party. Article 46 also indicated that in all elections the ten per cent quota must be respected on every list.'[94] In this same vein, Weitz (1982) notes that prior to the European parliamentary elections of 1978, Yvette Roudy argued that 30% of all PS candidates should be women.[95]

Efforts to obtain guarantees of numerical representation have also been pursued in the West German SPD. Somewhat ironically, early ASF activists argued against quotas for women in 1971, only to find that once the relevant statutes were removed, 'only two women were elected to the national executive at the following party convention – rather than the five who had served until then.'[96] This experience led to attempts within the ASF to reintroduce a guarantee of numerical representation in both 1977 and 1979. However, proposals to establish guidelines for party office and legislative lists were twice

defeated by a majority who argued that quotas would endanger the emancipatory movement, that women must become a political factor within the party to effectuate change, and that it would be insulting to women if they gained party positions on the basis of a quota system rather than their qualifications ... a quota system violated the principle of intra-party democracy and was not in women's interest. It would put a psychological burden on women seeking public office, who if elected would be labelled as belonging to a 'percentage' category.[97]

The ASF debate within the SPD thus echoed older, primarily North American arguments over the merits of formal affirmative action guarantees. While this particular controversy remains as yet unresolved, its close resemblance to other discussions of underrepresentation is notable, particularly in light of an earlier 1971 SPD decision to abolish quotas in favour of outright 'integration.'

DIRECTIONS FOR FUTURE RESEARCH

This cross-cultural discussion of the impact of women's history upon their attitudinal and participatory development has tended to confirm at least three significant hypotheses, each of which may help to inform future comparative and Canadian research on women and politics. First, we have proposed that political history holds empirically and theoretically meaningful implications for female politicization and partisanship. Second, our analyses have offered support for the argument that despite recent increases in female participation, higher echelons of party activity, particularly within politically competitive organizations (i.e., which hold or are in a position to challenge the reins of government), still include relatively few women. Third, and parallel with this last point, we have confirmed in cross-cultural terms a variation on the 'higher the fewer' rule, noting that women have often performed traditional gender-stereotyped party functions, including clerical positions at the local level as well as service- and socially-oriented work within older party women's associations.

These three main findings suggest a number of possible directions for future research. On an attitudinal level, our discussion has pointed toward the need for additional study, especially in systems other than that of the United States, of the following: Does contemporary feminism hold direct implications for the development of partisan and social attitudes? If so, to what extent can these implications be related in empirical terms to ideological (including left-right), generational, and organizational (including feminist group membership) variables? If feminism is continuing to shape public opinion among voters at large, then might it not also distinguish among male and female, older and younger, or left and right partisans? Preliminary analysis of this question in an Ontario provincial context suggests that feminist attitudes are indeed related to both ideological and generational factors, such that both the internal (e.g., affirmative action) and external policy positions of political parties may be linked to patterns of elite-level opinion formation.[98] More extensive, and perhaps cross-cultural study of this attitude / policy linkage within parties is necessary in order to begin to document some of the political consequences of contemporary feminism.

Also on an attitudinal level, our discussion of general obstacles to female legislative participation cited a variety of social psychological explanations. Among the most popular of these has been the view that expressive rather than instrumental orientations characterize the bulk of female partisans, who hold different political motivations and more limited ambitions than their male counterparts. Except in the United States, little consideration has been given to possible changes in this expressive / instrumental phenomenon. For example, few analysts have questioned whether younger, feminist, and presumably more assertive women join parties to fulfil service and support functions – or, indeed, whether established assumptions regarding role incompatibility apply to newer participants. In light of Kirkpatrick's (1976) research on American national convention delegates, both of these older explanations would appear doubtful, yet they are rarely examined critically in recent Canadian or comparative studies.[99]

Structural explanations of lower participation suggest an additional set of research questions, many of which are related to the broader public policy directions of Western democracies. On a very basic level, the structural view requires more extensive comparative documentation of female party participation: How much 'tracking' of women into marginal seats, clerical functions, and social tasks occurs in Western European and North American parties? On the basis of more systematic data sources, could an index of discriminatory party practices be developed, which would include such measures as the proportion of female relative to male candidates sacrificed by party, age, and election? This type of exercise might better inform discussions of longitudinal change in the treatment of women by parties of the left, centre, and right.

More systematic data collection and analysis could also inform contemporary debates over affirmative action within party organizations. Are specific quotas necessary at all levels of activity and, once implemented, how effective are these guidelines in enhancing female political mobility? From the perspective of organizational development, what is the impact of formal affirmative action rules upon party life? As Fowlkes et al (1979) observe, 'Women may well be accommodated by being given a share of the more important positions, but will men begin to share in carrying out the very important expressive functions at the base of the party? As women adopt less traditional gender roles and become less responsible for performing their traditional party roles, and if men cannot be encouraged to do the same, the party organization, which is already weak because of other reasons, may become weaker.'[100] This challenge to organizational development which is presented by contemporary feminism deserves careful study by American, Canadian, and Western European researchers, who have generally ignored the political, and especially institutional, implications of a changing role for women in parties.

A final and very crucial set of research questions which follows from this study concerns the policy consequences of growing female political participation. On a substantive or public policy level, will increased numbers of women as party delegates, elected legislators, or backroom advisers make a difference? Can a linkage be established between numerical or descriptive representation, on the one hand, and policy or substantive representation, on the other?[101] This problem is widely overlooked in existing women and politics research, although studies by Leader (1977), Frankovic (1977), and Sinkkonen and Haavio-Mannila (1981) have begun to address the policy impact of elected female legislators.[102] Each concludes that in light of legislative roll-call data, party women are generally more supportive of feminist issue positions (including the American Equal Rights Amendment, equal employment legislation, and abortion) than their male colleagues. However, as Leader acknowledges, 'Voting is only one kind of political activity and possibly not the most important. It tells us nothing about who initiates the introduction of feminist legislation and who leads the floor fight and mobilizes support ... The essential leadership role played by women legislators is not revealed by voting data.'[103] Again, the need for additional research in new directions is confirmed by Leader's policy-oriented study, which argues that while the systemic consequences of increased female involvement are theoretically and practically important, they remain unexplored in the scholarly literature.

Considered as a group, the directions for future research which we have proposed suggest that the relationship between contemporary feminism, public policy, and party organizations is increasingly complex and in need of systematic study. On what bases have younger women endorsed different political ideas and institutions than older females, and to what extent might the latter expect feminist policy directions to follow from their support? What efforts have been made to mobilize women by political parties, and for what purposes? Canadian and comparative research must begin to give rigorous attention to these questions, in order to relate the attitudes and experiences of women with the many pressing policy, and especially representational, issues confronting contemporary Western political systems.

7

Epilogue:
Prospects for Political Representation in English Canada

This study has addressed the political history, attitudes, and participation of women in English Canada, including several responses to underrepresentation by party activists. Yet, it has thus far set aside the complex and very frustrating question 'where are women in general to go?' If party politics remains a difficult challenge facing women in English Canada, then what prospects for improved representation exist in the 1980s? How might women as a group obtain an increased and, one hopes, equitable share of policy influence?

Existing impediments to female political involvement are well documented and provide a useful starting point for this discussion. With respect to social psychological barriers, analysts generally agree that both women and men are constrained by conventional patterns of gender role socialization, which define the former according to passive, private, and apolitical norms, and the latter according to aggressive, public, and political ones. Socialization thus restricts female access to elite positions in two ways: first, by defining women in a collective sense as properly outside of politics; and second, by perpetuating a masculine 'ideal type' of political activist.

Like their counterparts elsewhere in North America and Western Europe, Canadian feminists have responded to gender role norms by arguing against the use of stereotypes in advertising, school texts, career counselling, and political recruitment. Although these arguments have met with some opposition, including from groups of 'new right' women, the basic act of identifying socialization as an obstacle to gender equality remains crucial to future political mobilization.[1] That is, as greater numbers of Canadian women acquire the confidence and organizational ability which are necessary in order to confront school boards, advertising councils, party selectorates, and other bodies, they build an invaluable groundwork for subsequent political activity – including within parties. In this manner, small-scale feminist lobbies would seem to offer an attractive alternative to conventional (and, in light of this study, not very promising) constituency routes toward elite-level political involvement.

Similarly optimistic conclusions may be drawn from ongoing changes in a less apparent but, from the perspective of role socialization, no less important environment – the family. Long defined as a private realm which was immune to both social change and political analysis, the family has become a popular focus of research and debate during recent years. Contemporary studies point toward three trends which could hold positive implications for Canadian women and politics.[2] First, females who enter into stable, long-term relationships can expect a somewhat more egalitarian sharing of household and child-rearing responsibilities with their spouses and are more likely to defer child-bearing and plan smaller families than previous generations. This general pattern suggests that younger married women take their careers (including political careers) more seriously and organize their family lives more carefully than did either their mothers or grandmothers.

Second, demographers note that women of the baby-boom era in particular are more likely to remain single or, if married, to become separated / divorced than earlier generations of North American females. This trend away from the nuclear family model of the post-war period, combined with a third set of data showing the relatively high educational attainment and earnings of younger women, indicate that decreasing numbers of females are encumbered by conventional family and household responsibilities – either because they contract (with spouses), buy (with earnings), or opt (with single lifestyle) out of traditional arrangements. Taken together, these developments bode especially well for the career mobility of younger middle-class Canadian women, who possess the education and employment opportunities necessary to circumvent established family roles.[3]

Aside from the political limits imposed on Canadian women by gender role socialization and family roles, there are major constraints which flow from structural or systemic, as opposed to psychological, sources. Perhaps the most obvious structural barrier facing contemporary women in politics is money. Candidates for constituency-level nomination, party office, and party leadership benefit little from campaign finance reform, which helped to democratize the fund-raising process in general elections more than a decade ago. Female candidates are particularly affected by this absence of meaningful spending limits for party nomination and leadership campaigns, since employed women on average are paid less than sixty cents for each dollar paid to a man, at the same time as household labour (the overwhelming bulk of which is done by women) is virtually non-remunerative.[4] Therefore, an average woman contesting local party nomination, for example, can be expected to have at least 40% less income to put toward her campaign than an average man, even though whoever wins nomination can expect to raise funds under reformed campaign expenses legislation.

Clearly, then, the financial plight of women generally is closely tied with the specific issue of access to party elites. Canadian women as a group thus require equal opportunity and remuneration in employment, including affordable child care, along with systematic reform of the internal party election process. Constituency nominations in winnable seats, as well as contests for party executive and leadership, have become increasingly expensive pursuits, which effectively discourage all but the most well-heeled competitors. And we would argue that women suffer disproportionately as a result of income differentials combined with the absence of serious party finance reform.

An additional, but no less significant, barrier to female party involvement in English Canada is the practice, conscious or unconscious, of tracking women away from influential political positions. Known in common parlance as 'discriminatory treatment,' this phenomenon served historically to perpetuate a 'pink-collar' service corps which was responsible for social, clerical, and fund-raising activities, and which had little if any role in campaign strategy or internal policy-making. One possible response to this feminization of 'donkey work,' as Judy LaMarsh referred to it, is for Canadian women to pressure for an equitable distribution of both routine trench labour – including 'pink-collar' assignments – as well as the more challenging tasks of party policy, strategy, and leadership.[5] Such assertiveness on the part of female partisans, combined with greater egalitarianism among their male colleagues, is probably essential in order for political organizations to successfully recruit younger women – few of whom are likely to find fulfilment in tea parties, bake sales, or clerical assignments.

This discussion of obstacles to party involvement is inseparable from a number of more general questions concerning the future of women in Canadian politics. First, in simple tactical terms, should contemporary feminists concern or involve themselves with the activities of mainstream party organizations? Could not non-partisan interest groups or municipal-level political work serve a more direct and useful purpose? Given the long tradition of political independence among women's rights activists in English Canada, this point poses far more than an academic dilemma, since it addresses the very heart of the 'where should women go' question.

Viewed from the perspective of Canadian politics, the argument for non-partisanship or independence seems flawed by its adoption of an American interest group approach to what is essentially a party-based parliamentary system. Unlike the U.S. case, where feminist and other lobby groups can expect regular access to more clearly delineated legislative and executive branches, and where legislative party discipline is relatively limited, the Canadian political process is characterized by highly disciplined legislatures, dominant executives, and fewer established points of access for interest groups. In other words, the non-partisan interest group route on its own is unlikely to achieve the policy changes sought by Canadian feminists, since existing parliamentary arrangements establish parties as a pivotal actor within the legislative process. Moreover, the municipal alternative to female party activity runs the risk of ghettoizing women in the lowest paid, and arguably least powerful, echelon of Canadian politics.

Second, it is important to consider the very significant issue of whether electing more women to party and legislative elites constitutes a politically worthwhile exercise. That is, do these elites indeed wield power? And would more women make a difference?

In response to the former question concerning effective power, high-ranking public servants in Canada would appear to exercise greater policy influence than most legislators, and probably some cabinet ministers.[6] This pattern suggests that electing more women to the pinnacle of legislative office, the House of Commons, may prove futile in policy terms unless attention is given at the same time to recruiting females to senior-level bureaucratic positions, particularly within central agencies of the federal government.[7]

Finally, in terms of the relationship between numbers of women in politics and substantive changes in public policy, we would propose that this conversion is by no means automatic. Accounts of political women who oppose equal pay legislation, maintain that gender constitutes no barrier to career mobility, and, in the oft-quoted case of Prime Minister Thatcher, question 'What's [the women's movement] ever done for me' point toward a crucial distinction between the biological fact of sex and the political phenomenon of feminist consciousness.[8]

Yet these popular examples hardly constitute proof that as a group, women in politics make no policy difference. In fact, the limited research which is available in this area suggests precisely the reverse – i.e., that politically active women in Western Europe and North America are generally more supportive of feminist issue positions than either women in the general population or men who are active in politics.[9] This simple finding, limited as it is, offers hopeful encouragement for the political future of women in English Canada.

APPENDIX A

Data Sources

Five major types of empirical materials were gathered in the preparation of this book. In order to inform readers with methodological interests, particularly those seeking to design related studies, each main data source is described briefly in this appendix.

TYPE 1: PARTY RECORDS

Since a major research question in the area of women and party politics concerns constituency-, provincial-, and federal-level participation, party records were consulted in order to document – longitudinally, whenever possible – the extent of female involvement (see chapter 3). In some cases, party women's organizations had collected relevant data on their own and shared these figures openly. In most parties, however, such tabulations were not available, and the author therefore requested access to internal files on riding association, provincial, and federal office-holding. These files provided a wealth of useful information on the dimensions of major party participation in English Canada.

TYPE 2: OFFICIAL ELECTION RETURNS

Scholars frequently overlook the very detailed data which are compiled in official federal and provincial election returns. For the student of women and politics, these returns provide information on numbers of female candidates, their career backgrounds, and electoral success rates. Both provincial and federal returns were consulted in the preparation of tables in chapter 3.

TYPE 3: PUBLIC OPINION SURVEYS

Existing survey data from Canada, France, and the United States were analysed for this study, particularly for chapters 2 and 6, in order to document patterns of female politicization and attitude formation. Although secondary analysis of sample surveys is frequently a frustrating process, it offers a relatively inexpensive and, in the case of longitudinal research, unique opportunity to probe political attitudes.[1]

The main surveys employed in this study are as follows:

(a) *1965 Canadian National Election Study* Directed by John Meisel, Philip Converse, Maurice Pinard, Peter Regenstreif, and Mildred Schwartz, this study was based on a stratified random sample of 2,113 respondents, weighted to a total of 2,719 cases.

(b) *1979 Social Change in Canada Study* Directed by Tom Atkinson, Bernard Blishen, Michael D. Ornstein, and H. Michael Stevenson, this survey employed a multistage probability selection sample, weighted to about 3,000 respondents.

(c) *1958 French Election Study* Directed by Georges Dupeux, with the assistance of François Goguel, Jean Stoetzel, and Jean Touchard, this study sampled 1,650 respondents, weighted to a total of 1,870 cases, during three survey waves: pre-referendum, post-referendum, and post-election. Approximately two-thirds of the sample was interviewed in each of the three waves.

(d) *Euro-barometre no. 10, October / November 1978* Directed by Jacques-René Rabier and Ronald Inglehart, this survey sampled 1,038 French respondents, weighted to a total of 1,194 cases.

(e) *1978 NORC General Social Survey* Conducted by the National Opinion Research Center, this study sampled approximately 1,400 American respondents in February, March, and April 1978.

The above survey data were made available by the York University Institute for Behavioural Research, in co-operation with the Inter-University Consortium for Political and Social Research. Neither the original investigators, the IBR, nor the ICPSR is responsible for the calculations or interpretations presented here.

TYPE 4: CONVENTION DELEGATE QUESTIONNAIRE

During February 1982, the Ontario Liberal and New Democratic parties held leadership conventions, while the Ontario Progressive Conservatives organized both a women's conference (OPCAW, held in June 1982) and general meeting (held in September 1982). These four provincial political gatherings, attendance at which was based upon internal party delegation, presented a valuable opportunity for cross-party research on elite-level activism.

The author designed and distributed identical self-administered questionnaires to male and female delegates to the OLP, NDP, and PC meetings, and to female delegates to the OPCAW meeting, after the questionnaire had been pre-tested at a large Toronto constituency association meeting in January 1982. Overall, approximately 500 questionnaires were returned to the author for use in the data base, including those from about 175 NDP, 130 OLP, and 95 PC delegates. These returns yielded a response rate of about 10% in the three mainstream cases, compared with a rate of approximately 50% at the OPCAW meeting ($N = 96$). This difference in response rates may be attributable in part to the size of, and more carnival-like atmospheres which prevailed at, the three mainstream party meetings. Delegates to all four meetings were reminded at regular intervals about the questionnaires; these reminders appear to have been most effective in the OPCAW case.

While the NDP, OLP, and PC response rates are low by social scientific standards, demographic breakdowns within each subgroup suggest that the samples provide a fairly representative cross-section from each party. For example, NDP and OLP records show that convention delegates were 60% and 40%, and 60.8% and 39.2% male and female, respectively, while questionnaire samples were 55.2% and 44.8%, and 66.4% and 33.6%, respectively. Also, as might be expected, the OLP sample was the most rural of any group in the survey.[2]

A standard questionnaire was presented to all four groups of Ontario convention delegates:

DIRECTIONS: Please circle one (1) number to indicate your response to each question. In cases where a straight line is provided, please write your response in the blank.

Q1. Is this the first time you have attended a ___(name)___ Party convention? (*Circle one only*)

Yes, first time	1
No, attended *one* in the past	2
No, attended *two or more* in the past	3

Q2. Are you presently a member of the *local* Executive of your   (party)   riding association, either on the federal or provincial level?

Yes	1
GO ON TO QUESTION 3	

      No   2

Q2a. IF NOT, are you interested in holding a position on your riding Executive at some point in the future?

              Yes   1
              No   2

Q3. Are you presently involved on the *provincial* level of the Ontario   (name)   Party; for example, as a member of the provincial Executive Committee or as a member of any other provincial committee?

Yes	1
GO ON TO QUESTION 4	

      No   2

Q3a. IF NOT, are you interested in serving on the provincial level at some point in the future?

              Yes   1
              No   2

Q4. Have you ever been nominated as a   (party)   candidate either for the federal House of Commons or for the Provincial Legislature?

Yes	1
GO ON TO QUESTION 5	

      No   2

Q4a. IF NOT, are you interested in pursuing nomination for public office at some
point in the future?

Yes	1
No	2

Q5. To what extent would you say that you have been encouraged to participate
in the political process by the following:

	To a great extent	To some extent	A little	Not at all	
a. Your parents & immediate family when you were growing up	1	2	3	4	
b. Your peer group in early adulthood, such as in university	1	2	3	4	
c. Your colleagues at work	1	2	3	4	
d. Your spouse (if not applicable, circle 9)	1	2	3	4	9
e. Local ___(party)___ activists in your area	1	2	3	4	
f. The provincial ___(party)___ organization	1	2	3	4	

Q6. At what age, approximately, did you become politically active; that is,
participating in campaigns and attending political meetings?

Before age 18	1
Age 19-25	2
Age 26-35	3
Age 36-45	4
Age 46 and up	5

Q7.   When you were growing up, would you say that your parents and other members of your immediate family were interested and / or involved in politics?

Yes, very involved	1
Yes, involved to some extent	2
No, not at all involved	3

Q8.   Overall, as you view ___(party)___ activity in your provincial riding, would you say that

Women participate more than men	1
Men participate more than women	2
Both participate about equally	3

Q9.   Recently, efforts have been made to encourage greater political partici-pation by Canadian women. One approach has been to institute affirmative action plans which aim toward equal representation of women and men at all levels of party activity. Do you approve or disapprove of the intro-duction of affirmative action in the Ontario ___(name)___ Party?

Strongly approve	1
Approve	2
Neither approve nor disapprove	3
Disapprove	4
Strongly disapprove	5

Q10.   If you were to compare the importance of politics in your life at present with the importance of your family and social life, where would you rank politics on a scale from one (politics most important) to five (family and social life most important)?

Politics most important	1
	2
	3
	4
Family and social life most important	5

Q11. And if you were to compare the importance of politics in your life at present with the importance of your career, where would you rank politics on a scale from one (politics most important) to five (career most important)?

Politics most important	1
	2
	3
	4
Career most important	5

Q12. And in an overall sense, keeping in mind your other commitments, such as your career, family life, and leisure activities, how would you rank the importance of politics on a scale from one (most important) to five (least important)?

Politics most important	1
	2
	3
	4
Politics least important	5

Q13. The contemporary women's movement is concerned with establishing equality for women in all spheres of economic, social, and political life in Canada. Do you approve or disapprove of this movement?

Strongly approve	1
Approve	2
Neither approve nor disapprove	3
Disapprove	4
Strongly disapprove	5

Q14. Based on your own political experiences, would you say that women presently experience discrimination in the Ontario ____(name)____ Party?

Yes, to a large extent	1
Yes, to some extent	2
No, not at all	3

Q15. Are you presently employed for pay?

> Yes, work full-time   1
>
> Yes, work part-time   2

No, work full-time in the home	3
No, am retired, laid off, student	4

Q16. Could you please describe briefly your *main occupation?*

_____

Q16a. What sort of business or industry do you work in?

_____

Q17. Do you presently have any children living at home?

> Yes   1

No   2
GO ON TO QUESTION 18

Q17a. How many children living at home are of pre-school age?   _____

Q17b. And how many children living at home attend elementary school?   _____

Q17c. And how many children living at home attend high school or
university?   _____

Q18. What is your educational background?

> Some high school   1
>
> Graduated high school   2
>
> Some post-secondary training   3
>
> University degree   4
>
> Post-graduate study   5

Q19. What is your present marital status?

Married, living with companion	1
Separated, divorced	2
Widowed	3
Single, never married	4

Q20. In what area of Ontario is your provincial riding located?

Metropolitan Toronto	1
Southwestern Ontario	2
Eastern Ontario	3
Northern Ontario	4

Q21. How would you describe the rural-urban composition of your provincial riding?

Primarily urban	1
Approximately half urban, half rural	2
Primarily rural	3

Q22. What was your gross family income (before taxes) in the year 1981?

Under $10, 000	1
$10,000-19,999	2
$20,000-29,999	3
$30,000-39,999	4
$40,000-49,999	5
$50,000-59,999	6
$60,000-69,999	7
$70,000-79,999	8
$80,000-89,999	9
$90,000-99,999	10
$100,000 and up	11

Q23. What is your gender?

Male	1
Female	2

Q24. In what year were you born?   19____

TYPE 5: ELITE INTERVIEWS

More detailed information on the family background, recruitment, involvement, and attitudes of female party activists was gathered during a series of in-depth interviews. Using the general design of Jeane Kirkpatrick's study of American state legislators,[3] the author interviewed respondents from each of the three main parties who had experience in at least one of the following roles: constituency association activist, women's organization activist, legislator, or party official. Notably, most respondents had combined more than one of these activities within a single political career.

The strategy for selecting interview respondents combined positional and reputational methods, to form a 'snowball' technique.[4] Using information from party and parliamentary records, activists were identified in each of the constituency, women's organization, legislative, and party official categories. Once an initial positional sample was derived, activists were asked for the names of others who they believed were influential partisans.

Using combined positional and reputational lists, interview selections were guided by a desire to ensure roughly equal numbers of respondents from each party, to sample from a variety of age groups and career backgrounds, and to solicit information from persons with an interest in women and politics. In all, forty interviews averaging one and one-half hours each were conducted with a total of ten constituency activists, ten women's organization activists, ten federal and provincial legislators, and ten full-time party officials.

The following questions were covered in all interviews, with some variation in order and wording to accommodate individual career paths. Respondents were encouraged to speak freely about their backgrounds and experiences in politics, so that each probe should be considered open-ended. The author conducted all interviews in the presence of the respondent only. Given the sensitive nature of some questions, particularly those dealing with perceptions of discrimination inside the parties, none of the interviews was taped.

INTERVIEWS: Note that biographical data on each respondent were gathered from party and legislative records prior to interview.

PART A Background to Political Involvement

1. At what age, approximately, did you first become politically active, in terms of attending party meetings and working on election campaigns? What motivated you to become active in the ___(name)___ Party at that stage of your life?

2. Can you describe briefly the kinds of political activities in which you were involved in these early years? How do you view your development over time in the ___(name)___ Party organization? Would you say that your primary focus has been the local riding association, the (party) women's organization, legislative activity, or work as a party official?

3. About how long, roughly, have you been actively involved in party politics? Did you take a break in your political work to accommodate family responsibilities, other employment, etc.?

4. How did you become involved as a constituency association activist / women's organization activist / legislator / party official? Can you recall any particular individual or event which encouraged you toward participation at this level?

PART B Major Political Activity

5. Let's look more specifically at your work as a constituency association activist / women's organization activist / legislator / party official. What are the most important responsibilities attached to this position?

6. How would you describe your main contributions in this political role? In what areas have you been less successful?

7. It is often said that a congenial social atmosphere among political colleagues encourages political activity. In light of your work as a constituency association activist / women's organization activist / legislator / party official, how important is this social dimension? Have you ever felt frozen out of informal party / caucus networks?

8. Looking again at your own experiences as a constituency association activist / women's organization activist / legislator / party official, what issues would you say have concerned you most? Were you frustrated in your pursuit of these concerns?

9. What impressions, overall, do you have of your experiences in party politics? In your view, what are the major positive and negative features of work as a constituency association activist / women's organization activist / legislator / party official?

10. Turning to your political aspirations and ambitions, have you considered pursuing other types of party work in the future? Do you have career aspirations outside of politics?

PART C Women and Politics

11. What are the main activities in which you see women, as compared with men, participating in the ___(name)___ Party? Would you say that your own experiences are typical or atypical of other female constituency association activists / women's organization activists / legislators / party officials?

12. In general, how would you describe your treatment in the ___(name)___ Party? Have you been discriminated against at any point in your political career? Can you describe this discriminatory treatment to me?

13. In light of your work as a constituency association activist / women's organization activist / legislator / party official, how would you describe the attitudes of male partisans with whom you interact on a regular basis? Have these attitudes changed over time?

14. The contemporary women's movement is concerned with establishing equality for women in all spheres of economic, social, and political life in Canada. Do you approve or disapprove of this movement?

15. What reasons would you offer to explain the relative dearth of women in provincial and federal politics in Canada? Do you believe that, in the future, more women will become involved in Canadian party politics? At what levels? In your view, does affirmative action provide a useful method of increasing female party participation?

PART D Family Background

16. Were the members of your immediate family involved in politics when you were growing up? Did any relatives contest public office or hold party office?

17. To what extent has your spouse / family been supportive of your political career? How does party work affect your family and personal life? How old were your children when you first became active as a constituency association activist / women's organization activist / legislator / party official?

18. In conclusion, what advice would you offer to Canadian women who seek to become politically active? How would you solve the problems which you mentioned as having contributed to female underrepresentation in Canadian politics?

Acknowledgment of Informants

In any study of this type, the author relies very directly upon materials supplied by informants. Some of the following individuals kindly agreed to provide access to party records, personal archives, and their political memories, while others helped to facilitate interviews and a 1982 convention delegate study. To each, I am deeply grateful.

Ruth Archibald
Becky Barrett
Hon. Monique Bégin
Margaret Birch
Margot Bowen
Margaret Bryce
Marion Bryden
Hon. Iona Campagnolo
Jacquie Chic
Sheila Copps
Joseph Cruden
Ed Dale
Ranne Dowbiggen
Jim Evans
Hon. Ellen Fairclough
Hon. Susan Fish
Barbara Ford
Audrey Gill
Prof. Esther Greenglass
Jean Haliburton
Marianne Holder

Aase Hueglin
Mary Humphrey
Jackie Isbester
Nancy Jamieson
Janis Johnson
Reva Karstadt
Helen Lafountaine
Mary Lancitie
Margaret Lazarus
Morden Lazarus
Kay Macpherson
Kay Manderville
Hon. Lorna Marsden
Bari Maxwell
Hon. Lynn McDonald
Alexa McDonough
Mary McGowan
Irma Melville
Jack Murray
Hon. Aideen Nicholson
Bruce Ogilvie

David C. Peterson
Jean Pigott
Jan Port
Marilyn Roycroft
Laura Sabia
Iona Samis
Kathy Sanderson
Margaret Scrivener
Hon. Muriel Smith

Lynda Sorenson
Kay Stanley
Hon. Bette Stephenson
Anne Venton
Judy Wasylycia-Leis
Marjorie Wells
Elizabeth Willcock
Harriet Wolman

Notes

In a number of places in the text, reference is made to the date of publication of various sources. This information is provided in order to inform the reader concerning the recency of such publications and to serve as a shorthand guide to the extensive references which follow.

PREFACE

1 An excellent critique of the bias toward and neglect of women in conventional political research is presented in Thelma McCormack, 'Toward a Nonsexist Perspective on Social and Political Change,' in Marcia Millman and Rosabeth Moss Kanter, eds., *Another Voice* (New York: Anchor, 1975), 1-33. See also Susan C. Bourque and Jean Grossholtz, 'Politics an Unnatural Practice: Political Science Looks at Female Participation,' *Politics and Society* 4:2 (1974), 225-66; and Murray Goot and Elizabeth Reid, *Women and Voting Studies: Mindless Matrons or Sexist Scientism?* Contemporary Political Sociology series, ed. Richard Rose, vol. 1 (Beverly Hills: Sage, 1975).

2 Book-length historical studies published since 1970 include Janice Acton, Penny Goldsmith, and Bonnie Shepard, eds., *Women at Work: Ontario, 1850-1930* (Toronto: Women's Press, 1974); Veronica Strong-Boag, *The Parliament of Women: The National Council of Women of Canada, 1893-1929* (Ottawa: National Museums of Canada, 1976); Ramsay Cook and Wendy Mitchinson, eds., *The Proper Sphere: Woman's Place in Canadian Society* (Toronto: Oxford University Press, 1976); Susan Mann Trofimenkoff and Alison Prentice, eds., *The Neglected Majority: Essays in Canadian Women's History* (Toronto: McClelland and Stewart, 1977); Marie Lavigne and Yolande Pinard, eds., *Les femmes dans la société*

québécoise (Montreal: Boréal Express, 1977); Linda Kealey, ed., *A Not Unreasonable Claim: Women and Reform in Canada, 1880s-1920s* (Toronto: Women's Press, 1979); Barbara Latham and Cathy Kess, eds., *In Her Own Right: Selected Essays on Women's History in B.C.* (Victoria: Camosun College, 1980); Micheline Dumont, Michèle Jean, Marie Lavigne, and Jennifer Stoddart, *L'histoire des femmes au Québec depuis quatre siècles* (Montreal: Quinze, 1982); and Carol Lee Bacchi, *Liberation Deferred? The Ideas of the English-Canadian Suffragists, 1877-1918* (Toronto: University of Toronto Press, 1983). For a useful review of much of this literature, see Eliane Leslau Silverman, 'Writing Canadian Women's History, 1970-82: An Historiographical Analysis,' *Canadian Historical Review* 53:4 (1982), 513-33.

3 Economic and sociological studies of women in Canada include Gail C.A. Cook, ed., *Opportunity for Choice: A Goal for Women in Canada* (Ottawa: Information Canada, 1976); Pat Armstrong and Hugh Armstrong, *The Double Ghetto: Canadian Women and Their Segregated Work* (Toronto: McClelland and Stewart, 1978); Julie White, *Women and Unions* (Ottawa: Canadian Advisory Council on the Status of Women, 1980); Lorna R. Marsden, ' "The Labour Force" Is an Ideological Structure: A Guiding Note to the Labour Economists,' *Atlantis* 7:1 (Fall 1981), 57-64; and S.J. Wilson, *Women, the Family, and the Economy* (Toronto: McGraw-Hill Ryerson, 1982).

Relatively limited attention has been devoted in recent years to the empirical study of women and politics in Canada. In the area of political and feminist theory, see Lorenne M.G. Clark and Lynda Lange, eds., *The Sexism of Social and Political Theory* (Toronto: University of Toronto Press, 1979); Mary O'Brien, *The Politics of Reproduction* (London: Routledge and Kegan Paul, 1980); and Angela Miles and Geraldine Finn, eds., *Feminism in Canada* (Montreal: Black Rose Books, 1982). Research on women's political activity and attitudes is reported in M. Janine Brodie, 'The Recruitment of Canadian Women Provincial Legislators, 1950-1975,' *Atlantis* 2:2 (1977), 6-17; Jill McCalla Vickers, 'Where Are the Women in Canadian Politics?' *Atlantis* 3:2 (1978), 40-51; Naomi Black, 'Changing European and North American Attitudes toward Women in Public Life,' *Journal of European Integration* 1 (1978), 221-40; Margrit Eichler, 'Sex Equality and Political Participation of Women in Canada,' *Revue internationale de sociologie* 15:1-3 (1979), 49-75; Jerome H. Black and Nancy E. McGlen, 'Male-Female Political Involvement Differentials in Canada, 1965-1974,' *Canadian Journal of Political Science* 12:3 (1979), 471-98; Allan Kornberg, Joel Smith, and Harold D. Clarke, *Citizen Politicians –*

Canada (Durham, NC: Carolina Academic Press, 1979), chap. 8; Sandra D. Burt, 'The Political Participation of Women in Ontario' (PhD dissertation, York University, 1981); Sylvia B. Bashevkin, 'Women and Change: A Comparative Study of Political Attitudes in France, Canada, and the United States' (PhD dissertation, York University, 1981); M. Janine Brodie, 'Pathways to Public Office: Canadian Women in the Post-war Years' (PhD dissertation, Carleton University, 1981); M. Janine Brodie and Jill McCalla Vickers, 'Canadian Women in Politics: An Overview' (Ottawa: CRIAW Papers no. 2, 1982); Evelyne Tardy, et al., *La politique: un monde d'hommes?* (Montreal: Hurtubise HMH, 1982); and *Politique, Revue de la Société québécoise de science politique* 5 (1984).

4 See Catherine L. Cleverdon, *The Woman Suffrage Movement in Canada,* with an Introduction by Ramsay Cook (Toronto: University of Toronto Press, 1974), chap. 7; and Thérèse Casgrain, *A Woman in a Man's World* (Toronto: McClelland and Stewart, 1972).

5 This argument is presented in an attitudinal context in Sylvia B. Bashevkin, 'Social Change and Political Partisanship: The Development of Women's Attitudes in Quebec, 1965-1979,' *Comparative Political Studies* 16:2 (1983), 147-72.

6 See M. Jean, ed., *Québécoises du 20e siècle* (Montreal: Presses Libres, 1974); Yolande Cohen, ed., *Femmes et politique* (Montreal: Le Jour, 1981); and Lise Payette, *Le pouvoir? Connais pas* (Montreal: Québec-Amérique, 1982).

CHAPTER 1: INDEPENDENCE VERSUS PARTISANSHIP

1 *Woman's Century,* 1918, as quoted in Jean Cochrane, *Women in Canadian Politics* (Toronto: Fitzhenry and Whiteside, 1977), 37.

2 Agnes Macphail, 'Men Want to Hog Everything,' *Maclean's Magazine,* 15 September 1949, 72.

3 For a concise treatment of constraints upon female political participation, see Jeane J. Kirkpatrick, *Political Woman* (New York: Basic Books, 1974), chap. 1.

4 A useful definition of political power is provided by Robert Putnam, who suggests that power constitutes 'the probability of influencing the policies and activities of the state.' See Robert D. Putnam, *The Comparative Study of Political Elites* (Englewood Cliffs: Prentice-Hall, 1976), 6.

5 See Catherine L. Cleverdon, *The Woman Suffrage Movement in Canada* (Toronto: University of Toronto Press, 1974).

6 See Carol Lee Bacchi, *Liberation Deferred? The Ideas of the English-*

Canadian Suffragists, 1877-1918 (Toronto: University of Toronto Press, 1983), 26. Cleverdon (1974: 20) reports that the Toronto Women's Literary Club was established in 1876.

7 These subsequent organizations included the Canadian Woman Suffrage Association (CWSA), established in 1883; the Dominion Women's Enfranchisement Association (DWEA), founded in 1889; and the Canadian Suffrage Association (CSA), established in 1906.

8 On the international ties of the Canadian suffragists, see Deborah Gorham, 'English Militancy and the Canadian Suffrage Movement,' *Atlantis* 1 (1975) and 'Singing Up the Hill,' *Canadian Dimension* 10 (1975).

9 Richard Evans, *The Feminists* (London: Croom Helm, 1977).

10 The terms 'social' and 'hard-core' feminism were introduced in William L. O'Neill, *Everyone Was Brave: A History of Feminism in America* (New York: Quadrangle, 1971). A similar distinction between the 'expediency' and 'justice' claims of American suffragists was made earlier in Aileen S. Kraditor, *The Ideas of the Woman Suffrage Movement* (New York: Columbia University Press, 1965).

11 See Deborah Gorham, 'Flora MacDonald Denison: Canadian Feminist,' in Linda Kealey, ed., *A Not Unreasonable Claim: Women and Reform in Canada* (Toronto: Women's Press, 1979), 47-70.

12 J. Stanley Lemons, *The Woman Citizen: Social Feminism in the 1920s* (Urbana: University of Illinois Press, 1973), ix.

13 On the role of maternal feminism in Canada, see Linda Kealey, 'Introduction' to *A Not Unreasonable Claim*, 1-14.

14 Bacchi, *Liberation Deferred*, 35.

15 Cleverdon, *Woman Suffrage*, 111.

16 The pivotal role of these women's organizations is discussed in Veronica Strong-Boag, ' "Setting the Stage": National Organization and the Women's Movement in the Late Nineteenth Century,' in Susan Mann Trofimenkoff and Alison Prentice, eds., *The Neglected Majority* (Toronto: McClelland and Stewart, 1977), 87-103; and Wendy Mitchinson, 'The WCTU: "For God, Home and Native Land," ' in *A Not Unreasonable Claim*, 151-67.

17 See Cleverdon, *Woman Suffrage*, chaps. 6 and 7.

18 Allen Mills summarizes this position in his study of J.S. Woodsworth: 'In Woodsworth's view what was wrong with Parliament was the partisan system that destroyed the independence of the average Member of Parliament ... Government, he felt, should not be party government but a committee of the best minds.' See Allen Mills, 'The Later Thought of J.S. Woodsworth, 1918-1942,' *Journal of Canadian Studies* 17:3 (Fall 1982), 80.

19 W.L. Morton, *The Progressive Party in Canada* (Toronto: University of Toronto Press, 1967).
20 Ibid, 16.
21 Candace Savage, *Our Nell: A Scrapbook Biography of Nellie L. McClung* (Saskatoon: Western Producer Prairie Books, 1979), 26.
22 Ibid, 27.
23 Ibid, 83.
24 Ibid, 95.
25 On the early debate over federal enfranchisement, see Cleverdon, *Woman Suffrage*, 105-18; and Bacchi, *Liberation Deferred*, 134-9.
26 See Gloria Geller, 'The Wartime Elections Act of 1917 and the Canadian Women's Movement,' *Atlantis* 2:1 (Autumn 1976), 88-106; and Bacchi, *Liberation Deferred*, 139-43. On the background to this period, see Ceta Ramkhalawansingh, 'Women during the Great War,' in *Women at Work* (Toronto: Women's Press, 1974), 261-307.
27 Dr Margaret Gordon, as quoted in Geller, 'Wartime Elections,' 104.
28 See Savage, *Our Nell*; as well as Carol Bacchi, 'Race Regeneration and Social Purity: A Study of the Social Attitudes of Canada's English-Speaking Suffragists,' *Histoire Sociale / Social History* 11 (November 1978), 460-74.
29 Cleverdon, *Woman Suffrage*, 129.
30 See Geller, 'Wartime Elections.'
31 Savage, *Our Nell*, 171.
32 See Bacchi, *Liberation Deferred*, 129-31.
33 One major difference between the two cases, however, was that in the United States, the Woman's Party grew out of 'hard-core' feminist activities, while in English Canada, it developed from the social feminist NEFU. On the American experience, see Susan D. Becker, *The Origins of the ERA: American Feminism between the Wars* (Westport, Conn.: Greenwood, 1981).
34 See Lemons, *The Woman Citizen*, chaps. 2-9.
35 See Savage, *Our Nell*.
36 Elsie Gregory MacGill, *My Mother the Judge*, with an Introduction by Naomi Black (Toronto: Peter Martin, 1981).
37 Ibid, 104.
38 Diane Crossley, 'The BC Liberal Party and Women's Reforms, 1916-1928,' in Barbara Latham and Cathy Kess, eds., *In Her Own Right: Selected Essays on Women's History in BC* (Victoria: Camosun College, 1980), 229-53.
39 Smith was initially elected as an Independent in 1918, replacing her deceased husband who had sat both provincially and federally as a Liberal. She was re-elected in 1920 and 1924 as a Liberal.

40 See Crossley, 'BC Liberal Party,' 234-5.

41 Bacchi, *Liberation Deferred*, 32. On the reluctance to pursue public office among Western Canadian suffragists, see L.G. Thomas, *The Liberal Party in Alberta* (Toronto: University of Toronto Press, 1959), 177.

42 See Liane Langevin, *Missing Persons: Women in Canadian Federal Politics* (Ottawa: Canadian Advisory Council on the Status of Women, 1977).

43 According to Macphail's biographers, the local UFO riding executive 'was besieged by protests' concerning its choice of a candidate during the 1921 campaign and asked Macphail to resign. See Margaret Stewart and Doris French, *Ask No Quarter* (Toronto: Longmans, Green, 1959), 56.

44 Macphail, 'Men Want to Hog Everything,' 72.

45 See Stewart and French, *Ask No Quarter*.

46 In the words of Stewart and French (1959: 38-9), Macphail 'never took any part in the battle for votes for women ... She was so absorbed in farm problems and cooperatives that the struggle seemed a long way off. She was never a formal feminist, nor even an informal one in the conduct of her life. She blamed women as much as men for the inferior position of the female citizen.'

47 Macphail, 'Men Want to Hog Everything,' 72.

48 According to Stewart and French (*Ask No Quarter*, 170), Macphail walked out of a CCF Women's luncheon with the words, 'I'm sick and tired of all this "woman" business. In all the time I've been in the House of Commons I've never asked for anything on the ground that I was a woman. If I didn't deserve it on my own merit I didn't want it! That's all I have to say.'

49 Macphail, 'Men Want to Hog Everything,' 72. LaMarsh's memoirs were published in 1968 by McClelland and Stewart under the title *Memoirs of a Bird in a Gilded Cage*.

50 See Doris French, 'Agnes Macphail, 1890-1954,' in Mary Quayle Innis, ed., *The Clear Spirit* (Toronto: University of Toronto Press, 1966), 179-97.

51 Ibid, passim. A major snowstorm on the day of the 1940 federal elections also damaged Macphail's chances for re-election.

52 See ibid.

53 For details of this background, see Rudy G. Marchildon, 'The "Persons" Controversy,' *Atlantis* 6:2 (Spring 1981), 99-113.

54 See ibid, 103ff.

55 Rowell's activities as Ontario Opposition leader are summarized in Cleverdon, *Woman Suffrage*, 35-44. It is notable that Murphy learned of this provision through her brother, an insightful Ontario lawyer with Conservative political ties.

56 Marchildon, ' "Persons" Controversy,' 106.

57 Ibid, 111.
58 John Leslie Scott, 'Our New Woman Senator, The Honourable Cairine Wilson,' *Maclean's Magazine*, 1 April 1930, 97. See also A.R. Way, 'From Time to Time in the Queen's Name: The Story of the Honourable Cairine Reay Wilson' (MA thesis, Carleton University, 1984).
59 Ibid, 98, 97.
60 Ibid, 97.
61 Mary Vipond, 'The Image of Women in Mass Circulation Magazines in the 1920s,' in *The Neglected Majority*, 118; emphasis in original. On the idea of educated motherhood in the United States during this period, see Sheila M. Rothman, *Woman's Proper Place* (New York: Basic Books, 1978).
62 See Vipond, 'Image of Women.'
63 John Manley, 'Women and the Left in the 1930s: The Case of the Toronto CCF Women's Joint Committee,' *Atlantis* 5:2 (Spring 1980), 100-19.
64 See ibid, 111-13.
65 Ruth Pierson, 'Women's Emancipation and the Recruitment of Women into the Labour Force in World War II,' in *The Neglected Majority*, 125-45.
66 Ibid, 142. Under federal tax statutes, relaxed during World War II, husbands are unable to claim a married status exemption if their wives are employed for pay.
67 Ibid, passim.
68 Betty Friedan, *The Feminine Mystique* (New York: Dell, 1963).
69 Dean Beeby, 'Women in the Ontario CCF, 1940-1950,' *Ontario History* 74:4 (December 1982), 258-83.
70 See ibid, 275-9.
71 Kay Macpherson and Meg Sears, 'The Voice of Women: A History,' in Gwen Matheson, ed., *Women in the Canadian Mosaic* (Toronto: Peter Martin, 1976), 71.
72 Cerise Morris, ' "Determination and Thoroughness": The Movement for a Royal Commission on the Status of Women in Canada,' *Atlantis* 5:2 (Spring 1980), 6.
73 Macpherson and Sears, 'The Voice of Women,' 75.
74 Barry Craig, 'Women's March May Back Call for Rights Probe,' *Globe and Mail*, 5 January 1967, 1.
75 See Lynne Teather, 'The Feminist Mosaic,' in *Women in the Canadian Mosaic*, 308-10.
76 Morris, ' "Determination and Thoroughness," ' 11. According to Laura Sabia, 'The CFUW generally worked on scholarship funds, white-glove tea parties, and the like. They were a very proper and academic group ... whose membership and executive frequently objected to my activities on

behalf of the royal commission. One member even wrote to me and said that she was handing in her membership card because we were becoming too militantly feminist. Of course, when my statement about a march on Ottawa appeared in the *Globe and Mail*, the CFUW women were just appalled.' Interview with Laura Sabia (15 March 1983).

77 See Doris Anderson, 'Let's Find Out What's Happening to Women,' *Chatelaine*, July 1966, 1. The CEW brief was compiled by a Toronto lawyer, Margaret Hyndman. On the chronology of this period, see Morris, ' "Determination and Thoroughness," ' 8-14.

78 See Macphail, 'Men Want to Hog Everything,' 72.

79 See Morris, ' "Determination and Thoroughness," ' 14.

80 LaMarsh, *Memoirs*, 292.

81 Bird's account of the royal commission is presented in *Anne Francis: An Autobiography* (Toronto: Clarke, Irwin, 1974), esp. 294ff.

82 In her *Memoirs* (301), LaMarsh observed, 'There seems no one now within Government circles who is interested in seeing its recommendations take legislative form.'

83 See *Report* of the Royal Commission on the Status of Women in Canada (Ottawa: Information Canada, 1970).

84 One radical brief presented to the royal commission in June 1968 was prepared by Bonnie Kreps. See Kreps, 'Radical Feminism I,' in *Women Unite! An Anthology of the Canadian Women's Movement* (Toronto: Canadian Women's Educational Press, 1972), 70-5.

85 See Judy Bernstein, Peggy Morton, Linda Seese, and Myrna Wood, 'Sister, Brothers, Lovers ... Listen ...,' in *Women Unite!*, 31-9.

86 For a useful clarification of these various streams within the feminist movement, written from a Marxist perspective, see Charnie Guettel, *Marxism and Feminism* (Toronto: Women's Press, 1974).

87 The highlights of this conference are documented in a 1974 film by Moira Armour, entitled *The Status of Women: Strategy for Change*.

88 See *Report* of the RCSW, chap. 7.

89 Rosemary Brown, 'A New Kind of Power, 1973 Address to Women for Political Action,' in *Women in the Canadian Mosaic*, 291.

90 See '105 Potential Women MPs,' *Chatelaine*, October 1971, 33ff.; and Barbara Frum, 'Insiders' Tips on How to Get Women Elected,' *Chatelaine*, October 1971, 38.

91 It should be noted that, between 1968 and 1972, Grace MacInnis was the sole female MP in Canada.

92 This idea was advanced by Kay Macpherson at the Strategy for Change conference in 1972, where 'Ms. for M.P.' buttons were sold. See Armour's film, *The Status of Women*.

93 Interview with Margaret Bryce (14 March 1983). Similar interpretations of the period following 1972 were presented in interviews with Kay Macpherson (18 March 1983) and Helen Lafountaine (25 February 1983).
94 Interview with Margaret Bryce (14 March 1983).
95 An important exception to this trend was Laura Sabia, who ran as a Conservative candidate in the 1968 federal elections and 1981 Spadina by-election.
96 In March 1971, for example, Prime Minister Trudeau appointed a three-woman task force 'to investigate and report on the priorities which Liberals and others gave to the Royal Commission recommendations.' See Report from Liberal Party Task Force on the Status of Women to LPC Consultative Council, dated October 1971.
97 Interviews with Aideen Nicholson (11 September 1982) and Lorna Marsden (18 March 1983).
98 Interviews with Kay Macpherson (18 March 1983) and Muriel Smith (7 July 1982).
99 On the general absence of legislative progress, see *Ten Years Later: An Assessment of the Federal Government's Implementation of the Recommendations Made by the Royal Commission on the Status of Women* (Ottawa: Canadian Advisory Council on the Status of Women, October 1979). The recommendations of the LPC Task Force on the Status of Women were also shelved (see note 96, above), according to at least two of its members. Interview with Esther Greenglass (17 March 1983) and note from Jan Steele to Esther Greenglass, dated 30 July 1973.
100 Interviews with Laura Sabia (15 March 1983), Lorna Marsden (18 March 1983), and Esther Greenglass (17 March 1983).
101 Feminist Party of Canada, 'Towards a Canadian Feminist Party,' April 1979.
102 Ibid.
103 The 'Yvette' rally of about 15,000 women in Montreal, and a series of smaller gatherings of federalist women during the referendum campaign, were organized in response to statements by the PQ Minister of State for the Status of Women, Lise Payette. In March 1980, Payette stated that the period of the obedient little 'Yvette' of Quebec schoolbooks had passed and compared women who voted against sovereignty-association to passive 'Yvettes.' Furthermore, she commented that the leader of the 'No' forces in the referendum campaign, Liberal Claude Ryan, was himself married to an 'Yvette.' See Evelyne Tardy, 'Les femmes et la campagne référendaire,' in *Québec: Un pays incertain* (Montreal: Québec-Amérique 1980), 184-203.
104 CACSW member Florence Ievers, as quoted in Marjorie Cohen, 'Editorial: The Need for Independent Feminism,' *Canadian Forum*, March 1981, 4.

105 According to most accounts, approximately 1,300 women attended the Ad Hoc Conference. See Anne Collins, 'Which Way to Ottawa?' *City Woman*, Holiday 1981, 12; and Chaviva Hosek, 'Women and the Constitutional Process,' in Keith Banting and Richard Simeon, eds., *And No One Cheered* (Toronto: Methuen, 1983), 280-300. Additional studies of women and the 1982 constitution include Penny Kome, *The Taking of Twenty-eight* (Toronto: Women's Press, 1983); and Sandra D. Burt, 'Women and the Canadian Charter of Rights and Freedoms' (paper presented at Canadian Political Science Association meetings, Vancouver, 1983).
106 Interview with Lorna Marsden (18 March 1983).
107 See Collins, 'Which Way' and Cohen, 'Editorial.'
108 See Elizabeth Gray, 'Women's Fight to Get in from the Cold Political Wind,' *Globe and Mail*, 30 January 1981, 7.
109 Lynn McDonald, 'The Charter of Rights and the Subjection of Women,' *Canadian Forum*, June-July 1981, 18.
110 A more recent example of such a coalition is the Canadian Coalition against Media Pornography, formed in response to Playboy programming on First Choice Pay TV in 1983.

CHAPTER 2: PATTERNS OF FEMALE POLITICIZATION AND PARTISANSHIP

1 M. Benney, A.P. Gray, and R.H. Pear, *How People Vote*, as quoted in Mildred A. Schwartz, *Public Opinion and Canadian Identity* (Berkeley: University of California Press, 1967), 193-4.
2 Recent studies which tend to neglect the gender variable include Harold D. Clarke, Jane Jenson, Lawrence LeDuc, and Jon H. Pammett, *Political Choice in Canada* (Toronto: McGraw-Hill Ryerson, 1979); and Michael D. Ornstein, H. Michael Stevenson, and A. Paul Williams, 'Region, Class and Political Culture in Canada,' *Canadian Journal of Political Science* 13:2 (June 1980), 227-71. Others which give somewhat more consideration to gender include Robert I. Drummond, 'Voting Behaviour: Casting the Play,' in Donald C. MacDonald, ed., *The Government and Politics of Ontario* (Toronto: Van Nostrand Reinhold, 1980), 272-89. A growing body of research addresses the political attitudes of Canadian political elites, including female party activists. See, for example, S.D. Burt, 'Democracies in Conflict? A Comparison of Men's and Women's Relationships with Government' (paper presented at Canadian Political Science Association meetings, Ottawa, 1982); and Sylvia B. Bashevkin, 'Political Participation, Ambition, and the Development of Feminist Attitudes: Women in the Ontario Party Elites' (unpublished 1983).

3 Peter Regenstreif, *The Diefenbaker Interlude* (Toronto: Longmans, 1965), 96.
4 Schwartz, *Public Opinion*, 193.
5 Benney et al, as quoted in ibid, 194.
6 J.A. Laponce, *People vs Politics* (Toronto: University of Toronto Press, 1969), 37.
7 The 1965 Canadian National Election Study, directed by John Meisel, Philip Converse, Maurice Pinard, Peter Regenstreif, and Mildred Schwartz, was based on a stratified random sample of 2,113 respondents, weighted to a total of 2,719 cases. The 1979 Social Change in Canada survey, directed by Tom Atkinson, Bernard Blishen, Michael D. Ornstein, and H. Michael Stevenson, sampled approximately 3,000 persons. Both studies were made available through the York University Institute for Behavioural Research. Neither the original investigators nor the IBR bears responsibility for the analyses or interpretations presented in this chapter.
8 Regenstreif, *The Diefenbaker Interlude*, 96.
9 Ibid.
10 Benney et al, as quoted in Schwartz, *Public Opinion*, 193-4.
11 Schwartz, 193.
12 Laponce, *People vs Politics*, 92ff.
13 Rick Van Loon, 'Political Participation in Canada: The 1965 Election,' *Canadian Journal of Political Science* 3:3 (September 1970), 389.
14 See Jean Bethke Elshtain, 'Moral Woman and Immoral Man: A Consideration of the Public-Private Split and Its Political Ramifications,' *Politics and Society* 4:4 (1974), 453-73; Susan Moller Okin, *Women in Western Political Thought* (Princeton: Princeton University Press, 1979); and Lorenne M.G. Clark and Lynda Lange, eds., *The Sexism of Social and Political Theory* (Toronto: University of Toronto Press, 1979).
15 Thelma McCormack, 'Toward a Nonsexist Perspective on Social and Political Change,' in Marcia Millman and Rosabeth Moss Kanter, eds., *Another Voice* (New York: Anchor Books, 1975), 12.
16 Other relevant sources include John C. Courtney and David E. Smith, 'Voting in a Provincial General Election and a Federal By-election: A Constituency Study of Saskatoon City,' *Canadian Journal of Economics and Political Science* 32:3 (August 1966), 338-53; Pauline Jewett, 'Voting in the 1960 Federal By-elections at Peterborough and Niagara Falls,' in John C. Courtney, ed., *Voting in Canada* (Scarborough: Prentice-Hall, 1967), 50-70; Richard Laskin and Richard Baird, 'Factors in Voter Turnout and Party Preference in a Saskatchewan Town,' *Canadian Journal of Political Science* 3:3 (September 1970), 450-62; and John Meisel, *Working Papers on Canadian Politics* (Montreal: McGill-Queen's University Press, 1975), 12.

17 Responses to an item regarding 1965 federal vote tended to parallel closely the party identification figures, since 19.1% of men and 13.7% of women reported having voted for an NDP candidate in that election.

18 Ratings of Liberal Members of Parliament were as follows: 43.3% of women and 37.9% of men rated them 'pretty good,' 47.0% of women and 50.7% of men rated them 'so-so,' and 9.7% of women and 11.5% of men said 'no good.' Ratings of Progressive Conservative MPs did not vary by gender.

19 Notably, a similar result obtains using 1979 survey data, as reported in table 2.3.

20 The circumstances surrounding female enfranchisement in English Canada were described as follows by Charlotte Whitton, a prominent social welfare activist and mayor of Ottawa: 'Canadian women got the vote as a gift rather than a reward. Moreover it was granted not as a conviction so much as a concession on the part of the major technicians within the parties.' See Charlotte Whitton, 'Is the Canadian Woman a Flop in Politics?' (orig. pub. 1946), reprinted in Ramsay Cook and Wendy Mitchinson, eds., *The Proper Sphere* (Toronto: Oxford University Press, 1976), 329.

21 One problem in trying to interpret these data is that political independence (i.e., non-partisanship) and non-voting, as well as refusals and 'don't know' replies, are grouped in a single category of non-response. Given that these are the only data available, however, table 2.7 provides a useful overview of the non-response phenomenon.

22 This approach follows Karl Mannheim's work on the generational component of historical change, which argues that generations share a specific 'historico-social space – the same historical life community' (K.H. Wolfe, 'Introduction' to K. Wolfe, ed., *From Karl Mannheim* [New York: Oxford University Press, 1971], 1). The chronological groups to be considered in this analysis are described as 'birth cohorts,' who were born during a particular period in the history of English Canada and who matured to the point of formally entering the electorate as 'adulthood cohorts' approximately twenty years later. See Norval D. Glenn, 'Cohort Analysis,' *Sage University Papers on Quantitative Applications in the Social Sciences* (Beverly Hills: Sage, 1977).

23 Regina Manifesto, as reprinted in appendix A to Walter D. Young, *The Anatomy of a Party: The National CCF, 1932-61* (Toronto: University of Toronto Press, 1969), 304. For a history of the Canadian social gospel phenomenon, see Richard Allen, *The Social Passion* (Toronto: University of Toronto Press, 1971) and, on its linkages with social feminism, see

Beatrice Brigden, 'One Woman's Campaign for Social Purity and Social Reform,' in Richard Allen, ed., *The Social Gospel in Canada* (Ottawa: National Museums of Canada, 1975), 36-62.

24 Title of Part I of Draft Program of the New Party, as appended to Stanley Knowles, *The New Party* (Toronto: McClelland & Stewart, 1961), 9.

25 For data on comparative levels of paid employment and unionization among males and females, see Julie White, *Women and Unions* (Ottawa: Canadian Advisory Council on the Status of Women, 1980).

26 See Leo Zakuta, *A Protest Movement Becalmed: A Study of Change in the CCF* (Toronto: University of Toronto Press, 1964), 88ff; and Gad Horowitz, *Canadian Labour in Politics* (Toronto: University of Toronto Press, 1968), 37ff.

27 Betty Friedan, *The Feminine Mystique* (New York: Dell, 1963).

28 Gary Teeple, ' "Liberals in a Hurry": Socialism and the CCF / NDP,' in Gary Teeple, ed., *Capitalism and the National Question in Canada* (Toronto: University of Toronto Press, 1972), 237.

29 On differential patterns of male and female employment and unionization in Canada, see White, *Women and Unions*.

30 In the English-Canadian sample overall, 17% of women (171) and 9% of men (78) stated that much more government effort should be devoted to eliminating discrimination against women.

CHAPTER 3: THE HIGHER THE FEWER

1 Ontario Cabinet Minister Robert Welch, nomination speech for Marg Lyon, candidate for Eighth Vice-President of Ontario Progressive Conservative Association (September 1982).

2 Catherine L. Cleverdon, *The Woman Suffrage Movement in Canada* (Toronto: University of Toronto Press, 1950), 281.

3 Rosamonde Ramsay Boyd, 'Women and Politics in the United States and Canada,' *Annals of the American Academy of Political and Social Science* 375 (January 1968), 53.

4 Ibid, 57.

5 Early reports on political candidacy in Canada can be found in M. Janine Brodie, 'The Recruitment of Canadian Women Provincial Legislators, 1950-1975,' *Atlantis* 2:2 (part 1, Spring 1977), 6-17; and Jill McCalla Vickers, 'Where Are the Women in Canadian Politics?' *Atlantis* 3:2 (part 2, Spring 1978), 40-51. More lengthy reports on this research are presented in M. Janine Brodie and Jill McCalla Vickers, 'Canadian Women in Politics: An Overview' (Ottawa: CRIAW Papers no. 2, 1982); and M. Janine Brodie,

'Pathways to Public Office: Canadian Women in the Post-war Years' (PhD dissertation, Carleton University, 1981).

6 Existing studies of Canadian political parties, particularly those which address activity at the local level, tend to support this position. They include Frederick C. Engelmann and Mildred A. Schwartz, *Canadian Political Parties: Origin, Character, Impact* (Scarborough: Prentice-Hall, 1975); Conrad Winn and John McMenemy, *Political Parties in Canada* (Toronto: McGraw-Hill Ryerson, 1976); Allan Kornberg, Joel Smith, and Harold D. Clarke, *Citizen Politicians – Canada* (Durham, NC: Carolina Academic Press, 1979); and Henry Jacek, John McDonough, Ronald Shimizu, and Patrick Smith, 'The Congruence of Federal-Provincial Campaign Activity in Party Organizations,' *Canadian Journal of Political Science* 5:2 (June 1972), 190-205.

7 Judy LaMarsh, *Memoirs of a Bird in a Gilded Cage* (Toronto: McClelland and Stewart, 1969), 281-2.

8 Robert D. Putnam, *The Comparative Study of Political Elites* (Englewood Cliffs: Prentice-Hall, 1976), 33.

9 See Kornberg et al., *Citizen Politicians*, 14-15.

10 Harold D. Clarke and Allan Kornberg, 'Moving up the Political Escalator: Women Party Officials in the United States and Canada,' *Journal of Politics* 41:2 (1979), 475.

11 Kornberg et al, *Citizen Politicians*, 205.

12 Statistics Canada, *Census of Canada: Population by Mother Tongue* (Ottawa: Supply and Services Canada, 1982).

13 According to party records, Ontario Liberal riding executives do not include a specific membership secretary position.

14 According to party records, no riding secretary positions existed in the Manitoba Conservative organization.

15 See John C. Courtney, *The Selection of National Party Leaders in Canada* (Toronto: Macmillan, 1973); and Donald V. Smiley, 'The National Party Leadership Convention in Canada: A Preliminary Analysis,' *Canadian Journal of Political Science* 1 (1968), 373-97.

16 For further discussion, see Sylvia B. Bashevkin, 'Women and Party Politics: The 1982 Ontario Leadership Conventions,' in R. Schultz et al., eds., *The Canadian Political Process*, 4th edition (forthcoming).

17 See Courtney, *Selection of National Party Leaders*, 108; Carl Baar and Ellen Baar, 'Party and Convention Organization and Leadership Selection in Canada and the United States,' in Donald R. Matthews, ed., *Perspectives on Presidential Selection* (Washington, DC: Brookings, 1973), 59; and C.R. Santos, 'Some Collective Characteristics of the Delegates to

the 1968 Liberal Party Leadership Convention,' *Canadian Journal of Political Science* 3 (1970), 303.

18 By way of contrast, political scientists in the United States, United Kingdom, and Australia have given relatively greater attention to women's political representation, particularly in party organizations. See, for example, M. Kent Jennings and Norman Thomas, 'Men and Women in Party Elites: Social Roles and Political Resources,' *Midwest Journal of Political Science* 12 (1968), 469-92; M. Kent Jennings and Barbara G. Farah, 'Social Roles and Political Resources: An Over-Time Study of Men and Women in Party Elites,' *American Journal of Political Science* 25 (1981), 462-82; Shelah Gilbert Leader, 'The Policy Impact of Elected Women Officials,' in Louis Maisel and Joseph Cohen, eds., *The Impact of the Electoral Process* (Beverly Hills: Sage, 1977), 165-84; Lorraine Culley, 'Women's Organisation in the Labour Party,' *Power & Politics* 3 (1981), 115-22; and Marian Sawer, 'Women and Women's Issues in the 1980 Federal Elections,' *Politics* 16 (1981), 243-9.

19 Cleverdon, *Woman Suffrage Movement*, 60.

20 Kornberg et al., *Citizen Politicians – Canada.*

21 For further discussion of Ontario provincial party structures, see Sylvia B. Bashevkin, 'Women's Participation in the Ontario Political Parties, 1971-1981,' *Journal of Canadian Studies* 17:2 (Summer 1982), 48-50.

22 Constitution and Resolutions of the New Democratic Party of Ontario (June 1980), article 9, section 3.

23 For a journalistic treatment of this problem, see Charlotte Gray, 'The New Backroom Girls,' *Chatelaine*, July 1980, 25-6.

24 Brodie, 'The Recruitment of Canadian Women'; Vickers, 'Where Are the Women'; M. Janine Brodie and Jill Vickers, 'The More Things Change ... Women in the 1979 Federal Campaign,' in Howard R. Penniman, ed., *Canada at the Polls: 1979 and 1980* (Washington, DC: American Enterprise Institute, 1981), 322-36; Brodie and Vickers, 'Canadian Women in Politics'; Brodie, 'Pathways to Public Office'; Liane Langevin, 'Missing Persons: Women in Canadian Federal Politics' (Ottawa: Advisory Council on the Status of Women, 1977); and Cleverdon, *Woman Suffrage Movement.*

25 Vickers, 'Where Are the Women,' 46.

26 Brodie and Vickers, 'The More Things Change,' esp. 323, 326ff.

27 Brodie, 'Pathways to Public Office,' chap. 7.

28 Margaret Stewart and Doris French, *Ask No Quarter* (Toronto: Longmans, 1959), 63.

29 In the 1981 Ontario provincial election, for example, 27 out of 45, or 60%,

of female candidates finished third, compared with less than 30% of male candidates.

30 For a succinct discussion of constraints upon female participation, see Jeane J. Kirkpatrick, *Political Woman* (New York: Basic Books, 1974), chap. 1.

31 See Langevin, 'Missing Persons.' For more general treatments of legislative recruitment in Canada, see Allan Kornberg, *Canadian Legislative Behavior* (New York: Holt Rinehart & Winston, 1967); and Allan Kornberg and William Mishler, *Influence in Parliament: Canada* (Durham: Duke University Press, 1976).

32 Ibid, 37.

33 However, the 1982 election of Conservative MP Jennifer Cossitt, the widow of a former Tory MP, in the riding held previously by her husband suggests that 'widows' succession' continues to operate in Canadian politics.

34 Interviews with Muriel Smith (7 July 1983) and Judy Wasylycia-Leis (6 July 1983).

35 See Kirkpatrick, *Political Woman*, chaps. 7-8.

36 Interview with the Honourable Ellen Fairclough (6 April 1983).

37 LaMarsh, *Memoirs*, 283. It is notable that LaMarsh disliked the Secretary of State and Postmaster General positions offered to her in 1965 because both had been held earlier by Fairclough; LaMarsh wanted to avoid any such comparisons. See *Memoirs*, chap. 9.

38 The precise extent of female office-holding in these areas is difficult to document empirically given frequent shifts in provincial- and federal-level cabinet responsibilities, as well as in opposition critic assignments. Prominent women in social welfare, cultural, and status of women portfolios have included M. Bégin (federal Health and Welfare); J. Erola (federal Status of Women); M. Mitchell (NDP federal Status of Women critic); B. Robertson (New Brunswick Minister of Health); S. Dysart (Liberal health critic, New Brunswick); S. Copps (Liberal health critic, Ontario); Dr B. Stephenson (Ontario Minister of Education, and Colleges and Universities); M. Hemphill (Manitoba Minister of Education); E. Dailly (NDP education critic, British Columbia); L. Verge (Newfoundland Minister of Education); B. Firth (Yukon Minister of Education); G. McCarthy (British Columbia Minister of Human Resources); R. Brown (NDP human resources critic, British Columbia); S. Fish (Ontario Minister of Citizenship and Culture); M. LeMessurier (Alberta Minister of Culture).

CHAPTER 4: INCREASING REPRESENTATION ON ELITE LEVELS

1 *Report* of the Royal Commission on the Status of Women (Ottawa: Information Canada 1970), 333.
2 Hannah Fenichel Pitkin, *The Concept of Representation* (Berkeley and Los Angeles: University of California Press, 1967), 11.
3 Senator Chubby Power, quoted in John C. Courtney, *The Selection of National Party Leaders in Canada* (Toronto: Macmillan, 1973), 107.
4 Donald V. Smiley, 'The National Party Leadership Convention in Canada: A Preliminary Analysis,' *Canadian Journal of Political Science* 1 (1968),373.
5 Notable exceptions to this pattern include research on female political candidacies by M. Janine Brodie and Jill McCalla Vickers, as well as studies of urban party activism by Allan Kornberg, Harold D. Clarke, and associates. See text above, chapter 3.
6 See Lawrence LeDuc, Jr, and Walter L. White, 'The Role of Opposition in a One-Party Dominant System: The Case of Ontario,' *Canadian Journal of Political Science* 7 (1974), 86-100; and Donald C. MacDonald, ed., *The Government and Politics of Ontario* (Toronto: Van Nostrand Reinhold, 1980).
7 Previous female candidates for major party leadership included Rosemary Brown (federal NDP), Flora MacDonald (federal PC), and Muriel Smith (Manitoba NDP), while those for minor party leadership included Thérèse Casgrain (Quebec CCF), Alexa McDonough (Nova Scotia NDP), and Shirley McLoughlin (British Columbia Liberals). Notably, each of the former was unsuccessful, while all of the latter were successful.
8 Marguerite J. Fisher, 'Women in the Political Parties,' *Annals of the American Academy of Political and Social Science* 251 (1947), 87-93.
9 Frank J. Sorauf, *Party Politics in America* (Boston: Little, Brown, 1976), 123. See also Hugh A. Bone, *Party Committees and National Politics* (Seattle: University of Washington Press, 1958), 107-11; Louis Maisel, 'Party Reforms and Political Participation: The Democrats in Maine,' in Louis Maisel and Paul M. Sacks, eds., *The Future of Political Parties* (Beverly Hills: Sage, 1975), 202-8; and Robert J. Huckshorn, *Party Leadership in the States* (Amherst: University of Massachusetts Press, 1976).
10 Jeane Kirkpatrick, *The New Presidential Elite* (New York: Russell Sage Foundation, 1976), 43. On the background to American party reforms, see John S. Saloma and Frederick H. Sontag, *Parties* (New York: Knopf, 1972), 108-10.
11 See Carl Baar and Ellen Baar, 'Party and Convention Organization and

Leadership Selection in Canada and the United States,' in Donald R. Matthews, ed., *Perspectives on Presidential Selection* (Washington, DC: Brookings, 1973), 59.

12 Kirkpatrick, *The New Presidential Elite*; and M. Kent Jennings and Barbara G. Farah, 'Social Roles and Political Resources: An Over-Time Study of Men and Women in Party Elites,' *American Journal of Political Science* 25 (1981), 462-82.

13 Sorauf, *Party Politics*, 123.

14 For a summary of this situation, see M. Janine Brodie and Jill McCalla Vickers, 'Canadian Women in Politics: An Overview' (Ottawa: CRIAW Papers no. 2, 1982).

15 Walter S.G. Kohn, *Women in National Legislatures: A Comparative Study of Six Countries* (New York: Praeger, 1980).

16 Additional internal affirmative action programs which are considered below include the 'Action Plan' of the Liberal Party of Canada, as well as resolutions adopted by the federal NDP during 1981 and 1983 party conventions.

17 Examples of this less formal approach include a series of conferences called 'Access to Power,' sponsored by the National Progressive Conservative Women's Caucus. See Dorothy Lipovenko, 'Conservatives Seek More Political Muscle for Women,' *Globe and Mail*, 18 November 1982. On the treatment of 'women's issues' by the major parties during the 1979 federal election campaign, see M. Janine Brodie and Jill Vickers, 'The More Things Change ... Women in the 1979 Federal Campaign,' in Howard R. Penniman, ed., *Canada at the Polls: 1979 and 1980* (Washington, DC: American Enterprise Institute, 1981), 333-6.

18 Constitution of the Ontario NDP Women's Committee, section 2, paras. 1 and 2.

19 This discussion draws heavily on interviews with former Women's Committee President Marianne Holder, as well as on participant observation in the committee by the author during 1980-1.

20 See *Resolutions to the Tenth Convention of the Ontario NDP*, Guelph, 20-22 June 1980, W1-W13.

21 One staff member was appointed to the office of the party leader, while the other was assigned to manage an unsuccessful campaign in a Metropolitan Toronto riding vacated by an NDP incumbent. Both the women's coordinator and women's organizer positions were eliminated during post-election reorganization in the party.

22 This same calculation may have led NDP campaign organizers to avoid the issue of sexual preference during the 1981 provincial election.

23 See Brodie and Vickers, 'The More Things Change.'
24 See Marianne R. Holder, 'Notes re. Internal Affirmative Action' (prepared for the NDP Participation of Women Committee meeting, Ottawa, 5 July 1980).
25 See Sylvia B. Bashevkin, 'Women's Participation in the Ontario Political Parties, 1970-1981,' *Journal of Canadian Studies* 17 (1982), 44-54.
26 As defined in a 1983 report to the NDP federal council, 'Systemic discrimination refers to practices or systems which may appear to be neutral in their treatment of women and may be implemented impartially, but which operate to exclude women for reasons which are not related to the job to be done. In terms of the Party, there is no conscious intention of practising discrimination; the discriminatory impact on women is either not recognized or is assumed to reflect actual inadequacies (or unavailability) of women to do the job.' See *Report* of the Affirmative Action Committee of the NDP Federal Council (1983), 1.
27 *Resolutions to the Eleventh Convention of the Ontario NDP*, Toronto, 5-7 February 1982, 93-4.
28 See *Resolutions to the NDP Convention*, Vancouver, 1981, 165-6.
29 Donald C. MacDonald, 'Affirmative Action: Moving from Talk to Reality in the NDP,' *Toronto Star*, 31 July 1983.
30 See *Report* of the Affirmative Action Committee of the NDP Federal Council (1983).
31 See Women's Liberal Commission, 'Action Plan: Basic Elements and Strategies of an Affirmative Action Plan for Women in the Liberal Party of Canada' (mimeo 1982).
32 On the failure of voluntary remedies in an American context, see Nijole V. Benokraitis and Joe R. Feagin, *Affirmative Action and Equal Opportunity* (Boulder, Col.: Westview Press, 1970), 173-7.
33 According to some advocates of affirmative action in the United States, 'discrimination is more costly than remedial action' in an organizational context (ibid, 187).
34 This argument maintains that rather than resulting in a loss of institutional autonomy, affirmative action enhances the operation of organizations, especially because it improves (or rationalizes) internal decision-making. See ibid.
35 For a critique of affirmative action from the point of view of individual merit, see Lance W. Roberts, 'Understanding Affirmative Action,' in W.E. Block and M.A. Walker, eds., *Discrimination, Affirmative Action, and Equal Opportunity* (Vancouver: Fraser Institute, 1982), 159-62.
36 The argument that affirmative action is unnecessary because discrimination

remains unproved is presented in Walter Williams, 'On Discrimination, Prejudice, Racial Income Differentials, and Affirmative Action,' in ibid, 69-99.

37 According to the editors of the Fraser Institute study, little evidence is available to suggest that discrimination exists, and therefore 'what is needed for intelligent public policy is careful analysis, a measured and dispassionate outlook, well-documented research, convincing evidence, and a willingness to look at the world as it really is, and not only as we might like to see it' (ibid, xix).

38 A five-page questionnaire, developed and pre-tested by the author, was distributed to delegates at the convention. Approximately 10% of registered delegates returned questionnaires ($N = 173$). While this response rate is low by social scientific standards, the gender breakdown in the sample (55.2% male, 44.8% female) fairly closely approximated that in the convention as a whole (60.0% and 40.0%, respectively). Results of an identical questionnaire distributed to delegates to the OLP leadership convention, the Ontario PC Association of Women annual meeting, and the Ontario PC Association meeting are compared with the NDP data in Sylvia B. Bashevkin, 'Political Participation, Ambition, and the Development of Feminist Attitudes: Women in the Ontario Party Elites' (unpublished 1983).

39 See, for example, Alan Fotheringham, 'BC's Mrs. Thatcher Embarrasses Barrett,' *Toronto Star*, 14 February 1975; Malcolm Gray, 'Has Rosemary Brown's Socialist Image More Style than Substance?' *Globe and Mail*, 20 February 1975; and Lisa Hobbs, 'Why Is Rosemary Running?' *Chatelaine*, July 1975.

40 Linda Archibald, Leona Christian, Karen Detarding, and Dianne Hendrick, 'Sex Biases in Newspaper Reporting: Press Treatment of Municipal Candidates,' *Atlantis* 5 (1980), 177-84.

41 'Rosemary for Leader of NDP,' campaign literature, 1975.

42 On the initially dismissive attitude toward Brown's candidacy, see 'NDP Gathers Friday,' *Winnipeg Tribune*, 2 July 1975; Nick Hills, 'For Broadbent, the West Is the Test,' *Winnipeg Tribune*, 3 July 1975.

43 Stewart MacLeod, 'NDP Converges on City,' *Winnipeg Tribune*, 4 July 1975.

44 T.C. Douglas, quoted in ibid.

45 'Who Is Rosemary Brown?' campaign literature, 1975.

46 Interview with Muriel Smith (7 July 1982); Robert Matas, 'Pawley Supporters Eyeing Early Victory at Convention,' *Winnipeg Tribune*, 2 November 1979; and Robert Matas, 'Pawley Wins Easy Victory to Lead NDP,' *Winnipeg Tribune*, 5 November 1979.

47 Frank Jones, 'Flora Keeps Her Cool in "Chauvinist Country," ' *Toronto Star*, 23 February 1976; and Harry Bruce, 'The Lady Was for Burning: Why the Tories Gave Flora Their Hearts but not Their Votes,' *The Canadian Magazine*, 10 April 1976.

48 Pat McNenly, 'Make Abortion Available to All, MacDonald Tells Her Supporters,' *Toronto Star*, 2 February 1976; and Jones, 'Flora Keeps Her Cool.'

49 MacDonald's status as a 'girl' was emphasized in Tom Hazlitt, 'Girl's Fight for an "Independent" Canada,' *Toronto Star*, 7 May 1971. For references to her as a 'spinster,' see for example Frank Jones, 'Flora MacDonald Is Finding Her Kind of People,' *Toronto Star*, 1 March 1975; and Heather Robertson, 'Delivering Politics Back to the People,' *The Canadian Magazine*, 3 May 1975.

50 Robertson, 'Delivering Politics.'

51 MacDonald, as quoted in ibid.

52 For example, in the caption beneath her photo in McNenly, 'Make Abortion Available,' the candidate was described as 'Flora MacDonald, women's candidate.'

53 Mary Janigan, 'Prime Minister Flora MacDonald? Why Not!' *Toronto Star*, 1 February 1975.

54 Frank Jones, 'Flora Keeps Her Cool.'

55 Flora MacDonald leadership address, as quoted in Alvin Armstrong, *Flora MacDonald* (Toronto: J.M. Dent and Sons, 1976), 192.

56 During the months immediately following her election to the legislature in March 1981, Copps announced that she would propose independently the inclusion of sexual preference in the provincial Human Rights Code. As well, Copps organized her own filibuster against ad valorem gas tax legislation and was the sole MPP to argue publicly against legislative salary increases. See Robert Matas, 'Party Split, but Copps Plans Motion on Gays,' *Globe and Mail*, 16 May 1981; and Gordon McNultry, 'Sheila Not Afraid to Speak out on Controversial Issues,' *Hamilton Spectator*, 17 July 1981.

Copps also gained notoriety as a result of sexist behaviour directed against her by a number of Conservative MPPs. During an exchange in the legislature on 5 May 1981, a cabinet minister informed Copps that she was more attractive than a former female MPP in the Liberal caucus (Margaret Campbell). Copps's response to this comment was interrupted by a government backbencher, who stated that she should 'go back to the kitchen.' Later in this same legislative session, Copps was presented with written comments of a sexist nature from other government members. See Rosemary Speirs, 'Outraged MPP Told to Get Used to Sexist Remarks,'

Globe and Mail, 6 May 1981; 'When Copps Plays Hardball, MPPs Better Wear Helmets,' *Windsor Star*, 15 May 1981; and Sylvia Stead, 'Rookie Women MPPs: You Have to Develop a Thick Skin,' *Globe and Mail*, 8 August 1981. Copps wrote publicly about these experiences and observed that 'quite a few members take a somewhat dim view of women in politics.' See Sheila Copps, 'The Inside Story of a Rookie's Life at Queen's Park,' *Toronto Star*, 19 July 1981.

57 The 'men's-club mentality' phrase was used initially by NDP MPP Richard Johnston, in responding to comments directed against Copps in the legislature. According to her *Star* article (see ibid), Copps at the time had not yet recognized this 'mentality.'

58 The importance of these background factors was recognized by Copps and her major supporters. Interviews with Sheila Copps (18 December 1981 and 13 April 1982) and interview with Joseph Cruden, Copps's campaign manager (10 May 1982).

59 By way of contrast, speeches and campaign literature distributed by candidates David Peterson, James Breithaupt, and John Sweeney addressed 'women's issues,' including day care, affirmative action in the Ontario public service, and equal pay.

60 Hugh Winsor, 'A Dash of Spirit Is Added,' *Globe and Mail*, 8 December 1981. It is notable that press reporters and columnists gave relatively little attention to the age of Ontario NDP leadership candidate Bob Rae (33) during this period, nor did they consider that at the time of his election to the provincial Liberal leadership in 1976, Stuart Smith had spent less time than Copps had in the legislature.

Questioning of Copps's suitability as a woman was observed by the author during an informal poll of delegates at the convention. For press accounts of this phenomenon, see Bill Johnston and Bruce Stewart, 'Copps Didn't Keep Up,' *Hamilton Spectator*, 22 February 1982.

61 Winsor, 'A Dash of Spirit.'

62 On Copps's marital history, see Jonathon Fear, 'Five Hope to Beat the Tory Machine,' *Kitchener-Waterloo Record*, 19 February 1982; and Jean Sonmor, 'Sheila: The Next Hurrah,' *Toronto Sun*, 23 February 1982. The comparison with Mansfield and Joan of Arc appeared in the 24 November 1981 Slinger column in the *Toronto Star*.

63 Winsor, 'A Dash of Spirit.'

64 On the Sunday morning of the convention, a number of members of the provincial Liberal caucus announced that were Copps elected as party leader, they would expect resignations en masse from the caucus. Their statements, accompanied by the distribution of a list of 23 OLP MPPs who

were supporting Peterson, were apparently meant to counter the endorsements which Copps had received from seven federal cabinet ministers. Interview with Sheila Copps (13 April 1982) and with Joseph Cruden (10 May 1982).

Peterson had received the support of such party insiders as Senator Keith Davey, Jim Coutts, and Jerry Grafstein. See Paul Palango, 'Peterson Runs Hard to Stay Ahead,' *Globe and Mail*, 16 February 1982; Pat Crowe, 'MP's Presence a Mixed Blessing,' *Toronto Star*, 21 February 1982; and Douglas Fisher, 'More of Same,' *Toronto Sun*, 22 February 1982.

65 See M. Janine Brodie, 'The Constraints of Private Life: Marriage, Motherhood, and Political Candidacy in Canada' (paper presented at Canadian Political Science Association meetings, Halifax, 1981); Marcia Manning Lee, 'Why so Few Women Hold Public Office: Democracy and Sexual Roles,' *Political Science Quarterly* 91 (1976), 297-314; and Emily Stoper, 'Wife and Politician: Role Strain among Women in Public Office,' in Marianne Githens and Jewel L. Prestage, eds., *A Portrait of Marginality* (New York: David McKay, 1977), 320-37.

CHAPTER 5: WOMEN'S ORGANIZATIONS IN THE MAJOR PARTIES

1 Judy LaMarsh, *Memoirs of a Bird in a Gilded Cage* (Toronto: McClelland and Stewart, 1969), 281.
2 *Report* of the Royal Commission on the Status of Women in Canada (Ottawa: Information Canada, 1970), 348. Emphasis in original.
3 See Catherine L. Cleverdon, *The Woman Suffrage Movement in Canada* (Toronto: University of Toronto Press, 1974), 98, 114, 204.
4 In this same vein, Cleverdon (ibid, 273) remarks that the willingness of Canadian women to be restricted to 'ladies' auxiliaries in the parties ... has resulted in their doing much of the drudgery, with payment in the form of "window dressing" jobs and a gentle pat on the back.'
5 *Report* of the RCSW, 348.
6 See Joseph Wearing, *The L-Shaped Party: The Liberal Party of Canada, 1958-1980* (Toronto: McGraw-Hill Ryerson, 1980), 216ff.
7 Toronto Women's Liberal Association, Historian's Report, mimeo (undated).
8 See Florence Tilden Harrison, 'Fifty Years with the Ontario Women's Liberal Association, 1914-1965,' mimeo (undated).
9 Ibid, 7.
10 Cleverdon, *Woman Suffrage*; Elsie Gregory MacGill, *My Mother the Judge*, with an Introduction by Naomi Black (Toronto: Peter Martin, 1981); and

Diane Crossley, 'The B.C. Liberal Party and Women's Reforms, 1916-1928,' in Barbara Latham and Cathy Kess, eds., *In Her Own Right* (Victoria: Camosun College, 1980), 229-53.

11 See Patricia A. Myers, ' "A Noble Effort": The National Federation of Liberal Women of Canada, 1945-1973' (MA thesis, University of Waterloo, 1980), Introduction.

12 See ibid, chaps. 1, 2.

13 Ibid, title page.

14 Tuesday Luncheon Club, 25th Anniversary Certificate, 1973.

15 Interview with Mary Lancitie (1 March 1983).

16 Harrison, 'Fifty Years,' 14-15.

17 Ibid, 18.

18 LaMarsh, *Memoirs*, 5.

19 Gladys Taylor, *Madam President* (Ottawa: Progressive Conservative Women's Association of Canada, 1966), 9, 27.

20 Ibid, 10.

21 See ibid for a review of this period.

22 Ibid, 16.

23 Lucy Sansom, as quoted in ibid, 23.

24 Ibid, 23.

25 Ibid, 20.

26 Eva MacLean, as quoted in ibid, 14.

27 Ibid, 14.

28 See Margaret Aitken, *Hey Ma! I Did It* (Toronto: Clarke, Irwin, 1953).

29 See Taylor, *Madam President*, 21-2.

30 *Report* of the RCSW, 347.

31 John Manley, 'Women and the Left in the 1930s: The Case of the Toronto CCF Women's Joint Committee,' *Atlantis* 5:2 (1980), 100-19; and Dean Beeby, 'Women in the Ontario CCF, 1940-1950,' *Ontario History* 74:4 (1982), 258-83.

32 Rosemary Brown raised this point in her speech to an NDP women's conference, held in Winnipeg in July 1974. According to Brown, the work of women in the CCF and NDP is generally neglected in existing historical studies of the Canadian left.

33 See Walter D. Young, *The Anatomy of a Party: The National CCF, 1932-61* (Toronto: University of Toronto Press, 1969).

34 Interview with Marjorie Wells (1 March 1983).

35 Manley, 'Women and the Left,' 101.

36 Ibid, 111.

37 Ibid.

38 Caroline M. Riley, 'Women and the CCF,' as quoted in ibid, 116-7.

39 See Beeby, 'Women in the Ontario CCF.'

40 CCF 12th Provincial Convention, 1945 (Ontario), as quoted in ibid, 266.

41 Beeby, 'Women in the Ontario CCF,' 269.

42 It is notable that some of these opponents acknowledge that, in hindsight, the opportunities available to female recruits may have differed from those available to males.

43 Interview with Margaret Lazarus (5 April 1983).

44 Ibid.

45 Interview with Marjorie Wells (1 March 1983).

46 Beeby, 'Women in the Ontario CCF,' 278. This same period was characterized by a weakening of recruitment activities in the Ontario CCF generally. On the increased use of women as sacrifice candidates following World War II, see Leo Zakuta, *A Protest Movement Becalmed* (Toronto: University of Toronto Press, 1964).

47 'Women's Committees, New Democratic Party,' mimeo (August 1962), 1.

48 Ibid.

49 'New Democratic Party, Development of Participation of Women,' mimeo (January 1982), 1.

50 Ibid, 2.

51 Ibid.

52 Ibid.

53 See ibid, 2-3.

54 Brief submitted by the New Democratic Party to the Royal Commission on the Status of Women, 11 March 1968, 9-10.

55 See Krista Maeots, 'The Role of Women in Canadian Society and the Implications of This for the NDP' (paper presented to Federal NDP Council, 19 September 1970).

56 Interview with Marianne Holder (22 March 1983).

57 Minutes of the Executive Meeting of the Ontario Women's Liberal Association, 26 March 1969, 2.

58 Wearing, *The L-Shaped Party*, 218. A recommendation that older women's organizations in the Liberal Party be integrated was made in the 1972 Final Report of the Liberal Party of Canada Task Force on the Status of Women. According to a summary of Task Force recommendations, 'The Commission encountered the opinion that the political women's associations are a deterrent to women who would like to contribute to politics in significant ways.' See Esther Greenglass, 'Summary of Task Force Recommendations,' mimeo, 2.

59 See Women's Liberal Commission By-Laws (July 1980), paras. 5 and 6.

The national executive of WLC also includes provincial representatives, one French and one English vice-president, and the immediate past president of WLC.

60 Ibid, para. 2.
61 See, for example, 'Women for a Change' flyer (undated); 'Canadian Women Have Terrible Figures' fact sheet (May 1980); 'Exploding the Myths,' fact sheet (May 1980).
62 See 'Constitutional Amendments as Proposed by Kay Manderville, Chair LPC(O) Women's Committee,' mimeo, 4-5.
63 Jean Cochrane, *Women in Canadian Life: Politics* (Toronto: Fitzhenry and Whiteside, 1977), 60.
64 Interview with Elizabeth Willcock, then president of the National PC Women's Caucus (12 June 1982).
65 Constitution of the National Progressive Conservative Women's Caucus (as amended 26 February 1981), article 3.
66 Notably, 'the wife of the Leader of the Party automatically is to be an Honorary Member of the Executive as well as the wives of former Leaders of the Party.' See ibid, article 5, section 6.
67 On the background to Pigott's decision, see 'The Ottawa Scene: A Not so Fond Farewell to Politics,' *Globe and Mail*, 29 December 1980, 8.
68 By 1982, 28 such cities had been targeted for federal PC women's caucuses. See 'Politics Isn't Just a Man's Game,' Women's Bureau leaflet (undated).
69 Interview with Barbara Ford (22 April 1982). It should be noted that according to the terms of article 4, section c, of the National PC Women's Caucus constitution, city caucuses may each send four delegates and four alternates to vote at National Caucus annual meetings.
70 On the age, party participation, and feminist attitudes of OPCAW activists, see Sylvia B. Bashevkin, 'Social Background and Political Experience: Gender Differences among Ontario Provincial Party Elites, 1982,' *Atlantis* 9:1 (Fall 1983), 1-12 and 'Political Participation, Ambition, and the Development of Feminist Attitudes' (unpublished 1983).
71 'Progressive Conservative Associations of Women,' mimeo, last para.
72 Stephenson as quoted in Mary Trueman, 'Bette Stephenson Says Conservative Women's Associations "Outdated",' *Globe and Mail*, 12 April 1976. Stephenson stands by her earlier statement that 'the P.C. Women's Association is an anachronism ... I simply cannot see any reason for segregation on the basis of sex in political or professional associations.' Interview with Dr Bette Stephenson (5 October 1982).
73 Interview with Aase Hueglin, President of OPCAW (1 December 1981).

74 Elizabeth Willcock, address to OPCAW annual meeting, Downtown Holiday Inn, Toronto, 13 June 1982.
75 As of the 1982 OPCAW meeting, federal riding associations rather than the National Caucus had the power to recognize women's groups.

CHAPTER 6: COMPARATIVE PERSPECTIVES

1 Frances Dana Gage, 'A Hundred Years Hence,' reprinted in Aileen S. Kraditor, ed., *Up from the Pedestal* (Chicago: Quadrangle, 1968), 285.
2 Ibid.
3 Treatments of the Flora MacDonald campaign for federal Conservative leadership in 1976 reflect many of these assumptions. See, for example, Jonathan Manthorpe, 'Can Flora Become Thatcher Matcher?' *Globe and Mail*, 12 February 1975, and Mary Janigan, 'Prime Minister Flora MacDonald? Why Not!' *Toronto Star*, 1 February 1975.
4 See Sylvia B. Bashevkin, 'Women and Change: A Comparative Study of Political Attitudes in France, Canada, and the United States' (PhD dissertation, York University, 1981). For a detailed review of much of the older empirical literature, see Sylvia Bashevkin, 'Women and Politics: Perspectives on the Past, Present, and Future' (paper presented at Canadian Political Science Association meetings, Saskatoon, 1979).
5 Richard J. Evans, *The Feminists* (London: Croom Helm, 1977).
6 Ibid.
7 Margaret L. Inglehart, 'Political Interest in West European Women,' *Comparative Political Studies* 14 (1981), 299-326.
8 Ibid, 301. For a more detailed treatment of this historical background, particularly in reference to subsequent attitudinal developments, see Bashevkin, 'Women and Change,' chap 3. On its application to France in particular, see Sylvia B. Bashevkin, 'Changing Patterns of Politicization and Partisanship among Women in France,' *British Journal of Political Science* 15:1 (January 1985), 75-96.
9 Alan Grimes, *The Puritan Ethic and Woman Suffrage* (New York: Oxford University Press, 1967), passim.
10 For a more complete treatment of wedging in Catholic cultures, see Bashevkin, 'Women and Change,' 58-65.
11 On party realignments during this period, see Jorgen Rasmussen, 'Women in Labour: The Flapper Vote and Party System Transformation in Britain,' *Electoral Studies* 3:1 (April 1984), 47-63; David Morgan, *Suffragists and Liberals: The Politics of Woman Suffrage in England* (Oxford: Blackwell,

1975); Virginia Sapiro, 'You Can Lead a Lady to the Vote, but What Will She Do with It? The Problem of a Woman's Bloc Vote,' in Dorothy G. McGuigan, ed., *New Research on Women and Sex Roles* (Ann Arbor: Center for Continuing Education of Women, 1976), 221-37; and chapter 1, above.

12 On political instability during the Fourth Republic, see Philip M. Williams, *Crisis and Compromise: Politics in the Fourth Republic* (London: Longmans, 1964) and *Politics in Post-war France* (London: Longmans, 1958); and Duncan MacRae, Jr, *Parliament, Parties, and Society in France, 1946-1958* (New York: St. Martin's, 1967). For an overview of French constitutional crises, see Roy Pierce, *French Politics and Political Institutions* (New York: Harper and Row, 1973), chaps. 1-3, 5; and John S. Ambler, *The Government and Politics of France* (Boston: Houghton Mifflin, 1971), chaps. 1, 10.

13 François Bourricard, 'The Right in France since 1945,' *Comparative Politics* 10:1 (October 1977), 13. For a more general treatment of social change in France, see John Ardagh, *The New French Revolution* (New York: Harper and Row, 1968).

14 See François Sellier, 'France,' in John T. Dunlop and Walter Galenson, eds., *Labor in the Twentieth Century* (New York: Academic Press, 1978), 201.

15 See Guy Michelat and Michel Simon, 'Religion, Class, and Politics,' *Comparative Politics* 10:1 (October 1977), 159-86.

16 Henry W. Ehrmann, *Politics in France* (Boston: Little, Brown, 1976), 211. On the traumatic implications of 1968, see also Pierce, *French Politics*, 129-40; and Lowell G. Noonan, *France: The Politics of Continuity in Change* (New York: Holt, Rinehart, 1970).

17 On the development of contemporary French feminism, see Elaine Marks and Isabelle de Courtivron, 'Introductions' to *New French Feminisms: An Anthology* (Amherst, Mass.: University of Massachusetts Press, 1980), 28-38; Maité Albistur and Daniel Armogathe, *Histoire du féminisme français* (Paris: Editions des femmes, 1977), 447-73; Jean Rabaut, *Histoire des féminismes français* (Paris: Editions Stock, 1978), 333-80; Annie de Pisan and Anne Tristan, *Histoires du MLF* (Paris: Calmann-Lévy, 1977); and Naty Garcia Guadilla, *Libération des femmes: le MLF* (Paris: Presses Universitaires de France, 1981).

18 This hypothesis is drawn from Alain Lancelot, *L'abstentionnisme électoral en France* (Paris: A. Colin, 1968), 179.

19 Janine Mossuz-Lavau and Mariette Sineau, 'Sociologie de l'abstention dans huit bureaux de vote parisiens,' *Revue française de science politique*

28:1 (1978), 73-101. The levels of non-voting among women and men born before 1900 were 32% and 18%, respectively.

20 Georges Dupeux, Alain Girard, and Jean Stoetzel, 'Une enquête par sondage auprès des électeurs,' in *Le référendum de septembre et les élections de novembre 1958*, by Mattei Dogan, et al. (Paris: A. Colin, 1960), 119-93.

21 A report on one such experiment is presented in Madelaine Grawitz, 'Le comportement féminin à Lyon, d'après une expérience d'urnes separées,' in *Le référendum du 8 janvier 1961*, by François Goguel et al. (Paris: A. Colin, 1962), 205-9.

22 The 1958 French Election Study, directed by Georges Dupeux, François Goguel, Jean Stoetzel, and Jean Touchard, sampled 1,650 respondents (weighted to a total of 1,870 cases) during three survey waves: pre-referendum, post-referendum, and post-election. Approximately two-thirds of the sample was interviewed in each of the three waves. The Euro-barometre no. 10 study, discussed below, was conducted in October / November 1978, and directed by Jacques-René Rabier and Ronald Inglehart. The French sample in Euro-barometre no. 10 included 1,038 respondents weighted to a total of 1,194 cases. Both datasets were made available through the York University Institute for Behavioural Research, in co-operation with the Inter-University Consortium for Political and Social Research. Neither the IBR, the ICPSR, nor the original investigators bears responsibility for the analyses or interpretations presented here.

The first wave of the 1958 survey is employed in table 6.3 because it included the largest number of female respondents (N = 606), compared with 395 in the second and 522 in the third waves.

23 David R. Cameron, 'Stability and Change in Patterns of French Partisanship,' *Public Opinion Quarterly* 36:1 (Spring 1972), table 3. In 1968, non-response among men and women age 21-29 was 17.4%.

24 Historical research indicates that the early American women's movement was characterized by an important cleavage between 'social' or maternal and 'hard-core' or political interests. According to O'Neill and Kraditor, political feminists maintained that equal rights for women were the primary objective of the movement, and that these rights should be secured on the basis of political justice. In contrast, prominent activists also employed a more dominant social feminist argument, which elevated progressive social reform above demands for legal emancipation. See William L. O'Neill, *Everyone Was Brave* (New York: Quadrangle, 1971) and Aileen S. Kraditor, *The Ideas of the Woman Suffrage Movement, 1890-1920* (New York: Columbia University Press, 1965).

25 J. Stanley Lemons, *The Woman Citizen* (Urbana: University of Illinois Press, 1973), passim.

26 On the programs and policies of the League of Women Voters from its establishment through the late 1970s, see Ruth C. Clusen, 'The League of Women Voters and Political Power,' in Bernice Cummings and Victoria Schuck, eds., *Women Organizing* (Metuchen, NJ: Scarecrow Press, 1979), 112-32. For a more complete discussion of this thesis, see Sylvia B. Bashevkin, 'Social Feminism and the Study of American Public Opinion,' *International Journal of Women's Studies* 7:1 (January / February 1984), 47-56.

27 The 1978 NORC General Social Survey is part of a series of national studies conducted by the National Opinion Research Center and distributed by the Roper Public Opinion Research Center since 1972. The 1978 study was conducted in February, March, and April of that year, using 'an independently drawn sample of English-speaking persons 18 years of age or over, living in non-institutional arrangements within the continental U.S.' (James Allan Davis, *General Social Surveys, 1972-1978: Cumulative Data* [NORC 1978], 1). The data were made available by the York University Institute for Behavioural Research in co-operation with the Inter-University Consortium for Political and Social Research. Neither the NORC, the IBR, nor the ICPSR is responsible for the calculations or interpretations presented here.

Note that figures in table 6.4 are based upon analysis of white respondents only. Since the central concern of this section is the attitudinal impact of the early American feminist movement, which developed as an essentially white response to problems of urbanization, slavery, and gender inequality, we have considered whites only in the data analysis. Our decision is supported by a number of recent studies which show that the experiences of minority women in the United States have differed dramatically from those of whites and that, as a result, patterns of political attitudes and participation among white versus minority women have also differed substantially. See, for example, Sandra Baxter and Marjorie Lansing, *Women and Politics: The Invisible Majority* (Ann Arbor: University of Michigan Press, 1980), chaps. 5 and 6.

28 Three major sets of findings are as follows: first, women are more pacifistic than men on issues of war, defence spending, capital punishment, hand-gun sales, and granting amnesty to Vietnam draft evaders; second, women are more supportive than men of federal spending on income maintenance and social services including child-care and anti-poverty programs; and third, females are less likely than males to endorse

'hawkish' presidential candidates, such as Wallace in 1968, Nixon in 1972, and Reagan in 1980, at the same time as they have been substantially more supportive of Democrats McGovern and Carter in 1972 and 1980, respectively. See Gerald M. Pomper, *The Voters' Choice* (New York: Dodd, Mead, 1975), 78-89; Robert S. Erikson, Norman R. Luttbeg, and Kent L. Tedin, *American Public Opinion* (New York: Wiley, 1980), 186-7; Sidney Verba et al., 'Public Opinion and the War in Vietnam,' *American Political Science Review* 62 (1967), 317-34; Louis Harris and Associates, *The 1972 Virginia Slims American Women's Public Opinion Poll* (New York: Louis Harris, 1972); Baxter and Lansing, *Women and Politics*, 61-4; and Gloria Steinem, 'Feminist Notes: Now that It's Reagan,' *Ms.*, January 1981, 28-33.

29 See Baxter and Lansing, *Women and Politics*; Steinem, 'Feminist Notes'; Bella Abzug with Mim Kelber, *Gender Gap* (Boston: Houghton Mifflin, 1984); and Ethel Klein, *Gender Politics* (Cambridge: Harvard University Press, 1984), chap. 9.

30 Catherine L. Cleverdon, *The Woman Suffrage Movement in Canada* (Toronto: University of Toronto Press, 1950), chap. 7; and Thérèse Casgrain, *A Woman in a Man's World* (Toronto: McClelland and Stewart, 1972).

31 On Liberal reform legislation during this period, see Cleverdon, *The Woman Suffrage Movement*, 261-4.

32 The major empirical materials employed in this discussion are the 1965 Canadian National Election Study (directed by John Meisel, Philip Converse, Maurice Pinard, Peter Regenstreif, and Mildred Schwartz) and the 1979 Social Change in Canada Survey (directed by Tom Atkinson, Bernard Blishen, Michael D. Ornstein, and H. Michael Stevenson). The former study was based upon a stratified random sample of approximately 2,100 respondents, weighted to a total of about 2,700 cases, while the latter employed a multistage probability selection sample, weighted to about 3,000 respondents. Both studies were made available by the Institute for Behavioural Research at York University. Neither the IBR nor the original investigators bears responsibility for the analyses or interpretations presented here.

33 For a more detailed treatment of these data, see Sylvia B. Bashevkin, 'Social Change and Political Partisanship: The Development of Women's Attitudes in Quebec, 1965-1979,' *Comparative Political Studies* 16:2 (July 1983), 147-72.

34 See Bashevkin, 'Changing Patterns of Politicization and Partisanship among Women in France.'

35 For a review of this literature, see Bashevkin, 'Women and Change.'
36 For a comparative treatment of the 'law of increasing disproportions,' see Robert D. Putnam, *The Comparative Study of Political Elites* (Englewood Cliffs: Prentice-Hall, 1976), 33ff.
37 For one comparative account of party convention delegation, see Carl Baar and Ellen Baar, 'Party and Convention Organization and Leadership Selection in Canada and the United States,' in Donald R. Matthews, ed., *Perspectives on Presidential Selection* (Washington, DC: Brookings, 1973), 49-84.
38 On the development of this empirical literature, see Bashevkin, 'Women and Politics.'
39 Joni Lovenduski and Jill Hills, eds., *The Politics of the Second Electorate* (London: Routledge & Kegan Paul, 1981).
40 See Bashevkin, 'Women and Change,' chap. 3.
41 See Allan Kornberg, Joel Smith, and Harold D. Clarke, *Citizen Politicians – Canada* (Durham, NC: Carolina Academic Press, 1979); and Harold D. Clarke and Allan Kornberg, 'Moving up the Political Escalator: Women Party Officials in the United States and Canada,' *Journal of Politics* 41:2 (May 1979), 442-76.
42 Diane Margolis, 'The Invisible Hands: Sex Roles and the Division of Labor in Two Local Political Parties,' in Debra W. Stewart, ed., *Women in Local Politics* (Metuchen, NJ: Scarecrow Press, 1980), 22-41; Mary Cornelia Porter and Ann B. Matasar, 'The Role and Status of Women in the Daley Organization,' in Jane S. Jaquette, ed., *Women in Politics* (New York: Wiley, 1974), 85-108; Ellen Boneparth, 'Women in Campaigns: From Lickin' and Stickin' to Strategy,' *American Politics Quarterly* 5:3 (July 1977), 289-300; and Louis Maisel, 'Party Reform and Political Participation: The Democrats in Maine,' in Louis Maisel and Paul M. Sacks, eds., *The Future of Political Parties* (Beverly Hills: Sage, 1975). For additional material on women in major American parties, see Janet A. Flammang, ed., *Political Women: Current Roles in State and Local Government* (Beverly Hills: Sage, 1984).
43 Margolis, 'The Invisible Hands,' 26.
44 See Boneparth, 'Women in Campaigns'; and Martin Gruberg, *Women in American Politics* (Oshkosh, Wisc.: Academia, 1968).
45 Boneparth, passim.
46 Maisel, 'Party Reform and Political Participation,' 205.
47 Two exceptions to this pattern are the affirmative action resolutions passed by the Ontario NDP in 1981 and by the federal NDP in 1983. For details of

these resolutions, see chapter 4. Unfortunately, their effects upon party convention delegation are not yet ascertainable.

48 See Gruberg, *Women in American Politics*, 60ff. On the low percentage of female party delegates to British and Australian party conventions, see Lovenduski and Hills, *Politics of the Second Electorate*, chaps. 2, 5.

49 Maisel, 'Party Reform and Political Participation,' 207.

50 M. Kent Jennings and Barbara G. Farah, 'Social Roles and Political Resources: An Over-Time Study of Men and Women in Party Elites,' *American Journal of Political Science* 25:3 (August 1981), 462-82. Jennings and Farah base their longitudinal comparisons upon 1964 Michigan data reported in M. Kent Jennings and Norman Thomas, 'Men and Women in Party Elites: Social Roles and Political Resources,' *Midwest Journal of Political Science* 12:4 (November 1968), 469-92.

51 Jennings and Farah, 'Social Roles,' 481.

52 Jeane Kirkpatrick, *The New Presidential Elite* (New York: Russell Sage, 1976) and Gruberg, *Women in American Politics*.

53 Roosevelt as quoted in Gruberg, *Women in American Politics*, 62. See also Susan and Martin Tolchin, *Clout: Womanpower and Politics* (New York: Coward, McCann, 1974), 64.

54 See Porter and Matasar, 'The Role and Status of Women in the Daley Organization' and Clarke and Kornberg, 'Moving up the Political Escalator.'

55 See Margaret Stacey and Marion Price, *Women, Power, and Politics* (London: Tavistock, 1981), 146.

56 See Yann Viens, 'Femmes, politique, Parti communiste français,' in *La condition féminine* (Paris: Editions Sociales, 1978), 357.

57 Alzada Comstock, 'Women Members of European Parliaments,' *American Political Science Review* 20 (1926), 379-84; Maurice Duverger, *The Political Role of Women* (Paris: UNESCO, 1955); Emmy E. Werner, 'Women in Congress, 1917-1964,' *Western Political Quarterly* 19:1 (1966), 16-30; and Emmy E. Werner, 'Women in the State Legislatures,' *Western Political Quarterly* 21:1 (1968), 40-50.

58 Useful reviews of this growing literature may be found in Virginia Sapiro and Barbara G. Farah, 'Women as Political Elites: A Literature Review and Agenda' (paper presented at Midwest Political Science Association meetings, Chicago, 1976); Virginia Sapiro, 'When Are Interests Interesting? The Problem of Political Representation of Women,' *American Political Science Review* 75:3 (1981), 701-16; Wilma Rule Krauss, 'Political Implications of Gender Roles: A Review of the Literature,' *American*

Political Science Review 68:3-4 (1974), 1706-23; and Vicky Randall, *Women and Politics* (London: Macmillan, 1982), chap. 3.

59 Kathleen Newland, *Women in Politics: A Global Review* (Washington, DC: Worldwatch Institute, 1975); as quoted in Stacey and Price, *Women, Power, and Politics*, 144.

60 On the case for proportional representation, see Pippa Norris, 'Women's Legislative Participation in Western Europe,' in Sylvia B. Bashevkin, ed., *Women and Politics in Western Europe* (London: Frank Cass, 1986); Karen Beckwith, 'Structural Barriers to Women's Access to Office' (paper presented at Americal Political Science Association meetings, Washington, DC, 1984); Melville E. Currell, *Political Woman* (London: Croom Helm, 1974), 124-5; Walter S.G. Kohn, *Women in National Legislatures* (New York: Praeger, 1980), 166; and Wilma Rule, 'Why Women Don't Run,' *Western Political Quarterly* 34 (1981), 77. Australian evidence in favour of proportional representation is presented in Marian Sawer, 'Women and Women's Issues in the 1980 Federal Election,' *Politics* 16:2 (1981), 246.

61 Stacey and Price, *Women, Power, and Politics*, 147.

62 Ibid.

63 See Raisa B. Deber, 'The Fault, Dear Brutus: Women as Congressional Candidates in Pennsylvania,' *Journal of Politics* 44:2 (1982), 463-79; Tolchin and Tolchin, *Clout*, chap. 2; and Nikki R. Van Hightower, 'The Recruitment of Women for Public Office,' *American Politics Quarterly* 5:3 (1977), 301-14.

64 See Stacey and Price, *Women, Power, and Politics*; Beverly Parker Stobaugh, *Women and Parliament, 1918-1970* (Hicksville, NY: Exposition Press, 1978); Currell, *Political Woman*; Monica Charlot, 'Women in Politics in France,' in Howard R. Penniman, ed., *The French National Assembly Elections of 1978* (Washington, DC: American Enterprise Institute, 1980), 171-91; and Ingunn Norderval Means, 'Political Recruitment of Women in Norway,' *Western Political Quarterly* 25:3 (1972), 491-521. For an autobiographical treatment of this problem, see Edith Summerskill, *A Woman's World* (London: Heinemann, 1967).

65 Currell, *Political Woman*, chap. 5.

66 See Werner, 'Women in the State Legislatures'; and Irene Diamond, *Sex Roles in the State House* (New Haven: Yale University Press, 1977).

67 Currell, *Political Woman*; Stobaugh, *Women and Parliament*; Marian Sawer, 'Women and Women's Issues'; Marian Simms, 'Australia,' in Lovenduski and Hills, *Politics of the Second Electorate*, 83-111; Charles S. Bullock III and Patricia Lee Findley Heys, 'Recruitment of Women for Congress: A Research Note,' *Western Political Quarterly* 25:3 (1972), 416-

23; Irwin N. Gertzog, 'The Matrimonial Connection: The Nomination of Congressmen's Widows for the House of Representatives,' *Journal of Politics* 42:3 (1980), 820-33; and Diane D. Kincaid, 'Over His Dead Body: A Positive Perspective on Widows in the U.S. Congress,' *Western Political Quarterly* 31:1 (1978), 96-104.

68 For a more complete elaboration of this view, see Jeane J. Kirkpatrick, *Political Woman* (New York: Basic Books, 1974), 13-19.

69 See ibid as well as two subsequent book-length studies by Virginia Sapiro, *The Political Integration of Women* (Urbana: University of Illinois Press, 1983) and Susan J. Pharr, *Political Women in Japan* (Berkeley: University of California Press, 1981). Role factors are also introduced in a number of articles which address the impact of marriage and motherhood upon elite-level participation. See Marcia Manning Lee, 'Why Few Women Hold Public Office,' *Political Science Quarterly* 91 (1976), 297-314; Emily Stoper, 'Wife and Politician: Role Strain among Women in Public Office,' in Marianne Githens and Jewel L. Prestage, eds., *A Portrait of Marginality* (New York: David McKay, 1977), 320-37; and M. Janine Brodie, 'The Constraints of Private Life: Marriage, Motherhood, and Political Candidacy in Canada' (paper presented at Canadian Political Science Association meetings, Halifax, 1981). These studies generally conclude that although some changes may be occurring among younger women and men, many females remain constrained by household and particularly child-rearing responsibilities, such that increased representation on elite levels is unlikely without substantial shifts in role perceptions and duties.

70 On the resource limitations confronting female partisans, see Jennings and Thomas, 'Men and Women in Party Elites'; Jennings and Farah, 'Social Roles and Political Resources'; and Paula J. Dubeck, 'Women and Access to Political Office: A Comparison of Female and Male State Legislators,' *Sociological Quarterly* 17:1 (1976), 42-52.

71 Studies which address lower levels of female political ambition include Diane L. Fowlkes, Jerry Perkins, and Sue Tolleson Rinehart, 'Gender Roles and Party Roles,' *American Political Science Review* 73:3 (1979), 772-80; Virginia Sapiro and Barbara D. Farah, 'New Pride and Old Prejudice: Political Ambition and Role Orientations among Female Partisan Elites,' *Women and Politics* 1:1 (1980), 13-36; Kirkpatrick, *The New Presidential Elite*, 411ff; Jennings and Thomas, 'Men and Women in Party Elites'; and Jennings and Farah, 'Social Roles and Political Resources.'

72 Discussions of expressive versus instrumental orientations toward political work include Werner, 'Women in the State Legislatures'; Fowlkes et al, 'Gender Roles and Party Roles'; Edmond Constantini and Kenneth H.

Craik, 'Women as Politicians: The Social Background, Personality, and Political Careers of Female Party Leaders,' *Journal of Social Issues* 28:2 (1972), 217-36; and Clarke and Kornberg, 'Moving up the Political Escalator,' 458ff.

73 For Canadian treatments of the voter receptivity question, see Monica Boyd, 'English-Canadian and French-Canadian Attitudes toward Women: Results of the Canadian Gallup Polls,' *Journal of Comparative Family Studies* 6:2 (1975), 153-69; E.M. Schreiber, 'The Social Bases of Opinions on Women's Role in Canada,' *Canadian Journal of Sociology* 1:1 (1975), 61-74; and Naomi Black, 'Changing European and North American Attitudes toward Women in Public Life,' *Journal of European Integration* 1:2 (1978), 221-40.

An extensive American literature exists in this area, including Baxter and Lansing, *Women and Politics*, 139ff; Hazel Erskine, 'The Polls: Women's Role,' *Public Opinion Quarterly* 35:2 (1971), 275-85; Myra Marx Ferree, 'A Woman for President? Changing Responses, 1958-1972,' *Public Opinion Quarterly* 38:3 (1974), 390-9; Audrey Siess Wells and Eleanor Cutri Smeal, 'Women's Attitudes toward Women in Politics,' in Jane S. Jaquette, ed., *Women in Politics* (New York: Wiley, 1974), 54-72; Robert A. Bernstein and Jayne D. Polley, 'Race, Class, and Support for Female Candidates,' *Western Political Quarterly* 28:4 (1975), 733-6; Robert Darcy and Sarah Slavin Schramm, 'When Women Run against Men,' *Public Opinion Quarterly* 41:1 (1977), 1-12; E.M. Schreiber, 'Education and Change in American Opinion on a Woman for President,' *Public Opinion Quarterly* 42:2 (1978), 171-82; Ronald D. Hedlund, Patricia K. Freeman, Keith E. Hamm, and Robert M. Stein, 'The Electability of Women Candidates,' *Journal of Politics* 41:2 (1979), 513-24; Jerry Perkins and Diane L. Fowlkes, 'Opinion Representation versus Social Representation; or, Why Women Can't Run as Women and Win,' *American Political Science Review* 74:1 (1980), 92-103; Laurie E. Ekstrand and William A. Eckert, 'The Impact of Candidate's Sex on Voter Choice,' *Western Political Quarterly* 34:1 (1981), 78-87; and Susan Welch and Lee Sigelman, 'Changes in Public Attitudes toward Women in Politics,' *Social Science Quarterly* 63:2 (1982), 312-22.

Australian studies in this area include Malcolm Mackerras, 'Do Women Candidates Lose Votes?' *Australian Quarterly* (1977), 6-10; and Jonathan Kelley and Ian McAllister, 'The Electoral Consequences of Gender in Australia,' *British Journal of Political Science* 13:3 (1983), 365-77. For European treatments, see Elina Haavio-Mannila, 'Convergences between East and West: Tradition and Modernity in Sex Roles in Sweden, Finland, and the Soviet Union,' *Acta Sociologica* 14:1-2 (1971), 114-25; Elina

Haavio-Mannila, 'Sex Roles in Politics,' in Constantina Safilos-Rothschild, ed., *Towards a Sociology of Women* (Toronto: Xerox College Publishing, 1972), 154-72; Peter Foverskov, 'Women in Parliament: The Causes of Underrepresentation Exemplified by Denmark and Norway in the 1960s,' *European Journal of Political Research* 6:1 (1978), 53-69; Ottar Hellevik, 'Do Norwegian Voters Discriminate against Women Candidates for Parliament?' *European Journal of Political Research* 7:3 (1979), 285-300; and Jorgen Rasmussen, 'The Electoral Costs of Being a Woman in the 1979 British General Election,' *Comparative Politics* 15:4 (1983), 461-75.

74 Means, 'Political Recruitment of Women in Norway,' 517.

75 See Stobaugh, *Women and Parliament*; and Lorraine Culley, 'Women's Organisation in the Labour Party,' *Politics and Power* 3 (1981), 115-22.

76 Means, 'Political Recruitment,' 518.

77 Frank J. Sorauf, *Party Politics in America* (Boston: Little, Brown, 1976), 123. Other discussions of the conventional role of women's associations include Hugh A. Bone, *Party Committees and National Politics* (Seattle: University of Washington Press, 1958); Cornelius P. Cotter and Bernard C. Hennessy, *Politics without Power: The National Party Committees* (New York: Atherton, 1964); Robert J. Huckshorn, *Party Leadership in the States* (Amherst: University of Massachusetts Press, 1976); and John S. Saloma and Frederick H. Sontag, *Parties* (New York: Knopf, 1972), 108-10.

78 Sapiro, 'When Are Interests Interesting?' 712.

79 David I. Kertzer, *Comrades and Christians* (Cambridge: Cambridge University Press, 1980); and David I. Kertzer, 'The Liberation of Evelina Zaghi: The Life of an Italian Communist,' *Signs* 8:1 (1982), 45-67.

80 Kertzer, 'The Liberation,' passim; and Culley, 'Women's Organisation,' passim.

81 Kertzer, 'The Liberation,' 68.

82 Maria Weber, 'Italy,' in Lovenduski and Hills, *Politics of the Second Electorate*, 194. The feminist challenge to this lower status is discussed in Yasmine Ergas, '1968-79 – Feminism and the Italian Party System,' *Comparative Politics* 14:3 (1982), 253-79; Annarita Buttafuoco, 'Italy: The Feminist Challenge,' in Carl Boggs and David Plotke, eds., *The Politics of Eurocommunism* (Montreal: Black Rose, 1980); and Judith Adler Hellman, 'The Italian Communists, the Women's Question, and the Challenge of Feminism,' *Studies in Political Economy* 13 (Winter 1983), 57-82.

83 Culley, 'Women's Organisation,' 119.

84 See Jane Jenson, 'The French Communist Party and Feminism,' in Ralph Miliband and John Saville, eds., *The Socialist Register 1980* (London: Merlin Press, 1980), 121-47; and Gerard Braunthal, *The West German*

Social Democrats, 1969-1982 (Boulder, Col.: Westview Press, 1983), chap. 7.
85 Sorauf, *Party Politics*, 123.
86 Ibid. For an excellent case study of political caucus formation at the state level, see Barbara Burrell, 'A New Dimension in Political Participation: The Women's Political Caucus,' in Githens and Prestage, eds., *A Portrait of Marginality*, 241-57.
87 Sapiro, 'When Are Interests Interesting?' 712. This same dilemma is considered in a British context in Culley, 'Women's Organisation,' 121; and Stacey and Price, *Women, Power, and Politics*, 168. In the words of Stacey and Price, 'There are those who feel that the existence of separate organizations makes it possible for women to learn about politics, to speak and debate, and to thrash out women's affairs. Others argue that such separate organization reinforces the tendency of the male-dominated parties to see women's issues as trivial, secondary, and removable to another and powerless forum.'
88 Braunthal, *The West German Social Democrats*, 130.
89 Ibid, 134.
90 On the introduction of affirmative action in the U.S. parties, see Saloma and Sontag, *Parties*, 108-10, as well as Jeane Kirkpatrick, *The New Presidential Elite* and 'Representation in the American National Conventions: The Case of 1972,' *British Journal of Political Science* 5:3 (1975), 265-322.
91 Culley, 'Women's Organisation'; Monica Charlot, 'Women in Elections in Britain,' in Howard A. Penniman, ed., *Britain at the Polls, 1979* (Washington, DC: American Enterprise Institute, 1981), 241-62; and Jill Hills, 'Britain,' in Lovenduski and Hills, *Politics of the Second Electorate*, 8-32.
92 See Hills, 'Britain,' 18-19.
93 See Yvette Roudy, *La femme en marge*, with a preface by François Mitterrand (Paris: Flammarion, 1975).
94 Charlot, 'Women in Politics in France,' 190.
95 Margaret Collins Weitz, 'The Status of Women in France Today: A Reassessment,' *Contemporary French Civilization* 6: 1-2 (1981-2), 213.
96 Braunthal, *The West German Social Democrats*, 129.
97 Ibid, 131.
98 See Sylvia B. Bashevkin, 'Participation, Ambition, and the Development of Feminist Attitudes' (unpublished 1983). American studies in this same area include Susan B. Hansen, Linda M. Franz, and Margaret Netemeyer-Mays, 'Women's Political Participation and Policy Preferences,' *Social Science Quarterly* 56:4 (1976), 576-90.

99 See Kirkpatrick, *The New Presidential Elite.*
100 Fowlkes et al., 'Gender Roles and Party Roles,' 779.
101 See Hanna Fenichel Pitkin, *The Concept of Representation* (Berkeley: University of California Press, 1967).
102 Shelah Gilbert Leader, 'The Policy Impact of Elected Women Officials,' in Louis Maisel and Joseph Cooper, eds., *The Impact of the Electoral Process* (Beverly Hills: Sage, 1977), 265-84; Kathleen A. Frankovic, 'Sex and Voting in the U.S. House of Representatives, 1961-1975,' *American Politics Quarterly* 5:3 (1977), 315-30; and Sirkka Sinkkonen and Elina Haavio-Mannila, 'The Impact of the Women's Movement and Legislative Activity of Women Members of Parliament on Social Development,' in Margherita Rendel, ed., *Women, Power, and Political Systems* (London: Croom Helm, 1981), 195-215. Additional studies of the policy impact of contemporary feminism include Irene Tinker, ed., *Women in Washington* (Beverly Hills: Sage, 1983), and Joyce Gelb and Marian Lief Palley, *Women and Public Policies* (Princeton: Princeton University Press, 1982).
103 Leader, 'The Policy Impact,' 284.

CHAPTER 7: EPILOGUE

1 See Andrea Dworkin, *Right Wing Women* (New York: Putnam, 1983).
2 For a more detailed discussion of these and other changes, see Margrit Eichler, *Families in Canada* (Toronto: Gage, 1983).
3 Working-class women in Canada, by way of contrast, face limited educational and occupational opportunities as well as the conventional gender bias of such working-class institutions as trade unions. See Julie White, *Women and Unions* (Ottawa: Canadian Advisory Council on the Status of Women, 1980).
4 See Pat Armstrong and Hugh Armstrong, *The Double Ghetto: Canadian Women and Their Segregated Work* (Toronto: McClelland and Stewart, 1978).
5 Judy LaMarsh, *Memoirs of a Bird in a Gilded Cage* (Toronto: McClelland and Stewart, 1968), 282.
6 See Richard French, *How Ottawa Decides* (Toronto: Lorimer, 1980).
7 See Lucinda Sue Flavelle, 'Women Senior Civil Servants in Canada, the U.K., and the U.S.' (MA thesis, York University, 1982).
8 Thatcher as quoted in Donna S. Sanzone, 'Women in Politics,' in Cynthia Fuchs Epstein and Rose Laub Coser, eds., *Access to Power* (London: Allen and Unwin, 1981), 44.
9 See chapter 6, notes 101 and 102, above, as well as Susan B. Hansen, Linda M. Franz, and Margaret Netemeyer-Mays, 'Women's Political

Participation and Policy Preferences,' *Social Science Quarterly* 56:4 (1976), 576-90.

APPENDIX A: DATA SOURCES

1 For a general discussion of secondary survey methodology, see Herbert Hyman, *Secondary Analysis of Sample Surveys* (New York: Wiley, 1972). Some limitations of this technique for students of women and politics are considered in Thelma McCormack, 'Toward a Nonsexist Perspective on Social and Political Change,' in Marcia Millman and Rosabeth Moss Kanter, eds., *Another Voice* (New York: Anchor, 1975), 1-33. According to McCormack (1975: 12), most sources presently available for secondary analysis offer 'male-female differences to questions men have raised arising out of their own or other men's experience.'
2 For a more detailed discussion of the questionnaire and its results, see Sylvia B. Bashevkin, 'Social Background and Political Experience: Gender Differences among Ontario Provincial Party Elites, 1982,' *Atlantis* 9:1 (Fall 1983), 1-12, and 'Political Participation, Ambition, and the Development of Feminist Attitudes: Women in the Ontario Party Elites' (unpublished 1983).
3 See Jeane J. Kirkpatrick, *Political Woman* (New York: Basic Books, 1974), appendix.
4 See Robert D. Putnam, *The Comparative Study of Political Elites* (Englewood Cliffs, NJ: Prentice-Hall, 1976), 15-19.

Index

abortion issue 91, 92, 155; *see also* women's issues
Ad Hoc Committee of Canadian Women 24, 32
affirmative action 153, 154, 166; obstacles to 63-4; in ONDP 66, 84-9, 95-6, 113; in federal NDP 68, 84n, 87, 91, 95, 113; in U.S. 82-4, 88, 139, 151; in LPC 84n, 87, 95, 115; in Western Europe 151-2
Alberta 72, 74, 77, 104, 105
Anderson, Doris 25n, 31-2
Australia 61n, 136, 137, 142, 147
Axworthy, Lloyd 31-2

backroom strategists 64, 68-9
Bégin, Monique 29, 78, 79n
Bird, Florence 20-6
Borden, Robert 10, 11
British Columbia 61, 72, 74, 76-7, 98, 100, 101, 104, 111
British Columbia Women's Liberal Association 14, 98
Broadbent, Ed 29, 91
Brown, Rosemary 28, 29, 79n, 82n, 89-91, 93, 106n, 113
bureaucracy, women in 159

cabinet appointments 77-9
campaign management 69-70
Canadian Advisory Council on the Status of Women (CACSW) 24, 27, 30, 31-2
Canadian Coalition against Media Pornography 24, 32n
Canadian Federation of Business and Professional Women's Clubs 21, 25
Canadian Federation of University Women (CFUW) 21, 25
Canadian Suffrage Association (CSA) 5n, 7, 11
Canadian Woman Suffrage Association 5
candidacy for public office 70-4, 143-5
Casgrain, Thérèse 20, 23
Chatelaine magazine 25, 28, 32
child-care facilities 22, 30, 131n, 158; *see also* women's issues
class, impact of 49-50, 157
cohort analysis: of attitudes in English Canada 45-51; of comparative data 124, 126-7, 129, 133-4
Committee for the Equality of Women in Canada (CEW) 24, 25
conscription crisis 10-12, 41-2